Stagecoach and Tavern Tales
of the Old Northwest

Stagecoach and Tavern Tales of the Old Northwest

by

HARRY ELLSWORTH COLE
Late President of the State Historical Society of Wisconsin

edited by
LOUISE PHELPS KELLOGG

The Arthur H. Clark Company
Cleveland, U.S.A., 1930

To the one who gave assistance,
encouragement, and inspiration
My Wife, DOROTHY F. COLE
I affectionately dedicate this book

Contents

Illustrations

No! those days are gone away
And their hours are old and gray
And their minutes buried all
Under the down-trodden pall
Of the leaves of many years.

– JOHN KEATS

Preface

Since the advent of the automobile into American life and a renewal of travel by road instead of railroad, interest has been reawakened to a remarkable degree in methods of early travel. The Old Northwest was settled in the days of pioneer travel and our forefathers came hither on horseback, by ox or horseteam, over roads which would not today be dignified by that appellation. Along these roads were places of entertainment, first the log-house of the primitive settler, later as more settled conditions obtained the tavern became a center for the community and its affairs were those of the settlement. The stagecoach later supplemented the private means of travel as the inn superseded the hospitality of the pioneers. Tavern and coach filled an important function in the history of the growing communities that peopled the Old Northwest in the decades before the coming of the Civil war.

This phase of history forms a tempting field for any historian and especially for one enamored of the open road. Such a one was the author of this book. Nature lover and history lover, the tales of stagecoach and tavern days appealed to Harry Ellsworth Cole with especial force. For years he gathered material for this book during many personal journeys to old taverns and the homes of pioneer taverners. He laid under contribution his wide acquaintance with historical literature and pressed his many friends into the service. After his regretted death it was found that the manuscript for this book was finished, lacking only the revision he would have given it had he lived.

It has fallen to my lot to revise and prepare the manuscript for publication. Exigencies of space have required much of interest to be omitted, especially the pictures of many taverns which the author gathered with such loving care. Those not included in this volume have been deposited with the State Historical Society of Wisconsin, which Mr. Cole had served as president for several years. We have ventured to add to the title "the Old Northwest," for while concerned largely with the region between Lake Michigan and the Mississippi the tales are characteristic of all the states of the Old Northwest and may be said to relate also to Iowa and Minnesota, settled nearly simultaneously.

With the manuscript was found the following Foreword written by Mr. Cole, in which he outlined his purpose and made his acknowledgements.

LOUISE PHELPS KELLOGG

November, 1929

Foreword

In the following pages an attempt has been made to open the door of the days of the stagecoach and tavern in the region between Lake Michigan and the Mississippi river. Little has been the effort to extend the period covered later than the advent of the railroad, for the arrival of the locomotive changed the old order in hamlet and village. Passenger travel deserted the slow-going vehicle for the new and speedier mode of travel, so the glory of the stagecoach and tavern was soon a thing of the past.

Dilapidated taverns by the wayside recall the lore of the middle of the last century – snatches of old songs, music of the contra-dances, practical joking of the time, and tragedies of frontier days. Those inns which are not standing live in a fading memory – haunts of fellowship and freedom and the abode of travelers on a border journey.

It is impossible to present all the incidents, to mention all of the landlords, to tell the story of all the taverns. It has been necessary to exercise our prerogative more or less and flit here and there in presenting this picture of other times. The magic of it all lies in a day so different from the present – the unusual human-interest thread appearing again and again in the woof and warp of changing life movements.

Unlike the taverns of old London or of New England, we cannot approach these Midwest taverns in the reverential attitude that pertains to rulers and literati, for storied royalty and Concord authors were not of the western frontier. Again, unlike the snug places of entertainment in old London, secreted in some narrow court, those in the West were largely on the main streams of travel, at convenient distances apart for the accommodation of those weary of a seat on the stagecoach.

Many volumes in the rich storehouse of the State Historical Society of Wisconsin have been consulted, and I wish to acknowledge my indebtedness to several members of the staff – to Doctor Joseph Schafer for his interest in reading the manuscript, Miss Edna L. Jacobson for editorial criticism, Doctor Louise P. Kellogg and Charles E. Brown for incidents, J. H. A. Lacher's article, "The Taverns and Stages of Early Wisconsin," published in Wisconsin Society *Proceedings*, 1914, was a source of much information. O. D. Brandenburg of Madison has carefully edited the manuscript and A. O. Barton has contributed a number of incidents. Acknowledgements are also due to Judge Emil Baensch, Manitowoc; Marshall Cousins, Eau Claire; George E. West, Milwaukee; E. A. Gilman, Portage; W. H. Orvis, Madison; Doctor C. V. Porter, Viroqua; M. C. Crandall, Baraboo; W. G. Kirchoffer, Madison; W. C. English, Wyocena; W. H. Carlin, Palmyra; Mrs. May L. Bauchle, Beloit; Miss Agnes Sperry, Delafield; Guy C. Glazier, El Cajou, California; V. C. Hawks, Alameda, California; and many others.

HARRY ELLSWORTH COLE

Expanding Days

Days of the thirties, forties, and fifties were days of expanding ideas. For many decades public travel had been by slow coach with the place of entertainment an inn or a tavern. As civilization advanced from the eastward toward the Mississippi, in the years just before the advent of the railway, the coach and tavern reached the peak of their usefulness.

Migration into the region between the Great Lakes and the Mississippi had been dilatory until the decade previous to the Civil war. For a little more than twenty years prior to 1850, miners, merchants, taverners, and farmers had found their way into the northwestern part of Illinois and the southwestern portion of the future state of Wisconsin and had become well established. Many of them came up the Mississippi or across the prairies of Illinois into a land which had lead for a loadstone. Meanwhile at Lake Michigan ports in the northern part of Illinois and the eastern portion of Wisconsin, New York and New England, settlers arrived by the way of lake steamers or by covered wagons drawn by horses or oxen, along the southern shore of Lake Erie, across Michigan, and through Chicago to the new commonwealths in the course of development in the Northwest. Within this region the movement of white settlers was eastward from the Mississippi and westward from the Great Lakes, the two expansive migrations meeting near the center. It has been said that the carefreeness and excitement of a mining region, represented largely by Southerners and Cornishmen, united oddly with New Yorkers and New Englanders making "the oil and vinegar of a noble salad dressing."

As population increased, as new towns appeared, taverns and stagecoaches became a component and highly important part of the community. Often tavern and coach blazed the way, so necessary were these factors to the development of the new country. By the time the railroad appeared, many main traveled roads were beaded with taverns, sometimes not more than a mile apart. On the first fifty miles west of Albany, New York, there were fifty taverns; in the region of Sandusky, along the south shore of Lake Erie, they were as numerous; and on some of the main arteries projecting out of Chicago and Milwaukee they virtually were within sight of each other.

These were interesting days in the West, days filled with worldly profits, political debate, religious differences, patriotic fervor. In the expanding movement of the time landlords often deemed it their duty to encompass many acres about their places and this desire for land added not a little to their material prosperity. Acreage was easily obtained and, incident to enlarging activities, was advancing in value.

Political ideals were far from stable. Slavery was breaking old lines and creating new, all, however, widening the zone of freedom. In the very midst of the era of taverns and stagecoaches, the Republican party was born, and with its expansion Lincoln was swept into the White House. Jerry Rusk and others dropped the reins of their horses or deserted their taverns to cast their destiny with followers of the idea which was to reach fruition in the abolition of slavery. Days they were, not only of hard drinking, but of hard thinking, not only on slavery, but on money, banking, and many issues.

It was a period when evolution was beginning to be a mighty concept and when religious ideals were no longer of everlasting punishment in a furnace of fire. Some sects still purchased muslin for ascension robes, but these were never worn beyond a neighboring roof from which followers of the cult expected to be translated into another world. These were the days of the grain-cradle, the flail, the horse-power threshing machine, the tallow-candle or kerosene-lamp, house-raisings, rail-splitting, contra-dances, spelling-bees. It was the day of log houses, ox-yokes, and well-sweeps. Newspapers advertised a preparation known as water-lime and salt, also sozodont, cholera mixture, vitalized air, pictures printed by sun's rays, galvanic belts, Arabian liniment for neuralgia, coach-wheel quilts, buffalo robes, bootjacks, bed-cords, rafting cable, melodeons, ambrotypes, mozambiques, paper collars, hop-plows, hop-roots, hop-poles. A feather bed was not infrequently a bride's dowry, and money was so rare that skins of animals and jugs of whisky were often pressed into service as legal tender.

Judging by the medicaments advertised in the forties and fifties, people must have suffered continually from a remarkable variety of ailments. No one was ever operated upon for appendicitis or bought glands to make him young; microbes were unknown; the x-ray photograph was afar off. Yet folks lived to a good old age and walked miles to wish their friends a Merry Christmas or a Happy New Year.

Aside from the local newspaper the most popular periodicals of the day were Horace Greeley's *New York Tribune*, Godey's *Lady's Book, The Drawing Room Companion*, and Littell's *Living Age*.

Men usually wore homespun, and their boots had

tops sufficiently roomy to admit the insertion of the lower portion of their pantaloons. Stovepipe hats were popular with doctors and others belonging to the professional classes, and were so universally worn by them that the glossy covering became, in a way, a badge of the professions. Woman's wear was more picturesque than man's. Bonnets were capacious. Often those worn in summer, made of Neapolitan straw, were perishable affairs as far as holding the shape was concerned. They were gaily decked with bows of corn-colored ribbon or realistic artificial flowers, mingled with ribbons of rainbow hues. The capacious hoopskirt was in high favor for a number of years, and outer skirts of necessity followed its undulating contour. How the ladies of that day were able to make graceful entrance or exit through the doors of stagecoaches remains an enigma.

These days were circumstanced in dried apples, salt pork, baked beans, cornbread, all frequently irrigated with fluid from handy flagons. When a man sold fresh pork or beef he gave away the heart, liver, and certain other parts. Man worked ten hours a day or more and never went on a strike. No tips were given to waiters and the hatrack grafter was unknown. During this period a kerosene hanging lamp in the parlor became a luxury. It was the era of phrenology, of the first sulphur matches, of cascading tobacco juice on board walks, the romantic underground railroad, vast woodpiles and whittling in front of the general store.

This period witnessed caravans crossing the plains in the great gold rush, and more than one hopeful band went forth from a northwestern tavern to end its adventure in disappointment, despair, or death. All was not gold that glittered on western mountains. This, too, was the time when Mormon pilgrims traversed the treeless tracts to establish themselves in the Salt lake valley; and the battles of Cerro Gordo and Buena Vista were fought across the Mexican border.

The first fifty years of the nineteenth century was moving time. Through Albany thousands of New England people proceeded to the west – to Ohio, Indiana, and Michigan; and these in turn, joined by recruits from the east, migrated to Illinois, Iowa, and Wisconsin. Travel was by canal, the Great Lakes, rivers, stagecoaches, the covered wagon – the way toward the seemingly limitless West, much to the concern of the redskins. This westward movement in which the tavern and coach played so important a part was a grand pageant. America was in motion and in the making.

The Old Military Road

Waterways were the routes by which the great central valley of North America was reached during the first two centuries of its historic existence, and it was not until the coming of the Americans with their hunger for land that roads were necessary to the economy of the growing communities. Among these early roads, in the region west of Lake Michigan, then a part of the territory of Michigan, none was more important than the Old Military road, which crossed the land from east to west and connected the shores of Lake Michigan with the banks of the Mississippi.*

After Jolliet and Marquette made their remarkable journey in 1673 from Green Bay to the Mississippi by way of the Fox-Wisconsin rivers, for more than a century and a half that route remained the only one from Lake Michigan to the western border of Wisconsin. So far as history records, no white man had plunged into the unbroken forest along the inland sea to emerge on the shore of the Father of Waters, until the month of May, 1829, when James Duane Doty, afterwards territorial governor of Wisconsin, Henry S. Baird, a young Irishman who is said to have been the first to practice law west of Lake Michigan, Morgan L. Martin, prominent as an attorney in the courts as well as in politics of the later state, and an indian guide made a journey

---

*In 1925 Mr. Cole prepared for the *Wisconsin Magazine of History* an article entitled "The Old Military Road"; by permission of the editor this is introduced as the second chapter of this book. Some omissions have been made because of inclusion in other portions of this work.

on horseback from Green Bay to Prairie du Chien. This is the first recorded land pilgrimage by white men between the two extremes of the journey. These same gentlemen had made the trip in 1825, 1826, and 1828, traveling the route by way of the Fox-Wisconsin rivers. When they made the journey by land there were no roads, no habitations, no familiar landmarks, no bridges over the streams. They plunged into an expanse inhabited only by indians, and thus opened a way for travel which afterwards became known as the Military road.

Previous to 1829, however, mail had been carried over much of the same route by Joseph Crelie, a half-breed, who delivered the first mail at Dodgeville in 1828. Often he was obliged to go on snowshoes, braving the prairie winds and cold at the peril of losing his life. In 1832, during the Black Hawk war, James Halpin, a soldier, carried dispatches for General Zachary Taylor between Prairie du Chien and Green Bay over this route. He traversed the distance alone, crossing the larger streams by swimming his horse. These carriers made the journey either on foot or by horseback, frequently following indian trails. One of these, from Green Bay to Milwaukee, was worn to the depth of twenty inches in places, showing long usage by indian and white man.

In October, 1829, at a public meeting at Green Bay, congress was petitioned for a road to Chicago, and this was followed by petitions for other roads within the territory. With the establishment of Fort Howard at Green Bay, Fort Winnebago at Portage, and Fort Crawford at Prairie du Chien, a need was felt for a highway connecting the three military posts, since during the winter season it was impossible to transport supplies by water from one fort to another.

In 1830 congress made an appropriation for the survey and location of a military road from Green Bay to Chicago, and another from Green Bay to Prairie du Chien. Judge Doty and Lieutenant Alexander J. Center, the latter of the United States army, were appointed commissioners, and during 1831 and 1832 surveyed and located these roads. The road connecting the forts, projected in a diagonal direction across Wisconsin, extended from Green Bay, along the south and east side of the Fox river to about a mile above Wrightstown, thence across the southeastern portion of Outagamie county, in a serpentine course to Sherwood, along the east side of Lake Winnebago through Stockbridge and Brothertown to Fond du Lac, through the villages of Lamartine and Brandon, across the southwestern corner of Green Lake county to Fort Winnebago at Portage, thence to Poynette, to the northeastern shore of Lake Mendota, to Blue Mounds, along the ridge dividing the waters flowing toward the north into the Wisconsin river from those flowing south into other streams, across the Wisconsin river at Bridgeport, and into Prairie du Chien from the southeast. The route for much of the way was along well-trodden indian trails, and was traced on the government plats when the first surveys were made.

After the road was surveyed in 1831 and 1832, nothing more was done until April 1, 1835, when Lewis Cass, then secretary of war, issued an order for the construction of the road connecting the forts. The soldiers at Fort Crawford were ordered to build the road to Fort Winnebago, those at the latter fort to construct the road to Fond du Lac, and the troops at Green Bay to complete the task. The soldiers at the three forts composed the Fifth regiment of the standing army, and were under the command of Brigadier-general George Mercer Brooke.

The road from the Mississippi to Lake Winnebago was completed in the fall of 1835, but the task of building the northern portion through a dense forest of hardwood timber was much more difficult, and the thoroughfare was not open until about 1838. The Fond du Lac river was bridged and the bridge used by the natives and wild beasts for a number of months before the first white settlers arrived. The road, as constructed by the soldiers, was necessarily a crude affair. The work was done by cutting through the timber land, clearing a track about two rods wide, and on the prairies setting mile stakes. Sometimes mounds of earth and stones were thrown up. On the marshes and other low places, corduroy roads were made by placing small logs on the soft earth and sometimes covering them with brush or dirt. Rude bridges were thrown across the streams.

From Green Bay to Fond du Lac each detachment of soldiers worked a week in turn. Twelve miles of this road was made by Captain Martin Scott and his men, "as straight as an arrow, and at the time considered quite a feat."

This early trail was rudely defined by blazing trees along the way, that is, by removing with an ax, a piece of bark as large as one's hand. Near Sherwood, when the soldiers of Fort Howard were constructing the Military road, they cut faces in the bark of trees on a hill, and the elevation became known as Mask Hill.

It was a poor excuse for a road, according to present day standards, and could be used only in the winter when the ground was frozen or in summer when the weather was dry. Downpours submerged great sections of it and made other portions, as one writer expressed it, "as slippery as noodles on a spoon."

In early days the main street of Fond du Lac – this being a portion of the Military road – "looked like a vat of blacking." The mud held like an octopus, and when a wheel or foot ventured into the mass something seemed to grasp it with tenacious power, never to let go. In 1850 James Ewen, proprietor of the Lewis House at Fond du Lac, waded out into the street early in the morning, before the guests had arisen, and placed a pair of boots and a hat in the sticky mass in such a way that at a glance one would think an individual was disappearing in the earthy mucilage. Those passing thought a man had drowned on land.

The soldiers built huts at various places to protect themselves from the weather. When Henry Merrell was returning alone from Green Bay to Portage one season, he found a shanty erected by the soldiers seven miles southwest of Fond du Lac. The hut was made by setting posts in the ground, placing poles across the roof, and covering it with a little brush and straw. After sleeping in the hut during a rainy night, Merrell awoke to find his clothes soaking wet, even to his saddle skirts. The road was difficult to follow. In the timber the trees were blazed, but when a traveler crossed a prairie he had to judge as accurately as he could the course, and when he reached the timber, hunt up the blazes and proceed.

When the question of improving this highway arose Captain C. J. Cram made a report to congress, September 1, 1839, in which he stated that the portion of the road from Fort Crawford to the portage, a distance of about one hundred fifteen miles, would need the sum of

$5700 to be expended, chiefly in repairs, construction of small bridges, and the opening of ditches. The building of a safe and permanent road across the portage, about four miles, would require the sum of $5955. He spoke in his report of the overflowing of the land at the portage, making it necessary for travelers to take a circuitous route of about fifteen miles, crossing a lake on the way, in order to reach or depart from Fort Winnebago. Captain Cram estimated it would require the sum of $6320 to construct the road from Fort Winnebago to Fond du Lac – a distance of about sixty miles – and $17,292 to complete the task between Fond du Lac and Green Bay – about fifty-six miles. In conclusion, he said the whole amount required to complete the construction of the Military road from Fort Crawford, by way of Fort Winnebago, to Fort Howard, an extent of about 235 miles, would be $35,267. Contrast this with road making today, when a mile of an average concrete road costs nearly as much as the total estimated cost of a highway across Wisconsin in the thirties. The money for the improvement was never appropriated by congress.

No king trod this highway, but a prince traversed it; no president of the republic ever rode in state over the route, but future presidents are associated with it; no high military commander ever led his troops from Green Bay to Prairie du Chien, but generals, colonels, and captains in numbers are linked with its history, and here and there are human episodes of interest.

When the Northwest was being settled, it frequently happened that two or three men coveted the same piece of land. The lucky individual was the one who first reached the land office with his money to purchase the primitive acres from the government. Along the Old

Military road these contests of speed were known as "Green Bay races," the land office being at Green Bay. In 1844, at Oak Grove in Dodge county, three or four individuals desired a certain tract of timber. Two of the men, each believing that no one but himself knew his errand, started for Green Bay to enter the land. About dusk of the same day, it having become known that two men were on their way to the land office, both after the same piece of land, Richard F. Rising said to James Riley that he (Rising) would furnish the money and pay liberally besides to anyone who could reach Green Bay ahead of those already gone several hours, and enter the land. Mr. Riley replied, "Give me the money to pay for the land, and if I fail, it shan't cost you a cent." The money was provided; Mr. Riley secured a supply of crackers and cheese, and was on his way fifteen minutes after the words were spoken. Taking a kind of dog-trot, he plunged into the darkness of the night, and before the day dawned passed both the mounted men. The man on foot never halted except to drink from a spring or brook, traveled the ninety miles, entered the land, and the next day while on the way home met the two horsemen traveling toward a disappointing goal.

In February, 1848, as Mr. and Mrs. J. H. Warren and daughter were eating breakfast in their home in Mayville, Charles H. Taylor leaped into the room. In a breath he explained that Garwood Green, Rufus Allen, and George Varnum had gone to Green Bay to jump his claim — eighty acres of choice land on which he claimed a preëmption for a year or more. Each of the men wanted the land for himself, and fondly believed that no one knew the secret save himself. Their errand had become known early in the day, and as

soon as the information reached Taylor he hurried
to Warren to prevail upon him to purchase the
property for an iron company, believing he could
obtain more in the way of justice from the organization than from any of the men who had departed for the land office at Green Bay. A few
minutes after Taylor had informed Warren of the
situation, the latter was on his way to secure the land.
With only a light lunch he set out on the trail and
reached the Badger House in Fond du Lac, having seen
no one on the way. At the inn he found all three of the
conspirators, and slept not only in a room with them,
but in the same bed with one of them without exciting
the least suspicion. Warren hurried along the Military
road, entered the land, and was several miles on his way
home before he met Garwood Green and the others.
The iron company paid for the land and removed the
timber, which was converted into charcoal for the
furnaces.

On another occasion E. J. Smith and Jacob Swarthout desired the same tract of land in the town of Fountain Prairie, Columbia county. Early one morning
Smith left for Green Bay over the Military road,
thinking no one possessed the secret of his going. During the day Mr. Swarthout was informed of the fact,
and just before nightfall mounted an indian pony and
hurried toward the land office. When about halfway
there he made a temporary exchange with an indian for
another pony and hastened on his mission without stopping to rest. He reached the land office ahead of Smith
and thus secured the land.

The story of Ebenezer Childs's journey in 1837 over
a portion of this road from Madison to Green Bay is
interesting. The army surgeon from Fort Winnebago

had gone to Madison to give medical aid to the mother of A. A. Bird, and on a bitter morning Childs, the surgeon and others left on the trip to Fort Winnebago at Portage. Wallace Rowan and his family occupied the only house between the head of Lake Mendota and Portage at that time. When the travelers had gone about halfway, it was found that the surgeon was so cold, although buried beneath buffalo robes, that it was necessary to stop in the timber, clear away the snow, and build a fire. The surgeon, so chilled he could not speak, was carried to the fire, rubbed a long time, given a little brandy, and then was able to resume the journey. When the fort was reached the thermometer registered thirty-two degrees below zero. On the way from Fort Winnebago to Fond du Lac, Childs did not see a house, and he saw but one between Fond du Lac and Green Bay. Before reaching Lake Winnebago he overtook two Stockbridge indians, whom he carried in his jumper, the snow being deep, until the timber was reached, where a large fire was made for them. They probably would have perished on the prairie had they not received this aid.

In 1844 Captain Edwin V. Sumner and his command came over portions of the road from Iowa to Portage, and returned with a number of Winnebago indians who had escaped from Turkey river in the Hawkeye state.

In 1842, in describing a journey over that portion of the road east of Lake Winnebago, Mrs. Elizabeth Thérèse Baird says that one of the landmarks along the straight-cut road was the eagle's nest – in view long before reaching it and long after passing. Snow had fallen, and one was never sure of missing the stumps. "We were now," Mrs. Baird says, "in the Stockbridge settlement, where the log houses were rather near together for farms. There were many stumps in the streets of Stockbridge, and as they were covered with snow it was an easy thing to hit one. One of them upset us at Fowler's very gate. We were all well cared for at Fowler's. The next morning we again took an early start — so early that the stumps in the road were no more visible than the night previous. I was thrown against a stump and one arm was hurt, though no bones were broken. The pain from the injury, however, was severe. I was carried into a little hut where the people were just rising, and placed on a bed which some very untidy-appearing folk had just vacated. I would have preferred the floor." The journey was continued to Portage, where a physician was called to attend Mrs. Baird's arm.

One of the most pathetic and arduous journeys ever made over a western portion of this road was that of Thomas P. Burnett on October 25 and 26, 1846. He had been elected a delegate from Grant county to the first convention to form a constitution for a state government, but on account of illness was prevented from being present at the opening on October 5. His physical condition was such that he should not have left home, but feeling the high responsibility resting upon him, he made the journey from his double log cabin by the side of the Military road at Wingville, now Montfort, to Madison. Mrs. Burnett attended the funeral of her mother on October 19. About a week later her husband departed for the capital, and on the day following she was taken ill with typhoid, then prevalent in the region. In a few days her condition was such that a messenger, with Mr. Burnett's own team, hurried to Madison for him. On the night of October 25, after the weariness of a day in the convention, he left in the wagon for home, arriving there the following night. The distance was eighty-five miles, and the fatigue and exposure caused a relapse of his disease. When he reached home he found not only his wife ill, but also his mother, who a few months before had come to make her home with him. On November 1, the mother died, and on November 5, Mr. Burnett breathed his last, his wife dying three hours afterward. They were buried in the family cemetery but a few rods from the frontier home and primitive road.

The Reverend Cutting Marsh, a Congregational missionary to the Stockbridge indians, kept at one time a house of entertainment between Green Bay and Fond du Lac. Colonel Childs, Morgan L. Martin, H. S. Baird, and others journeying southward were once entertained over night at the home of the missionary. It was the custom of this propagator of religion to distribute Testaments to members of the family and guests before sitting down to the morning meal, and to read from the Scriptures. Alternate verses were read, each in turn, by those present. On the morning when his distinguished guests were there, the good missionary selected a chapter in "Timothy," read his verse, the members of the family each his own, Judge Martin his, and the time when Childs must read was becoming imminent. He could not find the place, and the succession actually reached him before he reached "Timothy" in the New Testament. However, he continued to struggle among the saints and the apostles, confused and mortified, and in his despair forgot the character of his host and the solemnity of the occasion. Finally he was heard to utter, "Where in h— is 'Timothy?'"

Perhaps no travelers on the Military road attracted

more attention than the Prince de Joinville, a member of the royal family of France, and his retinue, who journeyed in 1840 from Galena to Green Bay. Commenting on the visit of the prince, the newspapers of the time state that the landlords of Galena decided that the royal visitor was legitimate prey, and charged him enormously for the entertainment received. One of the items was five dollars for the use of a piano during the evening – something rarely encountered in hotel charges. It is said that Wisconsin territorial tavern keepers were more considerate of the prince's purse. The mission of this member of the royal family was to search for the lost Dauphin of France. About the only result of the visit was an interview with Eleazar Williams, which so impressed the missionary that he became obsessed with the idea that he was the Dauphin; and this in turn has resulted in much writing about this character.

Naturally the most traveled portions of the road were from Green Bay to Fond du Lac and from Madison westward toward the Mississippi river. At Fond du Lac the road was joined by one from Milwaukee, and west of Madison by one from Milwaukee to Galena and Prairie du Chien. When the full tide of immigration was flowing and when settlers were entering land, such places as the Fond du Lac House at Fond du Lac and Brigham's Tavern at Blue Mounds presented a lively appearance.

A journey the length of this primitive road in early days was almost like going today from London to Bombay. It was sufficiently hazardous to remind one that it would be well to prepare his last will and testament before penetrating the wilds before him. All the traveler could do was to move slowly along, guided by the trail of rude construction, often with Altair and Vega looking down from the azure spaces of night. There were but few footprints and few echoes of humanity along the pioneer road, which now pierces several cities and is flanked by a world checkered with fertile fields.

In that day when travel was so limited that there was no treading on one another's heels, there was an inexpressible charm about the deep solitude along the way — the prairies fragrant and fascinating with a burst of brilliant bloom, the radiant view gained after ascending a prominent elevation, the idyllic glory of the frontier region in autumn, and the delectable charm of the lakes shimmering in the sunlight. Wild fowl filled the air in migratory flight, deer in herds disappeared over many a hill, bears gave excitement from day to day, and at night the wolves uttered their nocturnal cry. Every day was rich in new experiences for the traveler.

With the abandonment of the three frontier forts and with roads established on sectional and intersectional lines, the Military road in places lost its identity. A territorial road from Fond du Lac, through Fox lake to Portage, was much traveled; also a more direct route was established from Poynette to Blue Mounds. The section from Green Bay to Fond du Lac has retained much of its location. From Blue Mounds to Fennimore the railroad first brought changes, and with the coming of the automobile new locations have been made in order to eliminate dangerous crossings. In other places trees again grow where there was once pioneer-passing, and frequently all trace of the road is lost in long cultivated fields. In these places the highway to the newer generations is but a tale of faded days.

Should a resurrection trumpeter blow his bugle along this road, what an assemblage would answer his call! In review would come venturesome explorers in quest of lands heretofore unseen; daring hunters whose ambitions were to be realized in an abundance of birds, bear, bison, beaver, and wild game; determined pioneers with mighty axes to hew out homes in the solitary woodlands; officers and soldiers standing guard over the indian as he looks with suspicious eye upon the encroaching whites; anxious traders with beads and baubles to barter with unsophisticated tribesmen; and travelers from many lands seeking adventure on the advancing rim of civilization. Indians, explorers, hunters, pioneers, troopers, traders, and taverners tramped over this rough road by day and camped beneath the stars by night.

Territorial Roads

Many of the first highways in the new region were adopted by accident. They extended across the country without regard to the cardinal points of the compass; they followed ridges and ravines in about as irregular a path as that of a cow across an unfenced prairie. At first they belonged to nobody but later they were placed for the most part on sectional or inter-sectional lines, the location they hold today. However, rough and muddy as the roads were, they led the traveler to many an embryo village or city, through many towns and counties. Each hill and valley, each bridge and stream, each farm and field is saturated with events of human interest which are the common legacy of those who travel them today. These roads and trails were not only essential to the beginning of the history of a new country but they were the interesting threads that reached out across the tapestry of life of that time and place.

The route between Chicago and Green Bay, passing through Milwaukee, was quite as important to the development of the Midwest as the Old Military road from lake to river. This north-and-south road was at first an indian trail, used by natives, fur-traders, and mail-carriers – the last required about a month to make the round trip. After the Black Hawk war, when immigration began to flow to the Northwest this trace became of prime importance and the government had a road surveyed along this line. This early road left Chicago at what is now the Michigan boulevard bridge and

ran north along the height of land, following approximately Rush street to Chicago avenue, thence to Clark
street and northwest along that to Ridge avenue, Evan-
ston. It swung around to the lake shore at what is now
Wilmette, at that time the residence of a French trader,
Antoine Ouilmette. The route then ran north along the
line of the present Sheridan road, swinging back three
miles west of Waukegan and entering the present state
of Wisconsin about five miles west of the lake shore. It
then ran directly north, touching Skunk grove in Racine county and entered Milwaukee over Kinnickinnic
creek. It crossed what is now the south side of that city
in a northeasterly direction to Walker's point where the
Milwaukee river had to be forded or ferried, thence it
led north to Juneau's post on East Wisconsin avenue
and East Water street. Leaving Milwaukee for the
north the road ran inland so that the lake was seen only
at the mouth of Sauk river and at Two Rivers, Manitowoc county. Thence Green Bay was reached by the trail
on the southeast side of the Fox river. Along this route
came much of the travel of territorial days. Provisions
for the garrison at Fort Howard often came this way.

In 1825 Colonel William S. Hamilton, a son of the
celebrated statesman, Alexander Hamilton, accompanied by four men, drove a herd of cattle for the garrison
of Fort Howard from near Springfield, Illinois, to
Green Bay, by way of Chicago and Milwaukee. When
they arrived at Chicago, the town was not occupied by
troops but was under the care of an indian agent. The
people there desired an animal for food, but, knowing
Hamilton would not sell, they cleverly contrived to
drown one of the herd in the river as they were swimming across. The animal, of course, was eaten with
appreciation. There were no white residents between

SAUGANASH TAVERN, CHICAGO

Built in 1831 by Mark Beaubien, at southeast corner of Lake and Market; named for the half-breed Potawatomi chief, Billy Caldwell, called the Sauganash (Englishman) because his father was English. This tavern burned in 1851; on its site was built the Wigwam, where Lincoln was nominated

Chicago and Milwaukee and at the latter place only
one person, Solomon Juneau. Juneau, being nearly
starved, was delighted to see the strangers and their
food. No settlement existed between Milwaukee and
Manitowoc, and the only persons seen were a few fishermen. The time consumed in reaching Green Bay with
the drove was a little over a month.

In the early part of the month of January, 1834, Mrs.
Solomon Juneau of Milwaukee was taken seriously ill,
and there being neither medicines nor physicians nearer
than Chicago, Albert Fowler was hurried off by Juneau on an indian pony, for medical aid. The journey
in mid-winter through eighty-five or ninety miles of
wilderness was one of great hardship, and one which
Fowler never desired to undertake again. The indians
predicted that he would perish, but due to a vigorous
constitution and a physique inured to frontier life, he
succeeded in reaching Chicago, obtaining the desired
aid, and returning. Juneau rewarded Fowler with the
gift of a new suit of clothes.

When the erection of the capitol at Madison in 1837
devolved upon Commissioner Augustus A. Bird, he
made the journey from Milwaukee to the new seat of
government accompanied by more than thirty workmen. They traveled by team, making a road as they
advanced, fording streams, and threading their way
through swamps. There were drenching rains and numerous delays, so that it was ten days before the destination was reached. The journey is now made by train or
automobile in less than three hours. This was the first
road into the future capital of the territory. Congress
had appropriated $20,000 for the capitol building and
the territory, a like sum. Part of this money had to be
brought from Green Bay, and Eben Peck performed

the duty of courier. On the journey to Madison he swam several rivers, saturating the paper money, and when he arrived it was more or less dilapidated.

In the forties and fifties many plank roads were built, especially from the ports along Lake Michigan. Although lasting but a brief period, they actually were of considerable importance, enabling farmers to haul generous loads to market at fair speed. As planks decayed, gravel was substituted, making roads more permanent and valuable.

Along these roads of mud or planks crept stage-coaches, teamsters with heavy loads, and prairie-schooners bound for new scenes. Frequently a hamlet owed its existence to the tavern and in turn the tavern owed its existence to the mud in the road. Much of the time in spring and fall a streak of ooze crossed and recrossed the territory in many directions – from Milwaukee to Galena, from Chicago to Green Bay. These roads wound about in sinuous fashion often becoming forked only to unite a fraction of a mile beyond, or diverging to various points of the compass. Frequently when they intersected, it was not at right angles, hence a stranger on a cloudy day with no sun to guide him was often in a perplexing situation. Houses were few and guideboards rare.

Early travelers on these first highways had many unusual experiences. Late in December, 1836, Edward Pier left Green Bay with a horse and supplies for the home of his brother at Fond du Lac. On Lake Winnebago he encountered low temperature and a raging storm. The horse broke through the ice, and when this happened a second time he was not able to rescue the animal. Wet to the waist, boots filled with water, he pushed on and after going a considerable distance reached the home of his brother to find hands and cheeks frozen. In the meantime, his brother had gone to Green Bay for provisions; but the air filled with snow having obstructed the view they did not see each other as they passed on the lake.

At times wild animals made life uncomfortable for travelers. In 1836 Isaac B. Judson, on his way, alone in the night, from Milwaukee to Prairieville (Waukesha), was pursued by a pack of wolves. He wore a heavy cloak for protection from the cold and when the fierce animals came uncomfortably close, he shook the garment vigorously. This frightened them and during the confusion he covered as much distance as his legs would carry him. He continued this process until the McMillan Tavern was reached, where he fell exhausted. A warm fire and a bowl of punch restored his well-nigh exhausted strength. At another time E. S. Purple lost a portion of the leg of a new pair of boots, eaten by wolves. Since he was able to save his own legs from the voracious animals he did not complain of the loss.

Doctor William Fox of Dane county, in making his professional visits, would often ride a horse so far on a rainy day that his boots would become filled with water. When traveling at night over a country where there were no habitations or known landmarks, one cheek would be held against the wind in order to keep the general direction.

Extreme confidence in strangers was characteristic of early times. When William Vroman was walking from Milwaukee to Madison, as part of his journey from New York to the west, he met a man on horseback. After a brief conversation, the rider learned that the pedestrian had a brother at the capital and insisted that the stranger ride the horse back to the seat of government. This was done and Vroman later learned that his generous acquaintance was Adam Smith, a member of the legislature, who continued his way to Watertown, and later returned. Smith told Vroman where to stable the horse that he might secure it when he reached home. The simple fact that Smith knew Vroman's brother gave him full confidence in the new acquaintance.

The condition of roads in the fifties may be judged by the following incident: J. C. Lewis and Nathaniel Waterbury desired to enter land near Shawano, about one hundred miles from their home. The former decided to make the journey on foot and the latter on horseback. Spirited wagers were made by their friends regarding which would win the race. The honor was easily carried off by Mr. Lewis. On the return journey he met Waterbury on a jaded horse several miles from Shawano. A writer, telling of the incident, said that Lewis rested himself by running when he got tired of walking, and by walking when he got tired of running.

Sometimes persons got lost in their own counties; apropos of this, an amusing incident is related of a citizen of Racine. While exploring, in the thirties, the western part of the county he lost his way but soon was rejoiced to see a log cabin. Riding up he made inquiry as to where he was. A tall, long-bearded seedy fellow replied:

"Why, you're in Wisconsin!"

"Yes, but what part of Wisconsin?"

"Why, I don't know. I only kim here last week. I lived in Indiany, but folks was gettin' so plenty thar, I just pulled up stakes and squatted down whar thar wa'n't no neighbors."

Allen Perkins, another pioneer, lost his way while

wandering over unmarked Walworth county; his experience resulted in the first attempt to provide a highway by dragging the top of an oak tree from the settlement at Spring Prairie to where Delavan is now located, a dozen miles or so. The expedient made a track easily followed, and this became the most traveled road between the two places. The main highway today follows this primitive route.

Swampy places were made passable by means of corduroy roads – small logs placed on the boggy earth. Over these rough structures vehicles loudly bumped. When the first turkey-shoot was held at the home of David Bonham in the town of Lisbon, Waukesha county, a keg of beer was among the expectations. Bonham and Thomas Bradford drove to Milwaukee for the beverage. On the way home the road became so rough that the keg was violently shaken, and the bung flew out. Needless to say no amber fluid was partaken by the turkey-shooters on that occasion.

Over a corduroy road five or six miles southwest of Waupun, two men with loaded wagons met late at night. One called out,

"Are you loaded?"

The reply came that he was. One wagon carried a load of corn in bags and these were removed, the vehicle gotten to one side so the other could pass, and the corn reloaded, both men assisting good-naturedly with the task; then they bade each other good-bye.

Prior to the days of the railroad there was much hauling of freight by means of wagons drawn by oxen and horses. Often the teamsters were rude, selfish, and profane. Frequently, it was every man for himself and the devil take the hindmost. Much lead from the southwestern section was taken to Galena or to ports on Lake

Michigan with "sucker teams," these usually consisting of three yoke of oxen, and so called because the animals were brought from Illinois, the "Sucker" state. Seventy pigs of lead made a load, each pig weighing about seventy-two pounds. In 1842 nearly two million pounds of lead and 2614 kegs of shot were shipped from Milwaukee, all of which had been transported by wagon across the territory from the lead region. The following year the amount was slightly greater. The teamsters were paid ten dollars per ton for hauling, and returned with a load of salt, lumber, shingles, and other freight. From three to five tons made a load, the amount depending on the weather and on the condition of roads and animals.

Where there were no habitations, it was the custom to have regular camping places where there was plenty of water and grass, the drivers cooking their meals over camp fires and sleeping in or under their wagons. Many favorite sites were beneath trees. One such was an oak standing a short distance west of Sun Prairie, known as the "Traveler's Home." It was a frequent occurrence to see ten or a dozen prairie-schooners anchored there for the night. Teamsters prepared their frugal meals on the greensward at the base of the oak; hotel charges were nil, and feed for the stock was abundant as the prairies were productive. Heavy with slumber the men lay upon the earth and dreamed away the hours in such heaven-sent rest as only the weary know.

In these early days the teamsters frequently traveled in parties. As a rule, horses were quite sure to crave water as they approached a tavern, and a stop had to be made to assuage their thirst. It was considered that the landlord of a tavern was not properly requited unless drivers entered the barroom and obtained a three-cent drink all round, after which the procession would start for the next watering place where another of the drivers treated; and so on throughout the day. There were greedy characters in those days, men who would empty full glasses, but not all by any means became intoxicated. All had hearty appetites. It was not always possible for teamsters to procure beds even of straw, and when they could not, they were satisfied to sleep in their clothes, on robes or blankets on the floor. Teamsters and travelers, when they reached a wayside inn, were not only weary but frequently wet to the very skin. They were quite ready for the warming influence of bar or dining room.

These drivers prided themselves on the possession of a good whip. The stalk was some five feet long, with a heavy lash which each driver could crack with a sharp report. Often there was much rivalry to see who could crack his whip the loudest; the one at the head starting the contest, the next doing his best, the third striving his utmost, and so all along the line, the noise being audible a mile or more. They were the kings of the road. Every vehicle had to yield to them until the stagecoaches made their appearance. The drivers of the coaches provided themselves with long poles, to the ends of which knives were fastened. When teams hauling lead came too near, they were raked with the knives and sprang quickly away from the stage. Only a single experience was necessary for the freighters; thereafter they gave the stage plenty of room.

Freight-hauling was not without its compensations. Drivers of the heavy wagons had a unique method of obtaining liquor to quench their thirst. Stopping by the side of the highway to rest a team after a long pull, one of the six or more hoops on a barrel of whisky would be raised by pounding, a small hole bored where the hoop had been, the bulging vessel then being tipped to one side, and a convenient jug filled to the neck. A pointed piece of wood was afterwards used to plug the hole and the hoop pounded back into its proper place, the entire operation being accompanied with sundry winks and smiles. The shortage of contents was a mystery to the consignee and in those cases where he reported the discrepancy to the shipper, the darkness deepened. To solve the secret by attempting to locate the hole beneath the protecting hoop was about as profitable a venture as searching for the buried treasure of Captain Kidd in the shifting sands of some island along the sea coast. Drivers never revealed the secret, hence consignors and consignees never were able to satisfy themselves respecting their losses.

Along these primitive highways there rolled the slow accumulation of wealth in trade, the products of the farm, ore from the mine, goods from the east. Hamlets became small cities; ideas and ideals spread from tavern to tavern, from community to community. The highways were the vanguards of progress.

Stagecoach Days

Looking at Wisconsin and other midwestern states, now gridironed with railroads and improved highways, retrospective imagination is required to visualize a country whose sole means of transportation was team-drawn wagons or lumbering stagecoaches, all depending on the rural tavern for entertainment. From log shanty to palatial hotel, and from packhorse to swift express or automobile, is a far cry. Man always has advanced, but never before in so limited a time has he achieved such wonders in modes of living and of travel.

Travel by stagecoach developed slowly even after roads had been made, for ferries must be provided or bridges built. Two hundred years passed after Jean Nicolet landed in 1634 near Green Bay before a stage line was established between that city and Chicago. In some sections when stages first were operated, there were no roads. In 1836, when W. P. Ruggles came from Massachusetts to Wisconsin, the stage had made but three or four trips between Chicago and Galena, and one could scarcely discern the wagon tracks in the long prairie grass. The meals served at taverns on this line consisted generally of bread, bacon, and coffee; the bed was a sack of hay, the pillow of like material if there was one, the covering was the blanket the traveler carried with him.

A great variety of vehicles was used in transporting mail and passengers over the early highways. The most imposing of these was the Concord coach which seemed so wonderful in its decorations of gold and various gay colors that in imagination it rivaled a modern circus chariot. Some coaches cost as much as three thousand dollars – a great sum for those days.

The aspect of the driver was usually rougher and more uncouth than a close acquaintance revealed him to be. A flannel shirt, corduroy breeches stuffed into high boots, a well-worn hat or cap, and a fur or leather coat in inclement weather made up the conventional costume. In personal appearance he might be tall and lean or short and stout, yet always he was alert to meet exigencies that might arise in the course of duty. He was likely to be under forty years of age, though occasionally older men assumed the responsibilities of guiding the destinies of a coach. His complexion, tanned by the winds, showed a ruddy hue, often heightened by frequent visitations to the tavern bar. In speech he was more picturesque than grammatical, often voicing choice bits of humor or arguments graphic and convincing.

When the nineteenth century was young, at the period when the stagecoach attained its greatest vogue in this country, men universally wore whiskers. This was the age of whiskers in American history, and the important functionary atop the old stagecoach was no exception in this particular. The driver of a stagecoach was so exposed to variations of weather that it was prudent for him to grow a more luxuriant beard than men in other occupations.

Not all stage drivers were graduates of the college of Jehu. An incident is related of a stage bounding down the north slope of the Baraboo bluff, striking the rocks with resounding impact, rounding the curves at reckless rate, and passing every other vehicle on the road.

ONE OF THE LAST STAGECOACHES IN THE NORTHWEST

Used at Black River Falls before the railroad came in 1870. The driver in this picture is Ed. Pratt, who drove for Congressman W. T. Price

The four horses seemed about to take the lead and let the driver follow when the ancient coach came to a halt at the foot of a long incline. The passengers, realizing their peril as the swaying vehicle threatened at every curve to overturn, rejoiced as the youthful driver descended to make some adjustment about the harness. An elderly lady, fearing a continuance of the uncomfortable rate of speed, thrust her head out of a window and exclaimed in a voice of distress:

"Will you not drive a little more carefully, please? This is the first time I have ridden in a stagecoach."

Surprise filled the minds of the passengers at the answer which came from the adolescent holder of the whip:

"Lady, you haven't the better of me. This is the first time I have ridden in one of the things myself, mum."

Of the driver of a stage in the lead mining region in 1837, G. W. Featherstonhaugh, the English traveler, wrote:

"The driver of our vehicle was a droll cockney Englishman, about five feet high and near sixty years old, born in London, who, by his own account had never had either father or mother that he knew, and who had picked up his living in the streets there from his fifth year. After knocking about here and there, he had at length reached what may be called the pathos of all human desires for an Englishman, the situation of driver of this most wretched stage, as he called it, which was dragged by two lame, miserable horses through a country without the vestige of anything like comfort.

"At the top of his strange physiognomy was stuck the filthy remnant of what had once been a fur cap; about his neck was a disgusting handkerchief that had never been washed; an old, ragged, red blanket coat, thrice too large for him, covered his person, and beneath its ample skirts appeared two odd boots that had been patched and repaired so often that, as he said, they had been made nowhere. One of them, he remarked, was so plaguy large that he had cut a hole in the foot to let the water out, that the other was such a blessed sight too small, that he had cut a hole in that to let his toes out. Everybody we met seemed to know him except one person who said, 'General, I guess it's a toss-up whether your horses or your stage break down first.' "

Jeremiah M. Rusk, later governor of Wisconsin and later still a member of the federal cabinet, was a picturesque driver of early days. He was almost a giant in stature, big featured, and strongly bearded. As his stage neared Viroqua one day, a horse fell ill. Rusk at once tied it behind the vehicle, seized the neckyoke himself, and with his herculean strength, aided greatly in getting the coach into town. One cold day Rusk stopped the stage at a tavern near Prairie du Chien that his passengers might warm themselves. When they entered, an innocent-looking horn lay on the counter and the youthful driver was invited to blow it. He did, but instead of musical notes radiating from the circular opening of the instrument, flour covered the face of the future governor. Of course, a treat for the onlookers was imperative.

It was esteemed a privilege to ride with such drivers as Andrew Bishop, better known as "the Elder," who afterwards became sheriff of Dane county; Prescott Brigham, who drove the first stage from Madison across the Wisconsin river to Sauk county; and many others. The driver formed many abiding friendships, especially with those who shared his seat on the coach. Albeit he outdid himself, particularly if he was a single man, when a young lady mounted the seat beside him. If he was loquacious, the fluency of his language and the marvelous attention displayed afforded much amusement to others aboard the coach. Some jehus were seasoned shellbacks, however, their faces mapped with the hard furrows of time. To tip a driver with a coin never was known, but a drink of intoxicating liquor frequently was offered and rarely refused. Rusk's biographer says, however that the future governor even while driving stage, never indulged in intoxicating liquors.

An amusing incident happened on the route between Madison and Prairie du Sac. John M. Meisser, later a resident of Baraboo, was the driver and on the way home from Madison one afternoon a keg of whisky consigned to Max Stinglhammer of Sauk City accidentally rolled from the stage. While the postmaster sorted the mail at a little hamlet between the terminals of the route, the driver hurried back in search of the missing property. By great good luck he had only gone a short distance when he saw the keg, resting upon the shoulders of a brawny individual, disappear behind a rick of wood by the roadside. Pulling horses and vehicle up near the wood, it was an easy matter to look over. There on the other side was an Irishman sitting on the precious keg.

"Hello, sir! Have you seen a keg of whisky?" queried the driver.

"Yes, sir; it is right here," answered the Irishman in decisive tones.

"I lost it from my load and would like to have it again."

"Well, sir," came the defiant reply, "you will have to be a bigger man than I am to get it."

It required some time to nuzzle the keg out of the finder, but finally the release was given upon the promise of a free ride to Madison at the convenience of the culprit.

The stage driver had to go through fair weather and foul. After managing to secure a few hours of necessary sleep, he often plunged into Stygian blackness to find his way as best he could. He learned to read the road not only by day but by night, as a scholar reads a book. From the sky he interpreted the meaning of the passing cloud or encircled moon, for the omens meant either comfort or discomfort to him and his horses in the hours ahead. In the thirties and forties there were no rubber goods, hence his clothing became more or less hygroscopic – dampened anew by each passing drizzle or rain. For him there was no protection when Jove's artillery was heard in the sky.

Death sometimes rode beside the driver when the mercury descended to the twenties below zero. One cold morning as the driver of a stage from Portage to Newport (now a deserted village below Kilbourn) was hurrying along, he was noticed by those at a farmhouse to be swinging his arms to keep from freezing. As the stage passed the farm, the man with the whip shouted about the frigid temperature, and those were perhaps his last words, for when the conveyance arrived at the Steele Tavern, Newport, he was found to be dead. How the horses negotiated the steep hill just before reaching the hostelry was a cause for wonderment; and to passengers the thought of the driver perishing in the bitter air of the early morn was gruesome indeed.

The weather was not always inclement, to be sure. There were glorious mornings in the spring, summer, and autumn when possession of the reins of four strong horses, well-matched and smooth-gaited, was a joyful occupation. Every day was rich in experiences, so varied, in fact, that the Odyssey of their adventures has never been told.

Artists of a century ago frequently pictured the horses of the stagecoach as prancing, fire-breathing steeds, but upon investigation it is found that much of this picturesqueness was imaginative. It required highly practical teams to pull the coaches loaded with passengers and baggage, and the long monotonous journeys conspired to produce conspicuous ribs, pronounced backbones, and other indications of arduous toil. The animals were toughened by hard hauls and usually were subdued in spirit and inured to heat and cold, as well as endowed with unusual patience necessary for the heavy burden man imposed upon them. Harnesses were often adorned with ivory, or imitation ivory, rings. These ornaments, especially of ivory, were somewhat expensive, and tempting to drivers on rival lines. More than one driver has gone for his team and found the harnesses stripped of their gee-gaws. Changing of horses demanded quick work, and, with fingers numb from excessive cold, buckles and snaps were frequently manipulated with much difficulty.

At the Hawks Tavern in Delafield the coach topped the hill as it approached the hostelry and then rolled down the grade, which permitted a gallant dash to the front door, the driver flourishing his long whip and he or a companion blowing the horn. All ended in a masterly stop. Then the hostler's bell rang, the hostler appeared, horses were stabled, mail bags exchanged, and after dinner four new horses were attached to continue the journey to the next tavern. It was the custom of the time for the driver, when he gathered up his lines, to crack his whip as a flourish for the departure with a great hurrah and whirring of wheels, and then lazily to creep along when muddy stretches or sandy wastes were encountered. Where meals were not taken, teams were changed as quickly as possible, and the vehicle hurried onward to its destination. At terminals the animals were given a rest, watered, fed, and curried. There, too, oil was rubbed on the harness, the coach washed and the wheels greased.

The blaring of a horn often presaged the arrival of the stage at a rural post-office or village inn. A single blast, particularly during the Civil war, was sufficient to throw inhabitants into intense excitement, so eager were they to receive news from the front. The sight of the coach always brought to the door housewives with barefooted children clustered about, exhibiting as much interest as might be expected if the stage were the advance van of a circus.

The opening of a stage line generally caused great rejoicing. In 1846, when the first stagecoach drawn by four horses arrived at Beaver Dam, "men tossed their hats in triumph, women waved their handkerchiefs in delight, the dogs barked in anger, and children hid in fear and amazement." Competition developed unusual situations among stage folk. Robert Baxter owned a hotel at Prairie du Sac and operated stage lines out of the village, one of which had Mazomanie, the nearest railway station at that time, for its terminus. Two brothers, Joshua and James Long, erected a competitive hotel at Prairie du Sac and secured the government contract for carrying the mail. This exasperated Baxter, and competition waxed so warm that for a time passengers were carried from Prairie du Sac to the railway station, ten miles distant, for fifty cents including breakfast.

ADVERTISEMENTS OF STAGECOACH LINES AND TAVERNS
Newport is now a defunct town; Baraboo and the Dells are yet noted for their hotels

Of course encounters of various kinds were unavoidable, and one day an amusing incident happened at a bridge near the village of Mazomanie. In the morning sun at Prairie du Sac two glistening silk hats adorned the heads of two young attorneys, Messrs. Stewart and Tripp. Both were waiting to go in the big Baxter stage to the station at Mazomanie and Joseph Johnson, driving another vehicle and knowing Tripp well, asked him if he was in a mood for a little fun. Not realizing what mischief was in the mind of the driver of the rival line the young attorney nodded affirmatively. Johnson, with his lighter vehicle, trailed the Baxter coach until near the bridge, when he cracked his whip and feigned to pass the other conveyance. The ruse worked, for at once the wheels of the big vehicle were spinning rapidly. When the wheels struck the plank – there being a rise of several inches – the owner of one of the plug hats sitting in the forward portion, found himself hitting the roof and his precious silk tile shoved in a dilapidated condition over his ears. To make the situation more embarrassing he was thrown rearward into the lap of a lady. The next instant the other lawyer, sitting at the rear, went to the roof, his beloved stovepipe being jammed down over his head and his body flung into the center of the vehicle. As the two disciples of Blackstone ruefully brushed their crushed tiles while standing on the railway platform at Mazomanie, they gave Johnson an angry glare but he was too busy with passengers to volunteer conversation or hear caustic comment.

There always was keen rivalry on the part of drivers on this line regarding which should reach the destination first. One day the big Concord coach owned by Baxter undertook to pass the lighter vehicle driven by Johnson. The latter, instead of permitting the larger conveyance to rumble by when its driver turned aside, pulled his horses in the same direction, sending the Baxter teams and swaying coach into the ditch. Both teams came to a dead stop. The driver of the Baxter coach was in a dilemma; he could neither back out nor drive ahead for Johnson's vehicle obstructed his progress. After hastily appraising the situation, he shouted to Johnson:

"What are you doing?"

"Letting my horses rest," was the complacent reply. After a few more words Johnson moved on and the heavy stage was pulled out.

On other lines personal encounters were not infrequent and much bad blood was displayed by competing drivers when they chanced to meet on the road. In awarding mail contracts it was not an infrequent custom for firms in other states to purchase many routes and sub-let these "star" routes, as they commonly were termed. One day when the stagecoach driver, William Tarnutzer, called for the mail at Sauk City he found a new stage driver ready to take the pouches. Someone evidently had made a lower bid. Tarnutzer collected what was due him and told the stranger to join in the excitement. Both stages were operated for some time but Tarnutzer, having a wide acquaintance with persons patronizing the route, won the war. During his latter years Tarnutzer received the microscopic sum of sixty-one cents for making the daily drive between the Sauk villages and Baraboo in order to carry the mail, a total round trip distance of some thirty-five miles. To be sure, there was a revenue from passengers, each individual paying from seventy-five cents to one dollar per trip.

The nearest approach to a consolidation of stage

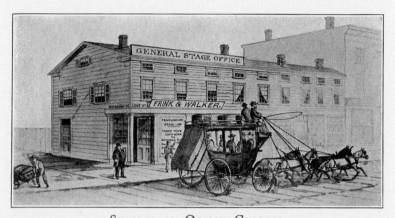

STAGECOACH OFFICE, CHICAGO

At Lake and Dearborn, whence Frink and Walker stages went to all parts of
the Northwest. John Frink sent out the first stage in 1836

TOLL HOUSE

Near Portage, Wisconsin, still standing in 1924

lines was in the days when Frink, Walker, Moore, and Davis owned routes in Illinois and Wisconsin. This firm was dissolved, Moore and Davis securing the mail contracts for Wisconsin; still later this firm also was dissolved, Moore retaining the business. Both partners had their headquarters in Milwaukee and operated lines over the greater portion of Wisconsin. When Moore died he left his wife a fortune (so considered at that time) of about twenty thousand dollars.

When the driver brought his stage to some hospitable inn where his tired passengers were to be refreshed, they were greeted by the landlord and smiled upon by the landlady, who, in anticipation, had prepared an appetizing meal. With the man of the whip at the head of the table, steaming dishes in abundance, and keen appetites, a happier picture was seldom seen. Drivers who loved their horses, who had friendly customers along the way, who found diversion at the rural inn, greatly deplored the passing of the ancient order. If there was exposure to storm, weary hours in the seat, there also was the romance in the human incidents which came under their observation or in which they played a part. Their story never has been adequately told.

Travelers' Experiences

The first travelers from the east to visit the great Northwest returned with marvelous tales of its surpassing beauty, of the regions of extensive forests, valuable water-power sites, and rich prairie land, all awaiting the coming of the settler. Throughout New York and New England especially were these reports absorbed with deep interest, and it was the aspiration of thousands, particularly of the younger generation, to migrate into the land of promise. They set forth with light hearts and came freighted with many hopes. They found but a slight veneer of civilization, naught but pristine conditions.

As these men and women from the east moved slowly along in stagecoaches or covered wagons, indian wigwams met their view in almost every direction, and inquisitive savages crept around that they might scrutinize the new arrivals and their baggage. The landscape, however, was one of infinite freshness and beauty; beautiful indeed was the panorama which greeted their vision. In summer the land was covered with a luxuriant growth of vegetation, the greater part new and strange to the newcomers. There were wild flowers of nearly every shade and color that fancy could paint or imagination conceive, and the tall prairie grass waved in luxuriance in the gentle breezes of balmy afternoons. There were crystal lakes and streams, bubbling springs and rivulets, wild animals, flocks of birds – a new paradise for man's inheritance. It was a land from which Pandora might lift a lid.

Travelers, when they reached the Northwest after the long journey on the Great Lakes, supposed they were in the far west; but in one instance this was found not to be the case. When John S. Frary reached Milwaukee he was accosted by a stranger:

"Do you want to go west, young man?"

"West!" cried the weary, homesick traveler. "West! for eighteen long days and nights have I sought the west on the fastest conveyances the country affords, and if you have anything further *west*, commend me to the first boat going *east*." He changed his mind, however, and on a rocking stagecoach moved into the interior of Wisconsin locating at the village of Oregon in Dane county.

The younger generation can scarcely realize the extent of travel across Wisconsin in the fifties. By that time much of the land east and south of the Wisconsin river had been settled, and emigrants arriving at Milwaukee and other lake ports outfitted for undeveloped regions farther west. It is estimated that during the fall and summer of 1850 more than ten thousand persons with teams and stock crossed the river at Portage. Immigrants came through in large wagons, to which were hitched four, six, or eight oxen. Often cattle, hogs, and sheep were driven along. This innumerable stream of life flowed past many a tavern, the Steele Tavern at Newport, the Red Tavern near Mauston, and numberless others along the route.

Pictures which illustrate the manner of traveling in pioneer vehicles indicate that if one were not accurately balanced in the crude conveyance his nether extremities were scheduled for sore punishment. It was quite possible that a passenger might be churned about until he longed, upon alighting at his destination, for the serv-

ices of a masseur, had this functionary been in existence at the time. On a protracted journey the coach was
liable to be dragged from one mudhole into another,
over rough corduroy roads and through rocky stretches,
up hill and down, until the patience of not only the
driver and passengers, but of the horses as well, was
near exhaustion.

The overturning of a stage was not as disastrous as a
modern train wreck; nevertheless, it provided plenty of
thrills. At the close of the Black Hawk war, the de-
feated chief and others of his tribesmen were taken by
stage over the National road to Washington in order
that they might recognize the futility of engaging in
war with the whites. At Washington, in Pennsylvania,
the horses ran away, thundered down a long steep hill
and before they were brought under control the vehicle
upset. Naturally, the indians were greatly excited; some
were injured, and as a crowd gathered Black Hawk
himself was the first to emerge from the wreck. The war
chief gave vent to his feelings with intensity.

Not infrequently passengers placed their trust in
Providence, especially when the ice across an impedi-
tive river was weak, the current cold and swift. It is a
miracle that so many escaped casualty, for drivers became careless of dangers which they encountered almost
daily along the way. When the river was open a ferry
was used in crossing, the rude floating device being attached to a cable in such a way that the current forced
it along. Occasionally the ferryboat broke from the
cable, landing the load perhaps far down the river. This
occurrence resulted in vexing delay and necessitated
much labor to bring the cumbersome vehicle back on
the highway.

When the stage over the line extending between Baraboo and Madison crossed the Wisconsin river at Merrimack on the ice, it was sometimes necessary to go on a gallop to keep from breaking through – a magnified "ticklish bender" of one's boyhood days. One wintry day Henry Cowles, the most famous driver on this line, did break through and his horses were extricated with the greatest difficulty. Timid passengers always walked across the ice and those more daring who ventured to retain their seats usually held themselves in readiness to leap to safety at any instant. Often it was necessary, when great cakes of ice came floating down, to use long poles to push the craft across, and during the fall when the Wisconsin was freezing over and when the ice was unsafe in the spring, the stage was driven to Prairie du Sac and the crossing made on a toll-bridge. Such an emergency left the village of Merrimack isolated.

Salmon E. Cowles was a driver in the fifties when his brother Henry owned the line and while driving four horses between Lodi and the present site of Waunakee, one of his wheel-animals deliberately lay down in the water and mud which filled the highway. The beast was stubborn. After much coaxing, threatening, and even punishing, it became evident that the coach with its load could not be pulled out. For passengers to step out meant to step into anything but a pleasant plight, the mud being well-nigh knee deep. For the ladies, especially, the situation was most embarrassing. At last a big, good-natured individual in the vehicle volunteered to relieve the predicament by carrying the passengers to dry land. One by one he removed the women and children, then with much maneuvering the teams were able to draw the coach upon firm ground.

When a stagecoach broke down, passengers were

compelled to sit in the cold and rain, if weather were inclement, until repairs could be effected. When a vehicle mired in a swamp or the load was too great for the teams negotiating hills, all hands must alight and help get the vehicle out of trouble.

When highways became snowy aisles through forest and farmland, and the sun looked down through flawless blue upon a world of glistening white, coaches were placed upon runners and the horses adorned with jingling bells. Passengers then rode through a landscape of immaculate loveliness free from dust and mud, their only inconvenience an occasional obstructive snowdrift. Great buffalo robes and a contrivance known as a footstove protected travelers measurably from wind and cold. The latter device was made of wood and metal combined in such manner that when live coals were placed within the stove it would radiate heat for a considerable time.

The baggage of the period was quite as unique as the mode of travel. There were queer carpetbags, strange trunks, curious boxes from foreign lands, and other nondescript pieces. Then, too, fair ones brought aboard the coach bandboxes of various kinds, some more or less attractive. In the feminine contraptions were the personal possessions of the owner, not only head-gear of various styles created through the passing years, but calashes, muskmelon hoods, and poke bonnets sufficiently large to hide pretty faces. In these pasteboard containers were likewise wigs, muffs, caps, and other wearing apparel necessary and unnecessary in the middle of the nineteenth century, the boxes filling the mission of the suitcase and wardrobe trunk of today. Boxes were of various hues and frequently elaborately decorated with pictures of Faneuil Hall, the old Philadelphia Capitol, or the Erie canal, contributing not a little to the picturesqueness of the outfit.

Early stages not only carried passengers, but express and freight. In the thirties a driver left Chicago having aboard a savage-looking wolf urgently wanted in Racine. Nimrods at that place had decided upon a hunting contest with Norman Clark as leader on one side and Marshall M. Strong on the other. These two individuals had "chosen up" and it was agreed that all kinds of game could be counted; a squirrel to equal a certain number of points, a rabbit another number, muskrat additional points. Deer were to count three hundred, a live wolf one thousand. It was further agreed that scalps of these creatures might be secured by fair means or foul, the heads of the animals to be in evidence on the designated day of reckoning. Clark and his companions heard of a deer hunter on Pleasant Prairie who had a generous collection of heads which were much desired. Without obtaining permission to use the animal, a horse belonging to Schuyler Mattison, a stranger in the town, was appropriated and driven hastily through the drifts to secure the collection by purchase. In the meantime the Strong contingent heard of a live wolf in Chicago and ordered it shipped by stage forthwith. When the stage reached the Willis Tavern, Captain Smith and a party of rollicking soldiers came out from Southport (Kenosha) and the captain ended the career of the wolf by striking it on the head with a bottle of gin. While this drama was being enacted Strong learned of a trapper at Milwaukee who had enough muskrats heads to fill a sleigh. When these were secured they out-counted everything in sight. The hunt was at an end and everybody was mad. Clark had ruined the Mattison horse and had to pay damages amounting to seventy-five dollars. Strong sued Captain Smith for killing the wolf with a bottle of gin. It was the first court action in Racine county, and the verdict was for six cents damages with costs. Stage drivers and taverners were important witnesses, the affair was one of much local celebrity.

During the middle of the nineteenth century the pendulum of life swung in wide arcs; slavery or no slavery was the paramount question. Freesoilers, Democrats, and Republicans contended at the ballot box. The Kansas-Nebraska bill, border warfare, the fugitive slave law, John Brown, and other topics were daily discussed. A storm was impending, hot human volcanoes were in eruption, and souls were set on fire by verbal friction. With an atmosphere thus surcharged, it was not surprising that passengers often found themselves in a turmoil as the old stage swayed and bumped along the road.

Among the passengers when stage lines were first opened were lawyers, doctors, preachers, newspapermen, lumbermen, traders, and settlers seeking to place their feet on the ladder of fame or gain a place of abode in the new country. In the fifties and sixties numerous raftsmen floated down the Wisconsin river to some snubbing post on the bank and resorted to stages for their return. During the Civil war soldiers were frequently passengers from railway stations to homes in the interior, bringing many thrilling tales of the sanguinary conflict. The fall of Vicksburg inspired citizens of Dodgeville to indulge in a brilliant celebration. The news reached the village from Mineral Point about midnight, the messengers riding their horses at a gallop and shouting the glad tidings. Soon the entire community was astir. Bonfires were built at street intersections and men toted combustible material from every quarter of the village. The band played, the crowd marched, and John Sagers served liquid refreshments with utter indifference to cost. The fanfare embraced the whole populace; it was a unique and grandiose celebration. In the midst of all the excitement the stage arrived bringing home William George, a soldier on furlough. Old friends gathered about and as he beheld the town ablaze his astonishment was complete. Thinking all the jubilation and illumination was in his honor he threw up his hands, exclaiming: "Great Heavens! how did you know that I was a-coming?"

Not infrequently there were aboard coaches individuals who were suspected of being horse thieves. They seldom had their eyes on the stage property, however, for there were more spirited beasts to be had in an open pasture or unlocked stall. Then there were peddlers with their packs, and speculators in prosperous dress. During the frenzied hop period, pickers arriving at stations were conveyed to the hop-yards, and of hop-pole pullers there were not a few.

Criminals and others making a hurried departure sometimes resorted to stagecoaches. In the early days of LaFayette county there was a dispute between two men respecting rights to a piece of mineral land. Both became angry, a crowd of miners gathered, and a duel followed. One contestant for the land drew an old pepper-box revolver and proceeded to fire upon his enemy. The other replied by seizing a rock and hurling it dangerously near his foe. By this time he of the weapon was ready to fire again only to find another boulder thrown defiantly at him. Back and forth, first pistol, then rock, the fray continued until the last ball had been fired when the holder threw down the gun and fled in the full belief that he had riddled his enemy with bullets. Rushing to the nearest village he mounted a horse that he found hitched to a post, saddled and bridled. Without leave of the owner he rode the animal with all speed a distance of ten miles to the barn of Frink and Walker on the stage route between Galena and Chicago, where he left the panting steed by the side of the highway and took hasty passage for the east. According to an early account of the affair the fellow did not cease his flight until he reached Rome, New York. As a result of the collision the man of the rocks, after making a thorough examination of himself, found there was a hole through the rim of his hat. Besides the perforation he secured the pistol as a souvenir of the affair with full possession of the "diggins" for future operations, and cheers from the approving crowd.

When officers were on the trail of a criminal, coaches sometimes made unusual speed. The distance from Madison to Baraboo is thirty-five miles by way of Lodi and Merrimack, and Salmon E. Cowles once drove it in six hours, the usual schedule being eight. A sheriff was aboard from Janesville and offered the driver ten dollars provided he reduce the time two hours. The stage reached its destination within the desired limit, the extra bonus was paid, and the criminal was apprehended.

Before the advent of the railroad in England, so many coaches were attacked by highwaymen that passengers frequently made their wills and said their prayers before setting out upon a journey. Britons insisted on carrying gold when traveling and this practice encouraged bold men to commit crime. In the western part of the United States gold carried as express on stagecoaches and by passengers was an invitation for the Jesse James style of bandit to gallop up, firing shots in the air as a warning to all to yield to his demands. In that section of the country, with its mountains and swiftly running streams, if passengers escaped with their lives from the great variety of natural dangers, there always was a chance of highwaymen stripping them of their money and leaving them injured or dying. Seldom were coaches disturbed in New England or in the Great Lakes region, as drafts and bills of exchange were largely used instead of cash.

When Moore and Davis operated a stage line between Galena and Mazomanie, then a railway station, a driver was discharged as the vehicle was near the Ruggles farm. Upon leaving he stole the mail pouch from the boot of the coach and this never was recovered. Years after silver coins were plowed up in a field some distance from the scene of the robbery and it is surmised that, in searching through the letters before burying the contents of the sack, the thief missed the coins. When these were brought to light the story of the theft was revived.

Raymond Holzse (pronounced Holsay and spelled variously) was a real bandit. He practiced shooting by mounting a horse and riding swiftly around a tree firing at a bull's eye. Sometimes he varied his program by tossing up hazel-nuts and cracking them with revolver shots. In the spring of 1890 a stage was held up between Pulcifer and Bonduel, the losses being small. The crime was thought to be the work of Holzse. About ten o'clock the morning of May 8, of the same year, as Herman Rafoth was driving a coach from the north toward Shawano, he heard an unusual sound behind and looking about beheld a revolver pointing at his face. Only two passengers were aboard, Thomas Ainsworth and a

RAYMOND HOLZSE

Bandit of northern Wisconsin, who planned several stage holdups

HERMAN RAFOTH

Driver of stage held up by Holzse, north of Shawano

Menominee indian. The driver at once brought his team to a stop and Holzse ordered the mail pouch thrown out. Rafoth asked Ainsworth what he should do and was advised to obey commands. After the mail had been surrendered the bandit bade the driver produce what money he had with him. Eleven dollars was passed over, the thief accusing the man of having more, which he denied. However, Rafoth did actually have forty-five dollars in his vest pocket and retained it by his equivocation. The bandit next turned to Ainsworth who was ordered to produce his money. The latter had nine dollars and seventy-five cents which Holzse threw upon the mail pouch lying on the ground. The indian was not molested. As the driver took up his reins to drive away, Ainsworth remarked to the highwayman that he was sorry he did not have an even ten dollars and told him to remember that he owed him a quarter. Holzse tartly commanded the man to close his mouth, to go down the road, and not to look back. After proceeding a short distance the occupants of the vehicle ventured to turn about and beheld the fellow ripping open the pouch with a knife. The loss was almost nothing as there were only two checks in the mail and these were worthless to the thief.

A number of episodes, some amusing, some of a serious nature, followed quickly. The driver, Rafoth, was taken by the sheriff to a neighboring town to identify a suspect and in his absence a youth was employed to drive the stage. On the return trip to Shawano a lumberjack suddenly appeared in the road and waved his pack as a signal for the conveyance to stop. Instead of bringing his horses to a halt the driver cracked his whip, and team and vehicle dashed by, leaving the expectant passenger standing in anything but a placid frame of mind. When later he accosted the driver demanding to know why he had not stopped, the boy declared he did not propose to be held up by a bandit. The suspect, taken by the officer, was not the highwayman who had stopped Rafoth.

Holzse might have given up his criminal practices but he was not of that kidney. Whether or not he ever had heard of Dick Turpin, it is a fact he had not far to go to emulate his fearless feats. He loved the limelight and his undoing was the consequence of his taking just one chance too many. Near Marquette, Michigan, he stopped a stage, warned all aboard there should be no shooting, but a passenger fired. At once Holzse sent ball after ball into the vehicle, killing one passenger, wounding another and twice piercing the hat of the driver. Following this he was captured and sentenced to the penitentiary for life, but later was paroled.

At one time stage lines crossed and re-crossed the state, linking hamlet and city in a network of communication. What has become of these hundreds of swaying, gilded vehicles? With the advent of the railroad they were either sent to remoter sections or became useless property. One of the last in Wisconsin, owned by W. T. Price at Black River falls, was permitted to fall to pieces in a barnyard.

Concerning some of these faithful old friends of our forefathers, the Concord coaches, W. W. Warner of Madison, in his youth a resident of Baraboo and its benefactor in death, wrote as follows:

"This was, I should say, about 1868-1869. Who among the boys who participated in that famous escapade, may ever forget? Be it known, there were fifteen or twenty antique, superanuated Concord stagecoaches which had been one after another placed, so to

speak, in dry dock and out of commission, having outlived their further transportational usefulness, and thus
they were housed in a rambling series of sheds, just
back of the present city hall. We young chaps, the day
after a Fourth of July celebration, conceived the idea
of decorating Oak street with the dilapidated vehicles.
Some of the chariots, I remember, bore euphonious
names – such as Argosy, Prairie Queen, and Western
Monarch. Those who remember the one-time resplendent coaches, gorgeous beyond the dreams of a Ringling
circus creation, will recall that they were integers connecting Baraboo with relatively near-by points of the
outside world, such as Madison, Mazomanie, Portage,
and Kilbourn. . .

"It was long after midnight when we scamps, as ex-
peditiously and as quickly as possible, hauled forth a
score of the nondescript vehicles from their moorings,
to the Western Hotel street corner, and thence made an
imposing string of them, reaching almost to the present
post office site, and a fine spectacle they presented early
next morning! Not many citizens of Baraboo were
aware that such antediluvian chariots were in existence,
much less that they were right here in Baraboo. The
general astonishment, therefore, may well be imagined.
What opportunities were lost in their destruction, short-
ly after this, their last appearance, for securing match-
less museum antiques! But soon trouble – our trouble –
began. Somehow the city officials and many of the older
and more staid, law-abiding citizens, did not take kindly to such deviltry, and public resentment was quite
general, while diligent efforts were at once put forth
to apprehend the several juvenile malefactors involved
in the disgraceful escapade."

Some of the principals in this adventure sought remote wheat fields and remained away from Baraboo until the turbulent state of the public mind had subsided. Perturbed parents in other cases paid modest fines.

A century ago not even the most envisioned citizen could have dreamed that the old stagecoaches on the great highways of the country would be relegated to oblivion. Such a conception was as impossible as could be the projective abolition of railroad or automobile to the present generation. The old stage routes were the arteries of communication between city and city, village and village, hamlet and hamlet. It was the accepted mode of travel. Especially did the sages of that day consider the bumping coach with plodding team the extreme of comfort and speed, and that no greater advance of transportation would ever be reached. These elderly gentry visualized the time when the traveler urged his horse along an indian trail or blazed way, fording unbridged streams, plunging through swamps, and penetrating forests beset with savages. No wonder they stood in admiration before a stagecoach with four sturdy steeds attached, ready to carry them in shelter from the torrid sun or bedraggling rain.

The Log Tavern

The type of public house, universal in the beginning of western frontier development, has all but passed away. Save for a few examples in the northern regions and those built at summer resorts to attract tourists, log taverns are but memories dear to the pioneer. Here and there through the country one may discover a little sward-covered mound where a chimney fell, but these are about all that remain of once busy places of entertainment.

Log taverns were built at a time when nature was resplendent and lavish with material and brilliant touches. The rude dwelling places arose among the monarchs of the forest where openings admitted sunlight and their shadows fell across stretches of grass dotted with wild flowers. The surrounding landscape was freshly beautiful and full of interest and wonder to the pioneer, but for most of the landlords and their families occupancy of a tavern meant a never-ending round of duties that left little leisure for contemplation of nature's attractions.

Naturally, these early taverns were of the plainest construction. No time was wasted in ornamentation. Simple homes they were in the wilderness, where the wayfarer might find needed rest and refreshment as he journeyed through the country. Rooms in these primitive places of entertainment were usually about fourteen feet square. Double log cabins were common. These consisted of two rooms with a hallway between, or if the cabins stood close together, with a single doorway connecting the two portions.

The construction of a log tavern was an important event in a neighborhood. Settlers came to assist with the work, frequently laboring without price, especially at the raising. Care was always exercised in cutting the trees that they might be of proper size and it was necessary that they should be straight. A day or two before the cabin was to be raised, the foundation was laid. The first logs were placed, and others to support the floor rested upon these. In case a puncheon floor – one made by splitting trees about eighteen inches in diameter, faced with a broadaxe – was to be used, the timber was selected, prepared, and often laid before the sidewalls of the cabin were erected. The puncheons were kept in place largely by their own weight. If boards were to be used as flooring, lumber was cut from logs for the purpose with a whipsaw. In rare cases the earthen floor without covering was deemed sufficient. On raising day, from far and near, men came to assist in the task. If enough helpers were present, cornermen were selected whose duty it was to cut notches in the ends of the logs as they were rolled up, that these might fit well together. The office of cornerman was quite important, so those chosen for this work must be men of experience, skillful with the ax.

After the first logs were in place the remaining ones were raised to the cornerman by means of skids, rolled up by men with handspikes and pikepoles. Shorter logs were used at the gable ends of the cabin, or in some cases boards were nailed over the triangular openings. Early builders had recourse to what are known as shakes or clapboards for roofing. Logs extending the length of the building provided a place on which to

LOG HOUSE NORTH OF BROTHERTOWN

East shore of Lake Winnebago. The logs were placed on end with plaster
between in old French-Canadian fashion

STEELE TAVERN AT NEWPORT

A deserted town on the Wisconsin river below the Dells. This tavern, built
in 1849, was razed about 1909

rest these, and they were held in position by means of long poles on the roof. Shakes were rived from straight blocks of hardwood about three feet long, their production involving many hours of labor. The best timber, generaly red oak, was used and the splitting was done with a frow, an iron tool with sharp edge and an opening at one end into which a handle was inserted. In appearance the instrument was not unlike a capital L. A wooden mallet served to drive the blade into the timber.

By cutting logs already laid or by using shorter ones doorways were made. Logs above the opening extended the full length of the cabin; those at the sides were held in place by nails or pins through the door jambs – boards placed at each side of the entrance. If sawed lumber was not available for doors, they were made of "splits" or long clapboards, rived from a log and fastened to crosspieces. Ends of the crosspieces of the door and two short pieces fastened at the side, each containing an auger hole, provided a way for hanging the door, which was accomplished by means of a long pin or two short ones thrust through these openings. Often no nails were used in the construction of these rude taverns, wooden pins alone being employed. In case nails were obtaincd they were usually the product of the forge of the local blacksmith.

Sometimes there was apprehension on the part of the taverner that sufficient help would not be on hand for the raising but usually fear was set at rest when the day arrived. People were only too glad to help get a tavern up, so there was rarely lack of willing hands. In that day the rule was: help one another. In no other way could important tasks be performed. Woe to the one who exhibited laziness on raising day. If he shirked, when the time came that he needed assistance, his punishment was sure. On the log tavern at Fond du Lac indians did much of the work and no doubt in other instances they gave needed aid.

In cutting shakes, the heart of the tree, a three-cornered piece, was always left. This was used to chink the cabin. After these small pieces of timber were fixed in the openings between the logs, the remaining apertures were filled with clay.

At one end of the cabin a chimney was built for the large fireplace, the more rapidly to burn the wood which was in abundance on every hand. The opening for the chimney was provided in the same manner as that for the door, by laying up short logs or sawing out the proper space. If brick was not at hand, stones were used for the hearth and for the sides and back of the chimney. Frequently the upper portion was constructed by laying up split sticks which were later covered with mud. When lime could not be secured, clay mixed with grass or straw was used. It was necessary to renew the clay from time to time, but even with this precaution fires were frequent. Chimneys built cobhouse fashion of sticks and mud were called "cat and clay" chimneys; others were made of sod plastered on the inside with mud, and occasionally flat pieces of sandstone or limestone were available for the purpose. When the last were used the crevices between were filled with mud.

Ventilation in these primitive homes was not lacking. The great open fire carried a constant current of air upward, and more often than not openings between the logs, which the chinking had not entirely closed, afforded generous drafts. To protect the rear portion of the fireplace as well as to throw the heat outward, a backlog of green elm or other slow-burning wood was rolled into the opening before a blaze was kindled. In front of this a roaring fire was built. It was ample exercise to cut logs and manhandle them for the fire; and as to split sticks, they afforded a fine assortment of splinters to irritate the fingers.

If, as sometimes happened, no chimney was provided light percolated into the cabin through an aperture left for the escape of smoke. Otherwise it shone through the large chimney opening, through a hole in the wall over which oiled paper had been pasted, or through small panes of glass, usually six in a sash, the panes ordinarily being eight by ten inches in size. Prior to the appearance of the kerosene lamp the open fire, the tallow candle, or a little oil lamp provided illumination at night.

No locks were on the doors of early taverns; simply latches. The wooden latch was placed on the inside of the door and a string was fastened to this which it was the custom to hang out during the day. The latchstring outside was an emblem of hospitality. At night the string was drawn in, barring the entrance. In case an unknown indian or any undesirable person approached, the latchstring could easily be pulled in, effectually preventing entrance. If it was considered desirable to lock the door during the absence of the taverner and his family, the latchstring was forced inside, through the small opening provided, and the door was opened by means of a wire which pulled the string outside. The latch also could be raised by means of this wire, which was kept secreted in a crevice or other hiding place near-by. Sometimes in the wall of the cabin near the latch a block was placed, easily removed by those in the secret. By this means a door could be opened without difficulty, the latch being within reach of the hand when the block was out. Only members of the family or near neighbors would be likely to know of the location of the block. It was the custom, however, to leave doors unlatched. Petty larceny was unknown in most communities. Travelers when they found no one at home were free to enter and eat and drink whatever was in sight, but they rarely carried away property.

Commonly, during the first summer of the erection of the tavern, doors and windows were merely indicated by openings. Blankets or quilts served to obstruct the view of curious indians at the doorways and to hinder the entrance of vexing mosquitoes.

Some of the taverns had primitive winding stairways which led to low-ceilinged attics. Frequently these stairways were nothing more than wooden pins driven into the logs which constituted the side of the cabin. Sometimes a rude ladder was used, made by splitting a sapling and inserting rounds of smaller saplings into the halves. The attics usually were only high enough to accommodate persons on their hands and knees; the floor was made of rough boards or poles. Thus it was only by dexterous use of hands and feet that one could reach the region above at nightfall and descend in the early morn. Sometimes the sides of a wagonbox were pressed into service as flooring of the attic and each time the wagon was used the boards had to be brought down.

On wintry nights the fireplace was piled with flaming logs and sticks. From the ends of the green timber there was much simmering of sap as it was driven out by the expanding heat. When storms prevailed and gales swept over the snow-mantled country, the tavern family and guests had to keep warm as best they could before the open fire. The men smoked, providing there was tobacco in the pouch, and the women plied their needles, if yarn was in the basket. Here guests related experiences or gave expression to hopes which stretched down the uncertain road of the future; mention no doubt was frequent of home and friends behind, the latter perhaps waiting for a convenient season to join the army of frontiersmen.

More often than not the household cat and dog managed to find comfortable resting places on the hearthstone, and children romped merrily or grouped themselves in fascinated attention as some one related with thrilling detail an encounter with indians, or boasted of his prowess in a bear hunt. When the fire burned brightly shadows were cast along the puncheon floor at the rear of the room, the heads of the company often dancing airily on the rough walls or beamed ceiling. As the blaze burned low and coals glowed between the andirons, the stories ceased and the old adage, "Early to bed and early to rise, makes a man healthy, wealthy, and wise," was voiced by some drowsy individual.

Sometimes it chanced that the fire was not properly covered when the taverner and his household retired and the last ember faded away during the night. In the morning it was necessary to send the children to a neighbor to borrow fire, which was frequently brought in a kettle or other receptacle, dry twigs being added to keep the embers aglow as they proceeded on the homeward way. If this was not done, it was necessary to kindle a fire with flint and tinder, matches not being abundant at that time.

Furniture in early taverns was of the simplest pattern. Landlords were far from being men of means, and had they been ever so able, rarely was it possible to purchase furniture in the new country. That not brought with the family of the taverner was likely to be homemade. Tables were often constructed by cleating puncheons together on posts, though occasionally a cabin boasted a table of boards. Sometimes a door between two rooms was used for the purpose, and as the cotton fabric which served as a table-cloth was apt to allow moisture from teacups or other dishes to penetrate, the door was often ornamented with a series of rings of varying sizes. These were suggestive of good dinners to those who understood the signs, but were perplexing to the uninstructed.

Not unusual was it to see on the lower floor of a cabin a bedstead standing on one leg. A forked stick usually served for this purpose; the ends of the rails supporting the bedtick being inserted in the logs of the wall, a single stick was sufficient to uphold the bed. In the earliest cabins no cords were tied from side to side on the rails, clapboards laid across serving instead. Often the clapboards were covered only with dry grass, sometimes humorously referred to as "prairie feathers." A bed thus constructed was given the unusual name of "catamount." Bedsteads were, however, usually corded, the ropes running backward and forward around short, upright wooden pins in rails and end pieces, forming squares about nine inches across. If rope was not available strips of twisted bark were substituted. On this corded base blue beech wood riven into fine splinters, after the manner of an indian broom, was placed to serve as a mattress.

Covering on tavern beds was apt to be scanty, often so lacking as to require the addition of the occupant's clothing for comfort. In corded beds there was commonly a sagging towards the middle that added not a little to the discomfort of the situation. Coverings of skins had merit in the minds of the toil-weary members of the taverner's family, as they did not have to be laundered.

These humble sleeping quarters were by no means as uncomfortable as might be imagined, especially when the thrifty housewife had placed a tick of marsh hay or dried grass on cords or clapboards, and perhaps had added a well-filled featherbed. Many times they won as sweet repose for the traveler as more pretentious couches have offered to his descendants.

Rude three-legged stools were common articles of furniture. They were constructed by boring holes in flat-sided pieces of timber and inserting legs. Sometimes a few chairs were brought by wagon with the family, many of these being of the "split-bottom" variety.

Two pins driven into the logs above the fireplace provided support for the mantel-board, and two inverted forks of small trees fastened above the mantel or over a door were useful as a resting place for the ever present gun. It will be noted that the tools necessary for the construction of the tavern were few – the ax, saw, hammer, adz, and frow being about all that were in use.

Some taverns were scrubbed and cleaned until they fairly shone. The floor of split puncheons or sawed boards often was worn smooth. It was not unusual to see the area about the fireplace flecked with black discolorations where hot coals had popped out to leave scars on the combustible wood. Much or all of the cooking in early log taverns was of necessity done before the open fire. Potatoes were baked in the ashes, meats were roasted by the blaze or boiled in a kettle, and bread was done to a turn before the fire or baked in a "dutch" oven.

Dishes were few, generally decorated in blue, brown, or the well-known mulberry coloring in various designs. In case there was a scarcity, additional ones were made by smoothing off pieces of timber, in which a slight depression was cut. The novelty of a plate of this kind often served as an appetizing spice to an otherwise ordinary meal.

Although timber was over-abundant in the country, some early taverners could not refrain from utilizing material found in indian wigwams. Potawatomi shanties near Waukesha for instance were quite substantial, being covered with bark and these were left intact when the indians made their annual journeys to deeper woods to pass the winters. When B. S. McMillan arrived at this place and erected his tavern and adjoining sheds, he decided that some of the material in near-by wigwams could conveniently be employed. Warned by his neighbors not to disturb the habitations, he insisted that the indians were not likely to return and if they should, would do nothing in retaliation. A few days later, however, some of them did appear, nor did they leave the same day as McMillan hoped they might. "Mac," as he was everywhere called, had a fine horse and was forewarned that the indians would be likely to depart with it sometime in the night. Fearing for the safety of the animal, he tied it to the doorlatch, declaring they could not take it without his knowledge. On peering through a crack in the door the next morning, the innkeeper found that his pony had disappeared along with other valued property, and the record goes

that never afterward did he see hide or hair of the
creature or catch a glimpse of the confiscated property.
McMillan never again appropriated indian belongings
without permission.

Most early taverns in the Northwest territory were
erected of logs and located near indian villages, far
from white neighbors. When Ebenezer Brigham established himself in 1828 at Blue Mounds, and Wallace
Rowan soon after built his rude hut on the western
shore of Lake Mendota, the two doughty adventurers
were so far on the frontier they did not know at what
moment the redmen might appear in full war panoply
of paint and feathers, brandishing scalping knives. In
fact, these two lowly meccas of entertainment were in
the very midst of exciting scenes of indian hostilities a
few years later, during the crisis of the Black Hawk
war. Naturally, too, these first tavern folk had strange
and ofttimes thrilling experiences with smaller groups
of the aborigines. Frequently the tribesmen were their
first visitors and came freely thereafter, so that occupants of taverns were of necessity brought into close
relationship with them.

Brigham, a bachelor, was imposed upon unwittingly
by two indians during his proprietorship of his famous
pioneer hostelry. He was born at Shrewsbury, Massachusetts, in 1789; came to Saint Louis while it was yet
but a straggling French settlement; reached Galena
where there was only a single cabin; and after a short
sojourn in Springfield, Illinois, came in 1827 to the
lead mining region of Wisconsin in the southern portion of the state. The next year he built a cabin at Blue
Mounds; and was there during the excitement of the
Black Hawk war and for a number of years after. In-

evitably he had much experience with indians. The following is but one of several recorded episodes in which redmen figured:

Caramaunee, an old Winnebago head chief, accompanied by a second indian, Chief Snake, had made a journey to Washington to consider matters of interest between the tribe and the Great Father. During their stay in the East, they had learned not a little English and also some of the etiquette practiced by white people. When ready to depart from the national capital, they were provided with new blankets, an abundance of trinkets, money to pay for transportation home, and likewise an order from the War Department at Washington to the commanding officer at Fort Dearborn, Chicago, for two horses to carry them to their native haunts in what afterward became the state of Wisconsin.

Filled with pride and loaded with new possessions, never were happier indians than the two chiefs as they proudly rode away from Chicago. The inflation of their vanity had not abated when they reached the log tavern on the sunny slope of Blue Mounds; and Caramaunee, knowing Brigham, it was decided that here was a splendid opportunity to display some of the politeness and shrewdness which they had learned from the palefaces.

They galloped up to the tavern, when the boniface was thus accosted:

"How! How! Brigham!"

Swinging from his saddle, the chief presented his companion:

"Brigham, Mr. Snake; Mr. Snake, Brigham."

Pointing first to the tavern, the chief said:

"Brigham, dinner." Next he pointed to the stable,

"Brigham, horses, corn. Big man, me."

There being no domestic help within many miles, Brigham did his own cooking and other work about the tavern. In order to please his important guests, he summoned one of his workmen to assist in preparing a meal for the hungry indians. From the rapidity with which the food disappeared, it was considered doubtful by the landlord and assistant whether the red travelers had partaken of refreshment since they left the fort at Chicago, a distance of almost two hundred miles.

Having satisfied their appetites, the indians arose from the table and Caramaunee called out:

"Brigham, horses." The animals were brought from the stable and the two chiefs mounted forthwith, Caramaunee shouting:

"Brigham, good-bye," as they departed at full speed.

Brigham was buncoed. All he could say was that having gone to so much trouble, they might have paid him for the meal, especially as the chief had made a display of a quantity of silver coin furnished by the government to defray expenses on the homeward journey.

Subsequent to the Black Hawk war Rowan removed from Lake Mendota and erected a log tavern on the Military road at Poynette; there he entertained Robert L. Ream, father of the sculptress, Vinnie Ream. Ream, then a boniface at Madison, was making a journey to Fort Winnebago and Portage. On his homeward way from the fort he remained over night at Rowan's, and at the dawn of day discovered what he thought was a small flock of sheep scattered around on the floor of the room in which he had slept; but on closer observation he found that they were indians. They had come in during the night from some trading post, where they had obtained new white blankets and had taken possession of the floor without disturbing the sleeper.

In 1836 James Duane Doty, afterward governor of the territory of Wisconsin, and other speculators purchased land where the city of Fond du Lac is located, made a plat, erected a tavern, and notified the world that a new municipality had been founded. The Fond du Lac House, as the inn was known, consisted of three log cabins united, there being an open hall between dining room and sitting room, with a kitchen at the rear. A number of Brothertown indians, partially civilized, who resided fifteen miles distant on the east side of Lake Winnebago, raised the building, the land company having provided funds for its construction. Colwert Pier supervised the work and became the first landlord of the hostelry. Mrs. Pier, his bride, did not arrive until some time after. When the boat which brought her had sailed down the lake and full realization came that she and her husband were alone in the wilderness, surrounded by hundreds of savages, the homesick woman sat down upon the ground and wept. Pier attempted to comfort his wife. Presently, they put up a stove and at last Mrs. Pier dried her tears and set about getting the primitive home in as habitable a condition as possible. The first guest at the new tavern was a squaw. The indian woman made Mrs. Pier understand that she desired to exchange feathers for flour. When the trade was made, the indian evidently thought she had the better of the bargain, for soon after the room was filled with squaws anxious to barter feathers for either flour or pork. No white visitors appeared until March of the following year.

To the erection of these early taverns, prior to purchase of rights from the indians and before government surveys, the redmen sometimes objected. When John Andrews and Henry H. Camp appeared at Mukwonago, the indian title not having been extinguished, the tribesmen would not permit the construction of a house in their village. The improvement was made a mile and a half away, however, and there General Henry Dodge and others were entertained. Delayed but not driven from their purpose the two white men continued negotiations with the indians and at last were permitted to erect a house within the village by giving two barrels of flour for the accommodation. A hut ten by twelve feet was built, and this became the lodging place of nearly all the early white settlers who came to that region.

The flavor of a night in a pioneer Wisconsin tavern is transmitted in a crisp description by the Reverend S. A. Dwinnell, a frontier minister, located for many years at Reedsburg. When this worthy man came to Lake Geneva in the fall of 1836, he was entertained at the Warren Tavern and his experience there is interesting:

"On the morning of November 15, 1836, I set my face toward the north, from Belvidere, Illinois, with a view of exploring Wisconsin. At 4:00 P.M. I entered Wisconsin at Big Foot prairie, an area of 16,000 acres, where not a furrow had been turned, soon after which I left the indian trail for the white man's dim track through the grass, and proceeded east on the south side of Big Foot lake, which was from time to time in view. As night set in, snow fell plentifully. At length, a welcome light from a distant window appeared, and I soon crossed a stream and a newly made mill-race, upon the north bank of which was a human dwelling.

"I had reached the outlet of Big Foot, as Geneva lake in what is now Walworth county was called – having traveled in solitude thirty-five miles without seeing a human dwelling. I knocked at the rude door of an equally rude log cabin, and heard the backwoodsman's welcome, 'Come in.' As I entered there seemed to be a poor chance for my entertainment. About a dozen men sat upon a backless bench before a hot fire of huge logs piled in the north end of the cabin. There was no chimney, and the smoke and sparks made their way through an opening left in the roof for that purpose. The floor of the cabin was of the natural earth and there was no chamber. The roof was made of shakes held in place by small logs laid upon the ends of them. Not a nail was in any part of the structure, I think. There were two chairs near the northeast corner of the room, in which two females were plying their needles. After an apology for the rude fare I could get, which I suppose was intended as a kind of bar against grumbling, I was permitted to remain. The meals were plain but bountiful and good.

"During the evening I wondered where they would lodge all their family and guests, as there was but one bed in the cabin and no other room apparent. My fears were removed at bedtime, however, by finding that there was a small room adjoining, over the door to which hung a blanket, which I had not distinguished from the clothing which hung in profusion around the room. In each corner of this sleeping room was a bedstead, which illustrated the truth of the proverb that necessity is the mother of invention; for each bed had but one leg, the rails at the other ends being inserted in the logs which composed the walls of the building. The bed was made of dried grass called prairie feathers, and laid upon shakes instead of cords. A bedstead thus constructed was known by the name of 'catamount.' A slight covering for it, to which the clothes of the sleeper were added, furnished a more desirable resting place than the wet ground on a cold stormy night; of which I then had a recent experience. A comforter was spread upon us before morning in the shape of a mantle of snow, sifted through the shakes of the roof over our heads."

The log tavern, homely but companionable, often impressed the traveler with a vague air of mystery. Landlords, however garrulous they might be in regard to current happenings, frequently exhibited a decided unwillingness to communicate anything of interest concerning years spent in former locations. This encouraged idle talk, which often resulted in rumors enveloping certain places of entertainment. Shadowy veils of comment, whether deserved or not, thus clung to many a hostelry. But the atmosphere of taverns usually was one of simple hospitality and good cheer. Like people they radiated personality, and names and certain attributes had their share, as well as the character of the boniface, in making them known as more or less inviting havens. However strange or rough their exteriors or interiors might be, frequently they were the only choice for the traveler of places of entertainment by day or night.

Taverns usually stood in neighborhoods or small hamlets where the inhabitants possessed about the same amount of worldly goods as the innkeeper. As to wealth or poverty, there was no classification. There were of course grades of society, if they might be so considered. There were people who came from good families, people of unclassified families, and people of whom no questions were asked. Everybody knew everyone, and notwithstanding past records which might be known, a comradeship existed among all who assembled in taverns.

Often the location of a tavern by a ford or spring was assurance of the success of the place of entertainment. Travelers then as now demanded shortening of distances, and this frequently meant the employment of a ford or ferry across a stream. Sometimes there was a contest for the retention of an old road; but inevitably changes were made, although they might cause the abandonment of one tavern and the establishment of another.

Quite remunerative were log taverns to those who desired to engage in the business of accommodating strangers. Their cost was low, and when well built the outlay for repairs over many years was negligible. No one ever suggested that a coat of paint would help their appearance; the plumbing needed no repairing, and the floors did not require a machine to wax them or a brush to give them varnish every year or two. In winter, wood from the near-by forests kept them healthfully warm, and when the season arrived for the appearance of the assessor, the owner felt no temptation to misrepresent their value.

Consideration of taverns of early times is like knocking at the door of yesterday. Soon the last of them will be numbered with things that were. Motorists passing swiftly along roads, once stage routes, rarely note these occasional weather-worn buildings whose shadows pattern the wayside; or if they do, only remotely realize the interest and romance that hover about these pioneer places of entertainment.

Taverns of a Later Time

Log taverns were ephemeral, giving way in time to those of frame, brick, stone, and gravel. Timbers of frame buildings were joined together with wooden pins forming sections to be elevated on the day of the raising, a notable affair in the community. Following the fashion of the time, invitations were sent to all in the country round to aid in the laborious task. The farmer left his plow, the blacksmith his forge, the teamster stabled his horses, and the housewife closed the door on domestic duties to join the merry company gathered from far and near to assist without price. Strong arms seized the canthooks, the handspikes, and pikepoles and soon the frame was upright. Dinner was free, and unless the proprietor was a temperance man, there was a liberal flow of liquor to add joyousness to the occasion.

Although timber was abundant, the ceilings in many of these early inns were so low that a person of ordinary height could scarcely stand upright in them. Sometimes suitable building material was not at hand even in Wisconsin's paradise of pine. In 1837 when Bininger, Smith, and Paine erected a tavern at Monroe, lumber was purchased in Pennsylvania, brought down the Allegheny and Ohio rivers to the Mississippi, then up the Mississippi to Galena whence it was hauled across country to Monroe. In 1844 T. T. Blauvelt began and David Green completed the first frame house in Fox Lake, the old Purdy House. The lumber for this was brought from Fort Winnebago twenty-eight miles to the west, and was drawn by a team owned by Q. H. Barron who made the trip in five days. It was said that the distance was so great and Barron so slow of movement that he had only a narrow margin of time to play "seven-up" on the road. In 1842 in order to erect the first tavern in embryo Elkhorn, Richard Hogablom, James Farnsworth, and Benjamin Arnold purchased a frame at Sheboygan, shipped it to Racine, and from that point hauled it to the chosen site. Unfortunately their hopes over-reached their powers as they were obliged to sell out on account of lack of funds. The purchaser was the Reverend Levi Lee, who completed the building. It stood for many years and had many bonifaces.

When a building was finished the day of the opening was almost universally celebrated with a dance, visitors traveling miles to be present at the important occasion. At the opening of La Belle House at Oconomowoc, September 11, 1850, a grand party was given. It was the first public gathering of the kind in the place as there was no building extensive enough to entertain a large company before the erection of the tavern. There were one hundred forty guests present and it is said there was not a gray head among them.

Occasionally a new sort of roof was attempted. When J. C. Cover visited Boscobel in 1856-1857 he "camped" at the Hall Tavern. The roof was of cement, which checked or cracked and permitted water to come through in a thousand places, he said. While doing the best he could with a menu of salt venison, cornbread baked in grease, and rye coffee without milk or sugar, he asked the waiter what was the matter with the roof. "Does it always leak like this?"

"No, sir, only when it rains," was the reply.

Sometimes the erection of early taverns was attended with more or less trouble. In 1837 theRacine House at Racine was built at a cost of ten thousand dollars, a munificent sum for those days. Not only was the expense unusual but the construction proceeded under difficulties. First, a clearing was made of sufficient scope. Everybody came to aid in the raising and of course had a good time. A portion of the lime was burned on a pile of logs by Lucius S. Blake, and for the product he received fifty cents a bushel, more than potatoes were worth at that time. Tom O'Spring, whose chief characteristic was procrastination, delayed the work so long that the whole community was exasperated, as the grand opening had to be thereby postponed. One Sunday morning O'Spring decided to attack the work but found the lime had not been delivered. It was deep in the woods and he had no team to bring it to the scene of operations. Paul Kingston and Stephen Campbell each had a yoke of oxen contentedly grazing, and it occurred to O'Spring that he might bring them into service. It would not do to ask the owners, for they were Sunday-observing citizens and at that very moment might be in the neighboring church. There was little else for O'Spring to do but to attach the oxen to the vehicle himself, which he did, but to no avail. The animals were not persuasive and the idea had to be abandoned for the day, because he had hitched the off ox of one of the owners to the off ox of the other owner. In due time, however, the Racine House was completed and, describing the opening event, an observer reports: "A celebration was had, and in the dancing room, which had been particularly prepared, from close of day until early morn a happy crowd danced away the night under the inspiration of music furnished by a hod-carrier on a three-stringed fiddle."

Sometimes a tavern was built and later moved. When it was thought that Sheboygan and not Milwaukee would be the metropolis of Wisconsin a tavern was erected at the former place. When Milwaukee began to grow the building was towed in the summer of 1843 along the lake shore by four yoke of oxen, under the direction of William A. Hawks; opened for business amidst new surroundings, it was called the Lake House.

An old hotel at Lone Rock had the longest trip on the Wisconsin river of any place of entertainment in the state. The building was first erected at Point Bas, some six miles below Wisconsin rapids, and was a popular hotel during the heydey of lumbering on the river. In 1871 when business was on the decline, the building was purchased by Albert M. Woodbury and rafted down to Lone Rock. The structure was framed like a barn, heavy timbers being used. When Mr. Woodbury re-erected the edifice at Lone Rock, he placed the upright timbers top end down, with the result that the rooms on the lower floor had lower ceilings than those on the upper floor; in other words, the top of the building was on the bottom and the bottom on the top. Fire destroyed the structure on October 15, 1925.

Some of the later taverns were built quite spaciously: the Wade on the Sheboygan-Fond du Lac road, the Oak Grove near Juneau, the Martin near Mukwonago, the Milton at Milton, one at Hale's Corners, and others having twenty or thirty rooms or more. Often the second floor of these old inns is a delightful maze of rooms that are connected now here, now there, now up, now down. As one turns a corner there are presented

LOG STABLE WITH STRAW ROOF

In the town of Greenfield, Sauk county

OLD HOUSE AT LONE ROCK

Used as a boarding house; not the tavern moved down the Wisconsin

the quaintest nooks, each tavern showing an individuality characteristic of the builder.

Guests frequently arrived before a place of entertainment was completed. The Dyer Tavern at Otsego stood the first summer without the roof being finished; and while the building was in this state many guests were entertained. On one occasion a traveler drove up during a storm, intending to stop for dinner. He found the light-hearted mistress seated in a rocking chair, with skirts tucked up, a baby on each knee, an umbrella over them to keep them dry, while the rain washed off the dinner dishes.

These taverns of frame, brick, or other material, were lighted with small window-panes by day, and at night by tallow candles in tin candle-holders or sconces, whale-oil lamps, or the new kerosene lamps. Kerosene, or coal-oil, as it was sometimes called, in those days of inferior refining, possessed the attributes of present-day dynamite and not infrequently exploded. When an accident of this kind happened there would be a lull in kerosene buying and a swinging back to the safer tallow candle. When Judge Hiram Barber in 1849 opened the Juneau House at Juneau, Solomon Juneau, who resided at Theresa, not far away, was present to congratulate the proprietor. The building cost three thousand dollars, and at the opening some fancy oil lamps were introduced, presented by Mr. Juneau. "It was a rare and luxurious sight," notes a chronicler, "tallow dips and candles had furnished light prior to that time, and the effect although not exactly electrical was very satisfactory."

At the head of the stairs in the Twin Island House at Knowlton was a recess in the wall where a supply of candles was always ready for guests. When one retired he selected a candle, lighted it and proceeded to his room. There was a similar arrangement for kerosene lamps in the Fox House at Columbus, except that the shelf was on the landing near the bottom of the stairs. The "handy man" about the hotel kept one or two of these lamps lighted all evening, and when a guest retired he took a lamp as he went up stairs. More were lighted as those in readiness were carried away.

Pioneer landlords had many duties to perform without digging wells, hence they usually located near a spring, stream, or lake. At Madison water for all purposes in the taverns was taken from the lakes until 1839, at which time a well was excavated at the American House. At the tavern at Beetown the guests washed themselves at a spring branch that crossed the street just below the hotel. Every morning, noon, and night the men ranged themselves on either side of the current and without washbowl, soap, or towel performed their ablutions by scooping the water into their hands, washing their faces as well as they could, and wiping them on their handkerchiefs or shirt sleeves. At many of the early taverns the family washing was done on the bank of a stream or near a spring, where wood and water were abundant. As late as 1845 there was but one well in Monroe.

About the tavern it was generally regarded as part of woman's work to carry water from the spring, creek or lake and when the building was a considerable distance from the source of supply this afforded plenty of exercise. What joyful calculations these women must have made when they contemplated the number of faces, windows, and dishes that a certain amount of water would wash, or how many potatoes and turnips it would boil. Sometimes the bearer would fall prostrate in the mud, losing the promising treasure. Not-withstanding all the difficulties in obtaining this house-hold necessity, the women of that day did not encour-age the men to drink anything stronger than water.

Bathtubs were unknown in early hostelries. No one thought of taking a bath even from a pail or small ves-sel during the winter and most persons refrained through the greater portion of the year. In early frame taverns the face and hands would be washed in a small tin basin at a wooden sink. Beneath the foul sink was a pail more foul, and it was the never-ending duty of the handy man about the hostelry to keep a watchful eye on the bucket that it did not overflow the surrounding territory. Near at hand were a dish of soft soap, a roller towel, and a comb which had lost not a few of its teeth. In those days but little time was consumed in making one's toilet.

In those days also every tavern housed a spinning wheel, which was busy much of the time. Spinning wheels and looms produced cloth that cost but little more than the time and effort required in its manufac-ture. In very early times men wore buckskin clothes, they themselves tanning the hides.

In taverns that boasted no patent clock on the wall the landlord and guests were dependent upon the sun to mark the passing hours. Early timepieces were invar-iably spoken of as patent clocks. Some of the interiors of these pioneer domiciles were papered with newspa-pers brought from the East. In inclement weather one might amuse himself by reading the news from the wall. Pictures on the walls were of the simplest kind. Mrs. Bingham in her *History of Green County* says:

Now and then a wall was adorned with a portrait of George Washington at which little boys were expected to look whenever

called on to give an account of themselves. A more common household treasure was one of a character similar to the epitaph which the
Vicar of Wakefield hung on the wall. It was a picture of a willow
and of a funereal woman pulling a child by the hand and leaning
over a tombstone, whereon were written the names of the departed.

The special delight of the tavern wives was pictured
dishes. In those days guests ate their pork and beans
and potatoes from plates adorned with scenes along the
Erie canal or views of Faneuil Hall in Boston or Inde-
pendence Hall at Philadelphia. There were also wil-
low-ware sets with fantastic decorations much coveted
in these later days. At the Beetown Tavern there were
but half a dozen pewter or block tin teaspoons, and
when the brown sugar was passed each guest stirred a
spoonful into his coffee and passed the spoon on to his
left-hand neighbor.

Festoons of pared apples and sliced pumpkin hung
about the fireplace in the beamed kitchen. Nearly every
tavern on the Milwaukee-Madison road harbored a
glass case of mounted birds, and usually among the
specimens was a pair of passenger pigeons. In some
buildings were natural history specimens and curiosi-
ties gathered from many quarters of the globe. On the
bar were China match-stands from which the frugal
helped themselves in anticipation of future smokes.
Conveniently near at hand were cloves useful in dis-
guising the odor of Old Bourbon or other brands of
liquor. The floor of the barrooms in the early taverns
was usually covered with sawdust, for mills were near
and their refuse was plentiful. Notched tissue paper in
various colors and in fancy designs clung to the ceilings,
forming an ornamentation and also a convenient habitation for flies. Wonderful and fearful were the sketches
made with soap on large frosted mirrors on the back of
the bar.

Noted Taverns and Taverners

Main roads into Milwaukee from the mining region and highways leading to the expansive pine forests of the north, at one time were dotted by a goodly array of inns. Something of the remoteness of these hostelries may be gained by recalling that in general they were erected before the Mexican war and soon will be crowding a century of age. Most of those standing today present a more or less forsaken appearance, their diminutive window panes and the glass bordering their front doors burdened with dust, a kerosene lamp in an entrance but faintly echoing the welcome of former days – the lace and ruffle epoch of the country's history.

Each of these aging meccas is something more than a simple relic of pioneer times. Each possesses individual interest. About their decaying timbers cling the traditions, romance, and history of the border, the essence of an interesting period in the development of the state. The log taverns are gone. These built of boards, brick, and stone have survived and stand like hoary sentinels amid the noise and bustle of an alien world. In some cases surroundings have so changed that the old tavern now looks out upon a landscape differing in every particular from that which originally encircled it. In the commercial districts of a city one will sometimes note one of these ancient landmarks standing a little apart from other buildings, suggesting by its aloofness the isolation of the rude pioneer past of which it was so important a part.

Entering one of these inns today, one is apt to experience a feeling of disappointment. Usually the fire-place yawns, as of old, which it is easy to visualize filled with blazing wood in defiance of chill winds; but the visitor must not be surprised if this has been closed with plaster or if the great dining room is divided by a partition. Frequently the ancient barroom has been altered to meet present day needs, and the modest window-sash, with its six or nine small panes of glass framing views of the country-side in early times, has given way to a modern landscape window.

In only a few of the taverns of the thirties, forties, and fifties is there any of the original furniture. Generations which it served are gone and many an interesting and historic piece has passed beneath the unemotional auctioneer's hammer, to be replaced by a later model. Very few of the old fourpost beds are in existence, mirrors have been carried away, candle-sticks retired in favor of kerosene lamps or electricity, and only now and then is a time-worn table or chair discovered with a history that can be traced to pioneer days.

Some of the taverns themselves have been changed and remodeled to such a degree that few traces of their antiquity are visible. Others stand in proud possession of their original outlines, their quaint doors and windows undisturbed and their verandas shaded as of old by friendly lilac bushes and stately forest trees.

As a coaching inn, the Hawks Tavern at Delafield is easily one of the foremost in interest, holding its own against claims of almost any similar place of entertainment in Badgerdom. From the day when Nelson P. Hawks, as landlord, greeted his first guest in 1840, until the coming of the railroad ended its popularity, this inn was celebrated far and wide for its excellent fare, glo-

FRANKLIN STOVE
Once used in Hawks's Tavern, Delafield

HALFWAY HOUSE, GREENBUSH, SHEBOYGAN COUNTY
Built in 1850, popular with travelers from the lake shore to Fond du Lac

rious liquid concoctions, and the unique character of its proprietor. Hawks was known the country over as a prince of high living and his tavern was a conspicuous center of village and neighborhood life. In many particulars it was typical of a goodly number of the inns of the day between the lake region and the Mississippi river. The building is little changed from the days of the Hawks régime, its colonial lines and dimensions identifying it even to the casual observer.

To the right of the long entrance hall is the old barroom and directly opposite a second public room. The ceilings are comparatively low and one may fancy the floors sawdusted. Two great Franklin stoves in which fires blazed merrily the winter through, ensured warmth and cheer during the boreal season. Besides the Franklin stoves a number of others of ordinary type were required for purposes of heating and cooking. These devoured fuel so freely that in winter two men were kept to feed them. About one hundred and twenty cords of hard wood usually were consumed. Help was inexpensive, maids labored long hours for a dollar and twenty-five cents a week, while men-of-all work often could be engaged for little beyond board and shelter.

In the cellar of the tavern are five rooms – an ice-house beneath the barroom, beyond a vegetable cellar, a preserve room, and a central space filled with shelves. In the remaining room soap was sometimes made and maple syrup boiled down. For a time one of the apartments boasted a fine well of unusually cold water.

Merry-makers were wont to gather in this tavern to dance the hours away in the spacious ballroom and joke and regale themselves with flip or other beverage. Its situation on the most prominent corner in the village aided in making the place a popular center but the personality of the landlord would have drawn custom in a less favored location.

Hawks never lost an opportunity of enjoying a joke. Late one afternoon a stranger appeared at his door seeking accommodation for the night. The jolly boniface, assuming a saintly air, told him in whispers that he had made a mistake, that the house was not an inn but a nunnery. He invited the prospective guest to step to the door of an inner room to see for himself that he was telling the truth. The two walked softly through a passage and sure enough, there could be seen a group of ladies garbed mostly in black apparently engaged in some useful work. Hawks directed the traveler to the tavern of Samuel Wells which was not far distant. Here the fellow told of his embarrassing mistake, insisting there could be no doubt about the place being a religious retreat as he had seen the old monk himself. Wells, roaring with laughter, finally convinced the stranger that he had experienced one of old man Hawks's jokes.

Hawks had a negro cook who had won the reputation of preparing a meal in a remarkably short time. One day when the stagecoach drove up, three professional men alighted and a wager was made that the negro could kill, dress, and have a chicken cooking on an open fire in three minutes. Purses were produced, Jack, the cook, was interviewed, and declared he could perform the feat. All repaired to the tavern kitchen where stood Jack holding a chicken aloft in his left hand, a knife in his right, with a kettle of boiling water on the hearth and a spit over the coals. The men held their watches. Hawks said, "Go!" The head of the bird was instantly severed on a block of wood, the body soused in the hot

MILTON HOUSE
Built in 1845 by Joseph Goodrich, eccentric tavern keeper

HAWKS TAVERN, DELAFIELD
Nelson P. Hawks, owner, a famous coaching station, still standing

water, a keen knife given a few passes, and the fowl was simmering within the alloted time.

Hawks was a generous provider and bought everything in the form of food that was brought to the kitchen door. Indians with berries, fishermen who offered strings of trout or bass, hunters with venison or wild fowl found a ready purchaser in the liberal-minded landlord. This genial host greatly enjoyed detailing episodes of his life. He was troubled with insomnia and often tarried late in the barroom recounting his experiences among the indians, his sojourn at Aztalan, and incidents of his days as a boniface in Milwaukee. So popular was the entertainment offered by this jolly landlord that patrons of stagecoaches always were anxious to partake of his hospitality, to enjoy his quips and jests which acted as a yeast-like leaven to any heaviness of heart with which they might be burdened. His contagious laughter has been stilled for many a year. He and his good wife sleep in the little churchyard hard by and strange faces greet the visitor at the old tavern.

Of all the taverns on roads from the mining region in the southwest to Lake Michigan ports, the long frame structure at Johnstown Center, east of Janesville, was one in which teamsters delighted to take refuge when climatic conditions were unfavorable for sleeping beneath wagons. The second floor of this building contains "the school section," where the weary traveler was permitted to enter and roll up in his blanket on the floor for the night, selecting "the best there was." Devoid of furniture, when the sleepers had folded their blankets or buffalo robes, the room was in order for a ball or other function.

The Stone Barn Tavern with its stone barn stands three miles west of Milton Junction, at the intersection of the highway and railroad. Both tavern and barn were erected by Joseph Kidder from limestone, gravel, and lime found in the neighborhood. Roofs, of course, are frame and the heavy timbers were first fitted on the ground, numbered, and placed in position above. The numbers are plainly visible today. The timbers were joined by means of dowel pins and roof-boards were cut from tamarack logs sawed near Watertown. No name was given this inn by its owner but from lake to river the place was known as the Stone Barn Tavern. Landlord Kidder, who was a good deal of an artisan with tools, wrought hinges and locks from small pieces of iron. The tavern contains fourteen rooms. Two immense fireplaces were noteworthy features of the building when it was erected.

In front of the ancient structure are four trees, three cottonwoods brought from Vermont by Mrs. Kidder when she came west behind an ox-team driven into what seemed a paradise of hardwood and pine, and a large bur-oak which sheltered waggoners when the tavern could not accommodate them. Teamsters were especially fond of this inn as it boasted a well of excellent water, cold and clear as crystal. Seated around a roaring fire within or lounging beneath the spreading oak, lead haulers and travelers sang and jested and otherwise made merry, through many years.

None but an unusual character would have built such an extraordinary structure as the Milton House at Milton. Constructed of lime and gravel, the tavern boasts a hexagonal tower three stories in height, the remaining portion two stories high stretching away to the south. A large chimney occupies the tower-like section and Joseph Goodrich, the landlord and owner, had in mind a plan to control the temperature of the rooms in winter by connecting stoves in the chambers with this central chimney. So many pipes were necessary that the interior of the tower was highly decorated. Asked his reason for building the tower, the landlord replied that it was to serve as a lookout for indians. Redskins, however, never appeared. The dining room in this inn is small in proportion to the size of the house. To economize space chairs with extremely low backs were purchased and were pushed beneath the table when not in use.

Goodrich was a jovial individual, enjoying any experience which furnished a laugh. Occasionally a stranger entering his tavern would ask the price of a meal. The landlord's invariable reply to the question was, "I'll fill your shirt for a shilling." A young fellow in playful mood once brought a shirt into the office and handed it to Goodrich with the request that he fill it for a shilling. The boniface opened the garment, pulled it down over his corpulent frame, almost splitting it from top to bottom in the endeavor, and with beaming face held out his hand with the question: "Where's your shilling?"

The Milton House was a strictly temperate hostelry. This and the fact that King Alcohol was unpopular in the village, made things a bit difficult at certain times. One day a stranger entered the tavern in a great hurry explaining that he was exceedingly thirsty and must have a glass of rum at once. Pointing to a pump at the side of the building the obdurate landlord replied: "There's the well. Help yourself to all the Milton rum you want."

The Milton House shared with other places in the village the debatable honor of being one of the stations on the "underground railroad" and aid and entertainment were given to many a fleeing slave. Upon one occasion Sojourner Truth, the well-known colored woman who spent her life laboring for the betterment of her race, was entertained at the tavern. The boniface, with his Seventh Day Baptist leaning, saw no virtue in tobacco and noticing she was smoking, said to her:

"Sojourner, do you not know that you can never enter the Kingdom of Heaven?"

"No, Massa Goodrich," replied the woman, "I do not know. How is that?"

"Well, you know that evil cannot enter the Kingdom of Heaven."

"Yes, Massa, I knows that evil cannot enter the Kingdom of Heaven."

"Well, you know that smoking is a sinful habit, makes a bad breath and in every way is evil."

Sojourner looked at the expectant landlord a moment, then replied:

"You see, Massa Goodrich, I 'spec when I comes to die I'll leave my bref behin'."

The landlord vastly enjoyed this story and would tell it with a roar of laughter.

The Milton House was built in 1845 and has withstood the frost and heat of eighty years remarkably well. At the rear of the tavern is a frame building, the side of which bears the sign,

MILTON HOUSE 1839

Beside this frame building is a log house in which the earliest visitors to the region were entertained. The three constitute an interesting trio in the evolution of the tavern in Wisconsin.

After the first railroad had been thrown across the state from Milwaukee to Prairie du Chien, the stage line from Galena to Mazomanie and the north became an important route. A famous stopping place of that period and one which still possesses the atmosphere of those days of slower travel, is the Ruggles Tavern, a short distance north of Ridgeway. At the end of the porch is the limestone mounting block and at the edge of the lawn stand two great stones on which hang gates that swung ajar in the early days at the approach of the stage. As the visitor drives up now he inadvertently looks for the old English sign:

> This gate hangs high
> And hinders none
> Refresh and pay
> And travel on.

A few rods distant are two other massive stones whose gates were flung wide as the team dashed away with the coach and its precious load. The large barn across the way is a relic of coaching days; with the old house whose green lawn stretches in front, in which bloom many old-fashioned flowers, it forms an interesting link between past and present.

Another tavern with venerable association is a salad-hued building in the village of Dekorra, a few miles south of Portage. Here the Wisconsin river approaches Lake Michigan more nearly than at any other point and the construction of a territorial highway between river and lake gave great hopes to the village. But rafting days came to an end, railroad supplanted stagecoach, and streets in Dekorra and country roads roundabout became little more than vagabond trails. The old tavern was built from timbers hewn on Pine island some miles above the hamlet and has defied wind and storm since 1836. The builder was Lafayette Hill, a member of the first Constitutional Convention and a person of importance in the locality. Many Scotsmen settled on either side of the river at Dekorra and on the ice of Rocky run, a small tributary of the Wisconsin, they were the first in the state to indulge in their favorite diversion of curling. They began by using flatirons from family kitchens, later had blocks made of wood, and finally treated themselves to granite curling stones. Naturally the tavern was the gathering place for the Scots of various clans; here their banquets were held, here they celebrated Robert Burns's birthday, and enjoyed various forms of merrymaking dear to the hearts of wearers of the plaid. Near the close of a feast, a hilarious occasion, it is told that one of the partakers, more or less in his cups, arose and proposed a toast to Tom Paine and Voltaire. To offer a toast to two such noted infidels was to explode a bomb in this company of hidebound Presbyterians. A near riot followed.

The Martin House, a martin bird-house proudly surmounting a tall pole in front as a sign, is located a few miles east of Mukwanago. In its day the old tavern was famous for foaming tankards, Virginia reels, post-chaises, flintlocks, tin lanterns, and for the number of hardy pioneers who sought shelter here. Leonard Martin, proprietor, was a lawyer, auctioneer, surveyor, merchant, postmaster, and operated a farm of some six hundred acres. A fire-eating Democrat was he and in his tavern local leaders of the party gathered during heated campaigns to arouse enthusiasm. Many stories are told of him. Once after a number of valuable animals had been stolen in the neighborhood, Martin organized a horse-owners' protective association and the criminals were so terror-stricken that from that time owners of live stock slept in peace.

The ballroom in his tavern where many a merry company gathered, occupies most of the space on the third floor. To reach it one must ascend an interesting winding stairway. On one side of the room is a railed platform for musicians.

The most popular daily event at the Martin House was the arrival of the mail pouch from Milwaukee. The neighborhood assembled on the porch waiting for the clarion notes of a horn which heralded the approach of the stage. No one with proper spirit would miss the excitement of its arrival. The gathering of a number of western enthusiasts, whose caravan was made up here for the journey to California, is an outstanding event in the tavern's history.

Jesse Smith's two and a half story cobblestone tavern near Mukwanago, with its engaging exterior, possesses much of the air of an old New England inn. The architecture of the building, the sloping lawn, and lovely pastoral environment all suggest comfort and a degree of seclusion and cleanliness offered by but few equally imposing hostelries. Within, the taproom is at one side of the entrance hall, a ladies waiting room being directly across. To the rear is a dining-room of generous proportions while beyond is the capacious kitchen. In the second story are bedrooms and the space above is occupied by the ballroom with its spring dancing floor, this last the pride of the proprietor and a joy to the merrymakers who frequented the tavern in the fifties. A few alterations have been made for convenience since the old days but these have not destroyed the outlines of the building or its broad porch nor changed the graceful proportions of hall and staircase and spacious rooms.

One of the oldest houses in Wisconsin and one richest in associations, is the Agency or Waubun House, stand-

ing on the bank of the canal at Portage. The building
was erected in the early thirties as a home for Mr. and
Mrs. John H. Kinzie. Mr. Kinzie came as indian agent
to Fort Winnebago, bringing with him to the frontier a
youthful bride, who, in a charming volume, *Wau-Bun,
the Early Day in the Northwest*, describes the life of the
locality at that early time. When no longer occupied by
the Kinzies, the domicile became a tavern with Mr.
and Mrs. James Ubaldine as landlord and landlady.
Ubaldine was Italian, his wife Irish. In 1836 T. J. Kingston and Samuel B. Pilkington were entertained at this
Agency House Tavern and describing the visit, the
former remarks that of the two, Mrs. Ubaldine was the
better man. Kingston further says that Ubaldine was
willing to acknowledge such to be the case when family
differences arose, which were not infrequent. The guests
remained at the tavern about a week, there being a
heavy fall of snow at the time. Before their departure
for Point Bas, the landlady presented them with a bottle
of medicine remarking:

"If you get frost-bitten, try this; it came from auld
Ireland."

On the Wisconsin river bank at Knowlton, half-way
between Stevens Point and Wausau, is the Twin Island
House which dates from 1849. Where the hostelry
stands, an imposing object on an elevation, the four-
horse Frink and Walker stagecoaches stopped, and every
pound of freight for Wausau or beyond had to pass the
building, either on the river at the rear or by team in
front. The Twin Island House was a place of importance; guests were numerous and often men slept three
in a bed although they might not have met before. It
was a favorite place for lumberjacks to indulge in
physical encounters on their way down the river or as

Mr. AND Mrs. SYLVANUS WADE

Owners of popular Halfway or Wade House in Greenbush, west of Sheboygan Falls. He was a promoter of plank roads

they returned to the pinery. On one of these fistic occasions a number of minor casualities occurred, one of which was the biting off of an ear of one of the combatants. An incident of the day was the fact that neither pane nor sash was left in the barroom windows when the frolic was over.

Another time a number of teamsters had congregated and there were not chairs enough to seat all. Orrin Maybe, who was left standing, opened the door and shouted, "A runaway, boys!" All quickly crowded outside to enjoy the excitement, only to find the runaway a hoax. When the chairs were again filled another member of the company was left standing.

When Sylvanus Wade built a log tavern at Greenbush, about half-way between Sheboygan Falls and Fond du Lac, his nearest neighbors were at those hamlets, now thriving cities. Wade, an Englishman, lived for a time at Fort Atkinson, later becoming a resident of Greenbush where he passed the remainder of his days. In 1850 he completed the Wade House, which is still a landmark in the village in the picturesque moraine region of eastern Wisconsin.

Wade was progressive and the first meeting to arrange for the building of a plank road from Lake Michigan past his door to Lake Winnebago was held in his tavern. After the planks were laid there ensued a series of unusual events which caused more debate in the old inn than politics, religion, or indians scares. Fond du Lac was ambitious to have a railroad and proceeded to build one. A locomotive was purchased in New England, shipped over the Great Lakes to Sheboygan, and hauled by means of several ox teams over the plank road to Fond du Lac. In order to prevent the flanges of the wheels from cutting the planks, wooden

felloes were placed about the wheels but the weight of
the iron horse was so great that serious damage resulted
as the treasured engine moved slowly along the plank
highway. Soon the owners of the railroad found that a
second locomotive would be necessary if the railway
was to keep abreast of the times, hence another machine
was ordered shipped to Sheboygan. The earlier experience of moving the engine on the plank had been
costly and the owners of the road seriously objected to
another piece of equipment taking the same course.
However, the charter of the road duly specified that
the highway was built for vehicles so when a number
of individuals climbed aboard making it a vehicle, the
locomotive passed the tollgate in triumph. Many times
did it break through the planks into the mud and when
it finally reached Fond du Lac the highway was for a
second time sadly in need of repair.

The Wade Tavern with its three stories and broad
verandas, not much changed from early times, is occupied to this day by descendants of the builder. Books,
pictures, furniture, and other articles of interest used
when the hostelry was opened may be seen there. This
is one of the few taverns that can boast many furnish-
ings of pioneer days.

The Denniston House at Cassville, the largest building of the kind erected in southwestern Wisconsin at
that time, was intended to be an imposing structure
worthy of admiration at the hoped-for new state capital. Its location on the bank of the Mississippi river
was considered especially desirable. But the territorial
legislature of 1836 selected Madison as the site of the
statehouse and the Denniston proved a folly for its
investors. Nelson Dewey, first governor of the state, was
heavily interested in the enterprise. He spent his last

days under its roof, passing away July 21, 1889, in his room on the second floor.

Diagonally across from the courthouse at Green Lake is an old tavern which has been the scene of many enlivening companies. There is a dancing hall in the building and this J. C. Mills, landlord for a number of years, was in the habit of referring to as the "school section." As many as could find accommodation on the floor were welcome to enter and when court was in session special efforts were made to have jurymen, witnesses, and others sleep behind the same door. For the landlord it meant more drinks sold at the bar and more fun for all concerned. One bitter day a bobsled with two occupants stopped at the tavern. The roughly dressed teamster opened the door and asked that his wife might enjoy a few moments' warmth while he refreshed himself with a drink. The man quaffed his rum and unnoticed by the landlord returned to his team which he untied and drove away. As soon as it was discovered that the fellow had forgotten his wife, the landlord aroused Louie, the hired man (sometimes called "King's Evil," from the roseate hue of his countenance) and sent him after the departing driver. Louie's horse soon overtook the derelict who returned to the tavern for his spouse. The woman vented her irritation in sharp words but took her place in the sled while the absent-minded companion vouchsafed the information that he knew he had forgotten something.

The tavern at Hale's Corners, just out of Milwaukee, has dispensed hospitality and good cheer since 1834. In the days when the Janesville plank road was a busy thoroughfare, farmers west and south stopped at the old hostelry over night, drove to Milwaukee the next morning to dispose of their products and purchase necessary supplies, and returned to the comfort of the inn at night. Lower prices ruled at this tavern than in the city, which was one of the reasons for its popularity. The Dreyfus family, father and son, have been operating the house for many years. Rooms are no longer available, but meals are served to many a merry party from the city as well as to passing travelers. The present owner has a penchant for marble-top tables and has succeeded in assembling a remarkable collection. With the exception of the front door, the building has undergone few changes during its more than ninety years of existence. Before the days of the Volstead act, two joyful individuals returning from Milwaukee one night, stopped at the tavern and endeavored to arouse the landlord. The hour was late and the host refused admittance. After arguing the matter to no purpose, one of the men advised his companion to kick in the door. The suggestion was promptly adopted and his foot went crashing through the panel. The following day a new door was purchased by the intruders and this has been functioning ever since.

The Oak Grove House is located two miles from Juneau, Dodge county. One brown October day in 1841 Major Thomas Pratt drove an ox-team attached to a clumsy, rumbling cart along the territorial road from Milwaukee until he arrived at the site of this historic inn. He first erected a log tavern but in the late forties supplanted it by a more commodious frame structure. A type of generosity not unusual among early settlers was a trait of Major Pratt. This was manifest when a meeting was held in the tavern to decide upon the location of a new courthouse for Dodge county. Pratt had secured a large farm from the government at the price of a dollar and a quarter per acre and in the course of the discussion he said, "The land here cost me but little and if you locate the county seat here it will cost you but little." The seat of government, however, went to Juneau.

One of the frequenters of the Oak Grove tavern was an individual known as Crazy Joe. For some time he was a teamster along the road leading from Milwaukee to Watertown, Oak Grove, and the north. At Watertown a landlord by the name of Valentine wanted some small pigs to consume the waste from his table and he delegated Crazy Joe to procure them. Along his route Joe noticed a number of fine young pigs on a farm, secured a small box on his return trip, made it convenient to pass the place under cover of darkness, and soon delivered the whole litter of young porkers to the Watertown landlord. When Joe was asked the price of the animals, he replied:

"Oh, that's all right, Mr. Valentine. The account is small. Just give me credit on my account for what they are worth."

Valentine placed the animals in a sty and soon they were thriving on a change of diet. A few mornings after, Valentine was a much surprised boniface. When he went to the sty it was empty and there was no hint by which he might solve the mystery. On his return from Milwaukee Crazy Joe made it convenient to pass the Valentine tavern at night, shoved the pigs into the same box in which they had been brought, placed them in his wagon, and returned them to the rightful owner.

When Joe registered at Watertown the next trip he asked with all solemnity how the porkers were progressing.

"Follow me," said the landlord.

Out to the sty they went but not a pig was in sight.

When the boniface marveled that such little pigs could escape over the top of the pen so high, Joe replied, "Well, you know, Mr. Valentine, them pigs is great climbers."

A dismal-looking building is the Kellogg Tavern six miles west of Kenosha. Here on the rim of civilization Sereno Fowler, a Harvard graduate, ambitious to have a college in the far West, erected several buildings and opened a school. Fowler's wife was Lemira Tarbell, a relative of Ida Tarbell, biographer of Lincoln. A few years after the school began, Fowler died and the educational work was abandoned. Several of the school buildings were razed, and one converted into a tavern. Not long after the demise of her husband the widow married J. M. Kellogg. There was another tavern a short distance to the north and persons traveling from Woodworth to Kenosha were obliged to go a bit to the east and back again if they desired to be refreshed at the Kellogg place. Kellogg owned all the land between the two taverns and promptly closed the north-and-south highway to the west of his building and opened a new road farther east. This turn of Kellogg's invested his tavern with additional importance and resulted in the rival place across the fields slipping out of the public ken.

In 1847 Lyman Clark built the first tavern in Baraboo, the Baraboo House, which stood on the south side of the river at the terminal of the stage line from Madison and Prairie du Sac. In that early day roads followed the course of least resistance. The East Sauk road from Prairie du Sac, after it descended the bluff, should have continued due north into Baraboo, but Landlord Clark so influenced the surveyor that the highway was deflected in order that travelers might more directly reach the tavern. The thoroughfare afterward became the Warner Memorial highway and it still retains the angle caused by the artful taverner.

At the Mansion House, near the railway station in Mineral Point, many celebrities have been guests. The Prince de Joinville in his journey across the state; Mrs. Alexander Hamilton when she visited her son, William S. Hamilton; and General Henry Dodge of indian fighting fame, were entertained here. It is probable that Zachary Taylor, Jefferson Davis, and others connected with the early military affairs of the territory sought refreshment in the old hostelry. Moses M. Strong, Judge A. A. Jackson, and Judge Charles Dunn, well-known pioneers, were familiar personages in the hotel. Of all its landlords Abner Nichols was the most famous. He was a popular host and beneath the roof of the Mansion House the traveler not only found bed and board but plenty of amusement as well. Miners who worked like moles during the week, doffed their rough clothes when Saturday came and sought the Mansion House to stake their savings at the faro bank or roulette wheel. Visitors came forty and fifty miles at the week-end to mingle with the varigated company which gathered in the long, historic hostelry. The landlord was resourceful and always found room for travelers, even if sometimes he put them to sleep, as he did Judge Dunn on one occasion, under the counter among bottles and barrels.

The Astor House, a two-story brick building, rests on the river bank at Sauk City like a child which fears to venture into the stream. This was a favorite rendezvous for rivermen and many rafts were snubbed at the rear and many groups from the pinery tarried here for the night. The Astor House was appropriately named, for it looks upon the stream where floated down, in 1810, the John Jacob Astor expedition bound for Astoria, Oregon, so vividly described by Washington Irving.

Berry Haney was a rough and ready westerner. Amongst the indians he erected a log tavern at Cross Plains, resided at Sauk City for a time, and later returned to Cross Plains where he built a stone tavern about a mile east of the present village. In a quarrel at Madison he shot Joe Pelkie, a Frenchman, then nursed him back to health. There was much drinking and carousing before an open fire in the basement of the old stone inn. A legend prevails that victims of Haney's wrath are buried beneath the floor of the old tavern. Be this as it may, timid persons hesitate about entering at night the rooms and recesses below, fearing spook or goblin. Bricks now fill the fireplaces above and below but the chimney remains to suggest blazing fires and rough hospitality.

In addition to the buildings mentioned above, the following may be found of interest to the visitor providing the destructive hand of man has not come as a visitation upon them after these lines were written: The Wilson Tavern west of Poynette; the quaint building at Fairwater; the McFarland at the village of that name; the Vermont House at Neenah; the Ceresco building at Ripon where the Phalanx people sometimes entertained; the Stagg or Terrill Inn at Mineral Point; the American House at Fairplay; two inns at Beetown; the Melchoir, with its antiquated brewery in one end, at Trempealeau; the Mag Lawe and Beaupré places north of Shawano; the Okauchee House at Oconomowoc; the Union House at Rochester; Brick or Circus Hotel at Delavan; Runkel at Germantown; Hotel Mukwanago at Mukwanago; Hinkley Tavern south of

Oconomowoc; Dodgeville Hotel; American House at Benton; Tyler House north of Hazel Green; Phoenix Hotel near Waukesha; Kingston Hotel at Kingston; Exchange at Waupun; East Troy House (1836) at East Troy; Spring Tavern near Madison; Winkley House at Wausau; Mount Breeze, Newhouse, County Line House, and Michael Herr places on the Green Bay road between Sheboygan Falls and Manitowoc; "Bavarian Heaven" in Sheboygan; Sheboygan Falls Hotel (1844); Four Mile House east of Trempealeau; Mayne Hotel at Wiota; Brayton at Exeter; Empire House at Hazel Green (grave of James G. Percival nearby); Bay State House at De Soto; the Vosler at Delton; Israel Stowel, now a residence at Delavan; two taverns at Butte des Morts; the Bragg at Gratiot; Junction House at Elmo; City Hotel and Potosi House at Potosi; Ball Tavern near Evansville; Harrisburg near Black Hawk; Dousman near Waukesha; William Tell at Oconomowoc; and several north of Milwaukee. This list is not complete, yet it records a partial roll of taverns which extend to the Civil war or before.

Off main roads many an old-time tavern which had outlived its usefulness as a convivial place of entertainment has become a prosaic residence or, sad to say, barn, garage, or warehouse. Some are empty and dingy with age. In rooms once vivid with life cobwebs in festoons dangle from low ceilings; the counter once reeking with beer, is now covered with dust; shelves erstwhile glowing with colored bottles and scintillating glasses betray the ruin wrought by time, and untrodden floors are buried under the accumulation of the departed years. Great rambling, queer old places some of them are, with commodious dance halls, spooky passages, antiquated staircases, and suggestions for a hundred ghost stories.

Taverns in the Shadows

A few taverns of early territorial days merit especial consideration in these pages. Once neighborhood nuclei, they have all long since disappeared as landmarks and must be viewed through the mists of remembrance of half a century or more.

Judge J. P. Arndt, after he came in 1824 from Pennsylvania to Green Bay, kept the village inn in the remodeled Langlade house. Of this house in *Historic Green Bay* we read: "It was constructed of square hewn logs, so nicely adjusted that it seemed one solid block, stucco or whitewash, but always retaining its soft gray color, so mellow and restful to the eye. Barely a story and a half high, its length was quite a hundred feet. Over the door of the main entrance was a sort of hatchment, which caught the first morning sunlight as it glimmered through a line of luxuriant lilac shrubs that stretched along the dwelling's entire front. There was no hall or vestibule, the outside door opening direct to one of the living rooms. On the western side a long, low-roofed piazza extended the length of the main building, and sitting under its pleasant shadow one could see all that was passing between fort and village, for traffic and pleasure alike took the river highway. In the center a door opened to the one large apartment of the house, used as parlor and reception-room, plainly furnished in old-fashioned style; a lounge covered with plain chintz, a generous sized sideboard, a two-story, cast-iron Canadian stove, a mirror hung over a small table. From the adjoining dining room, which occupied the very center of the building, an enclosed stairway led to the low-ceilinged upper story. There were queer little nooks, crannies, and dusky passageways that one was obliged to travel through in reaching the most attractive part of the dwelling, the great, generous kitchen, rallying point alike for the visitors and family. So many were the windows on the river side that when a clear sunset shone on the lilliputian panes it gave the impression of being entirely made of glass. An immense fireplace and huge brick oven nearby filled the south end of the room, while larders, store-rooms, and mysterious little pantries were here, there and everywhere. No swinging crane or crooked pot hooks ever held more delicious menus for the inner man, nor even a richer store of snowy loaves; for the mistress of the old-time hostelry inherited all the thrifty instincts and excellent housewifery of her Holland ancestors.

"In those days, not to be a notable provider and *chef de cuisine* was considered a serious misfortune, for unexpected guests came often, trained servants were not to be had, and not only were dainties for the table prepared by the house-mistress, but she must be an adept as well in the plainer branches of culinary skill. The indians were the purveyors of the settlement, bringing to the door all sorts of fish and game. Each French family had its own dusky retainers, who idled about the premises and partook of the good cheer as in feudal times."

Another early tavern at Green Bay was the Astor House, thus described by Deborah B. Martin in the *History of Brown County*:

"Daniel Whitney had before the erection of the Astor House, built a less pretentious structure directly across from Fort Howard on the site of the present Beaumont Hotel, calling it the Washington House. Fierce rivalry existed between the little towns and the prospect of a new and elegant hostelry for the accommodation of many guests attending land sales must have caused as great excitement as did the transference of property.

"When the work was actually completed and in all the imposing majesty of its three stories and crowning cupola, the Astor House, glistening with fresh white paint stood in the morning sunshine, as a beautiful object to the partial eyes of the dweller in Astor. A stranger might hardly have considered it an architectural gem. It was large and square, and quite guiltless of any adornment or frivolous device. Its many windows were provided with bright green blinds to temper sun and wind to the lambs gathered within its walls. Mrs. Mary Mitchell, whose memory goes back to pioneer times, writes of the early hotel:

" 'It was a fine structure for the time in which it was built and perhaps considered a work of art. I well remember the airs our little burg put on when it was said the hotel is finished.'

"When the last touch had been given to the house, furniture splendid beyond anything seen before in the West was sent to fill it. Old settlers were wont to wax eloquent in describing the soft carpets, the mahogany tables, chairs, and sofas, the abundant shining silver — knives, forks, and spoons; two tea sets, not plated, but real sterling silver, and the finest damask. As a last and crowning addition to the edifice its owner sent from New York a man to fill the responsible and difficult position of landlord, described as one of exceptionally fine appearance, with cultivated, genial manners,

Charles Rogers by name. Thomas Green and others followed as landlords. It was during Green's occupancy that the Astor House was honored with a royal guest, the son of the French king, Louis Philippe, the Prince de Joinville, with his suite, a gay party. They spent a few hours here dining sumptuously and conferring lasting distinction upon the house thereby.

"Here were held the important political meetings – the formation of the Whig and Democratic parties were first accomplished within the walls of the old hotel. Here, too, were given the Masonic balls and parties for many years. The Mexican war put a stop to the merrymakings and carried to the front the men, who through months of familiar intercourse had endeared themselves to the citizens of Green Bay."

When the Mexican war ended bonfires flared in the streets and dancing lent old-time gayety to the Astor House. Its first proprietor, Charles Rogers, was killed on the streets of New York. Several attempts were made to destroy the house, one of which was successful when in August, 1857, after twenty years of usefulness it was burned to the ground.

Frequently a frame addition was joined onto a log tavern. A typical tavern of this kind was the Exchange of Mukwanago, built in 1842 by Henry Camp. The bar was in the log building and the tavern proper in the frame. Describing this early place Camp's son Dan says:

"Tallow dips in tin reflectors hung on the wall near the bar, but usually no other light but that from the fireplace was needed. On one side of the fireplace was piled half a cord of dry maple and on the other was the sink where the guest of high or low degree performed his ablutions with plenty of hard water and a cake of yellow laundry soap. If we ran out of bar soap there was plenty of soft. Over the wooden sink there was a seven-by-ten-inch mirror, flanked by a comb and a brush suspended by chains.

"The new tavern was heated by four fireplaces, two on each floor, placed at each end of the building. There was a small cook stove in the kitchen. How my good mother ever accomplished the cooking for all the hearty eaters that came to our tavern, besides getting supper for forty or more couples that attended the dancing parties, is a mystery to me.

"The upper floor was made into one large room except for a long tier of bedrooms, six-by-seven, on one side of the building, which were reserved for guests of high degree and maiden ladies. The large hall which my father called the steerage, was lined on one side and down the center with beds, like a hospital ward. When a ball was slated, all these beds had to be removed and placed temporarily on the large veranda at the front of the building. The festivities concluded, my father, who had been a seafaring man, sent everybody aloft to put the beds back in shipshape order, whereupon they spliced the main brace in the aforesaid barroom.

"The steerage, when thus transformed into a ballroom, and trimmed with cedar boughs, with six candles on each side backed by bright tin reflectors tacked against the wall, together with the light from the fireplaces, presented a most cheerful appearance, and became a favorite resort for dancing parties."

Among early Milwaukee taverns were the Cottage Inn, a log house built in 1835 and kept by Jacques Vieau; the Bellevue House, built by Juneau and Martin; and the "Shanty Tavern," erected by the Lelands. The house kept by Vieau, sometimes known as the "Triangle Tavern," because a large instrument of that shape was placed on the roof instead of a bell, was a miserable excuse as a place of entertainment, the principle diet being a "terrifying mixture called hash." Since there was for a time no other hotel on the east side, the place generally was crowded. There was compensation for the wretched fare, for the guests were allowed to "have fun" and the owners of the hostelry did not hesitate to participate in the levity. The building had an unusual aspect – small in size, squat-looking in architecture, and green in color.

Of all the early taverns, the Bellevue, later the Milwaukee House, is the richest in memories. During the first years of its existence it was filled with a care-free set of happy fellows, not a poor man in the lot. They were so burdened with riches that currency with them was actually a drug on the market. This was the time of "wild-cat" money. They liquidated their obligations with the landlord by paying him in bundles and when a fiddler came from Chicago to provide music for a dance they heaped upon him fifty dollars for his services. They never complained if a bill loomed high because of a pyramid of charges: out came wallet and the amount was promptly paid. Alexander F. Pratt has related that Juneau was scheduled as worth one hundred thousand dollars and that he was known at one time, to take ten thousand dollars from his money drawer, thrusting the paper into his hat. Soon after the head piece was playfully knocked off while the owner was in a crowd, the money flying in every direction and nobody thought it worth picking up! This paper money with "wild-cat" characteristics was of no great value.

Because of the exceptional character of the landlord and from the fact that it became a temperance house, the Milwaukee House became the most famous of all hostelries in Wisconsin in its day. Caleb Wall was the boniface who gave it much distinction, and of both houses and landlord A. C. Wheeler, in his *Chronicles of Milwaukee*, has written as follows:

"The old Milwaukee House, that stood for a number of years at the corner of Main and Wisconsin streets, fell into good hands in 1842. Caleb Wall came from Springfield, Illinois, with the determination of starting a temperance hotel. His eye fell on this stately building, and he commenced a 'dicker' with Messrs. Hurley and Ream, then its proprietors. The result was, he bought them out and commenced his operations for the establishment of a hotel on moral principles.

"The place was refitted and thoroughly replenished with all the modern accessories of comfort. Before throwing open the doors, a code of laws for the government of the establishment and its happy inmates, was made out. This code was drawn up carefully, and among other excellent things expressly stated that all guests of this hotel shall be in at ten o'clock every night, it being a maxim with the host that those who could not comply with so simple and judicious a condition, were unworthy of the hospitalities of the institution. The starting of a hotel on such a plan attracted considerable attention. The temperance people, as is customary, said a great many fine things in praise of the proprietor, and then put up at another house. The moral men pointed to Mr. Wall as an example worthy of imitation in other cities, and then concluded it wouldn't pay.

"The proprietor, undeterred by insinuations, pushed forward his humanitarian plan and caravansary, posted his code conspicuously, put on an inviting but implacable air, and swung open his doors. It is curious to look

over the old register of that hotel at this day, and see
the names of men who have since become governors,
mayors, justices, aldermen, and M. C.'s, and to learn
that they utterly failed to comply with the reasonable
request, that they should be in bed by ten o'clock post
meridian. The proprietor was firm in his resolve, and
punctually at the appointed hour locked and barred the
doors. But it appears, the guests, while they admired the
system, were unable to comply with its demands. Long
confirmed habits were not to be broken like reeds, and
unable to enter in at the door, they had recourse to lad-
ders and ropes at night, by which they got in at the
back windows.

"It is said that on waking one night, and looking out
of his window, the worthy proprietor was so astonished to see half his boarders at work raising a heavy
ladder against the piazza, that he modified the code and
gave them another hour. It had hitherto been understood that the guests should not only be in at a reasonable hour, but that every man in the garrison should
present himself in a certain accountable condition to
avoid scandal. This was another breach in confirmed
habits. However, the modification in regard to the hour
led to others, and by insensible degrees the house under-
went a transit from one extreme of temperance to the
other extreme of intemperance, until it became the most
notoriously jolly and reckless institution in the town –
the boarders doing just exactly as they pleased and the
old building itself reeling night after night with the
mad revelry of gay parties and gushing music. The
temperance hotel at last rejoiced in a bar with decanters
and then it was discovered that a majority of the guests
had suddenly reformed in one particular and evinced

a decided reluctance to being out late, and some of them were opposed to being out at all.

"The Milwaukee House, under Mr. Wall's administration, bore the name of being the most comfortable and homelike institution in the western country. The proprietor spared no expense to make the house popular. The table groaned under luxuries brought from Detroit — in a word, the proprietor was altogether more liberal than the law of number one allows, and sunk several thousand dollars in the place, or, to use a parliamentary phrase, laid them on the table. It was, however, sustained for a long time in the very best style. What is known in the newspapers as the youth and beauty of the town assembled here at the then fashionable parties, the music being furnished by a negro band, composed of the cook and barber with their assistants. Mr. Wall retains a very pleasing recollection of these halcyon days, and insists that he never heard better music than those darkies discoursed.

"Caleb frequently made a trip to Chicago (whether to enjoy the scenery, of which he is an ardent admirer, or to do a little running for his popular house, is now uncertain) with his friend, Captain Howe. On one occasion there was a large party on board returning from that city; and among them were many distinguished strangers. Inquiry was made of the captain as to which was the best house in Milwaukee. The polite and affable captain (captains as well as hosts are, theoretically, always polite) referred interrogators to the proprietor of the best house in the town, who fortunately was aboard.

"Caleb made a speech. He did not commence with the creation of the world, and trace the history of all the hotels from the time that Abraham entertained the angels unawares to the successful establishment of the Milwaukee House. He was utterly regardless of the splendid opportunity to put in a few sentences on hospitality, but contented himself with a concise welcome, a brief description and a delicate reference to *the* hotel, 'where,' said he, 'it is customary for all the big bugs to stop.' The subsequent experience of the strangers at the Milwaukee House so fully corroborated Mr. Wall's statement in regard to the big bugs that a series of resolutions bearing witness to the truthfulness of his statement were drawn up. This may have been one of those little things which have helped to establish that gentleman's reputation for veracity."

When Mrs. Peck arrived at Madison in April, 1837, she found the log tavern she was to occupy far from completion, and all she could do was to sit in the wagon, beneath a tree, twenty-five miles from the nearest white resident at Blue Mounds, and almost one hundred miles from the mere handful of settlers at Milwaukee. A temporary habitation was constructed until the larger building could be floored and plastered, which was quickly done.

Guests soon filled the log building. Milwaukee and far-away New York were represented by visitors, and even England contributed its quota to the roll of occupants. The comforts of the establishment were substantial from the first, although necessarily the bill of fare consisted of such articles as could be transported from considerable distances; but very soon the table was a marvel to beholders, and cleanliness, the first requisite toward elegance, was a welcome feature from the beginning. The grand dining room was as well ventilated as the winds of heaven would make it, the hospitable

board being spread in the open air to meet the require-
ments of some fifteen new arrivals. Judge Doty, Colonel
Brigham, and Commissioner Bird, with others whose
names are historical, were frequent visitors, and the
unfinished building was tapestried with bed sheets to
furnish sleeping accommodations. The men who sought
accommodation then in Madison made themselves completely at home, hunting, fishing, during their leisure
to increase the variety of the table. Judge, afterwards
Governor Doty, gave an excellent example of helpful-
ness by assisting a party of amateur plasterers to make
the kitchen habitable, and one day's work under his
direction effected much.

The cheery spirit thus indicated was worth more than
all material aid, as it served the sturdy matron to master
the situation. Before long the sounds of gaiety within
that building would have been a surprise to the languid
pleasure seekers in much more costly mansions. Really,
at all times, the pleasure that can be found in palace
or cottage depends upon glad hearts, and not upon the
presence of luxurious viands.

Merry were these early tavern days at Madison.
Mrs. Peck's fiddle rang out sweet and clear on many a
social occasion and the evening was at its height when
some beaming couple led off with "Hunt the Squirrel,"
or "Virginia Reel." That was prior to the days of wide
spreading hoops and less space was required for nimble
feminine feet than in the years which were to come.
Quite frequently, however, the company gave space for
an agile dame or lassie who extended her skirts with
both hands as she performed a lively double-shuffle or
stood aloof as some athletic youth "cut a pigeon-wing"
over most of the available space on the floor.

The following observations are from *A Canoe Voy-*

age up the Minnay Sotor, written by G. W. Featherstonhaugh, who came to Mineral Point in 1837 for the
purpose of making a geological survey of the lead and
copper mines. After a hard ride from Galena he finally
reached Mineral Point, or, rather, its suburb where
there were various small wooden houses. "With difficulty, we procured a room to sleep at the postmaster's
and, it being evening, had scarce got our trunks out of
the vehicle when we were marched to his brother's,
who was an apothacary, to supper. The supper consisted of fried ham, coffee, bread and butter, and treacle
served up in a cleanly way, and, being hungry with our
drive, we made a very hearty meal. . .

"Mineral Point contained two taverns, into which I
ventured to enter for a moment, both of which seemed
to be very full. A court of justice, being held at the
time, had collected a great many parties and witnesses.
We had been referred to those taverns for lodging, as
the postmaster had told me it was not possible for him
to give us quarters for more than one night; but I was
not sorry to learn that none were to be had, being thoroughly disgusted with the appearance of everything;
and then such a set of 'generals, colonels, judges and
doctors' as were assembled there, was anything but
inviting, and most of these dignitaries, as I was informed, were obliged to sleep on the floor. This was
exactly what I had to do at the postmaster's, whose
house was at any rate, clean.

"On awakening the next morning, I found it exceedingly cold, and asked to have a fire lighted. An un-
shaven but confiding looking fellow walked into the
room with nothing but his nether garments on, and
immediately turning his back to the fire, engrossed it
all to himself. His free and easy way was not at all to

my taste and threatened to interfere very much with my
comfort. Under other circumstances I should not have
hesitated to have turned him out; but situated as I was,
it was far from a safe proceeding, or, indeed, a justifiable
one. It was certainly very cold, and I had been treated
hospitably, and the least I could do, was to be hospitable to others; besides, my bare-footed friend had an air
about him that imparted something beyond the low
swaggerer, something that smacked of authority – for
authority is a thing that from habit or from dignity
inherent in it, has a peculiar, inexplicable way of re-
vealing itself. This might be the governor, or some
great man, *en deshabille*; so I thought it best to meet
him in his own manner, by slipping a pair af pantaloons
on, and then addressing him in a friendly way. It was
most fortunate that I acted just as became me to do; for
he soon let me know who he was. He was no less a personage than 'the Court,' [Judge Dunn] for so they generally called the presiding judge in the United States,
and was beyond all question the greatest man in the
place. He was, in fact, the personage of the locality for
the moment, and it turned out that the postmaster had
given to him his only bedroom, and that he good-naturedly had given it to me for one night, and had taken
the majesty of the law to sleep behind the counter, in a
little shop where the post office was kept, with blankets,
crockery, cheese, and all sorts of things around him,
and had very naturally come to warm himself in his
own quarters.

" 'The Court' and myself now got along very well
together. He had been bred to the law in the western
country, did not want for shrewdness, was good-natured,
but evidently a man of low habits and manners."

After dressing and eating, our testy Englishman went

out with a scientific friend to make a regular survey and ascertain the real geological structure and nidus of the metallic contents of the rocks. After wandering about the whole day, they finally got back in the evening to the customary ham and treacle. They were then informed that the "good-natured Court" declined to repose behind the counter a second night, that not being according to the ideas of the majesty of the law and therefore Mr. Featherstonhaugh and his friend had to come down to the realities of their situation, and take lodging on the floor in the eating room with the "gin-nerals, colonels," etc., for company. He says, "Everything was makeshift at Mineral Point," and adds, "but certainly we found everybody very obliging." Thus it appears, at the last, that the kindness of the people had penetrated the cuticle of his sensibilities and extracted an acknowledgement.

"The sole topic which engrossed the general mind," continues the narrative, "was the production of galena and copper, especially the first, upon which they relied for everything they consumed, no one possessing capital beyond that which a transient success might furnish him. It was, in fact, a complete nest of speculators, with workmen following in their train; traders again upon their traces, to sell goods and provisions; doctors to give physic and keep boarding-houses; and lawyers to get a living out of this motley and needy population."

After collecting a quantity of fossils and minerals, Mr. Featherstonhaugh departed, but not without a parting anathema:

"A more melancholy and dreary place than this Mineral Point, I never expect to see again. We had not tasted a morsel of fresh meat, or fish, or vegetables, since we had been here. There was not a vestige of a garden in the place, and the population seemed quietly to have resigned itself to an everlasting and unvarying diet of coffee, rice, treacle, and bread and butter, morning, noon, and night, without any other variety than that of occasionally getting a different cup and saucer."

At Blue Mounds, Featherstonhaugh stopped with the bachelor taverner, Ebenezer Brigham, who served hard boiled eggs and stale bread, for which Featherstonhaugh says he was charged ten times what they were worth.

The traveler wrote of his experiences in the Peck tavern at Madison, an abridged account of which follows:

"Having secured our horses, we entered the grand and principal entrance to the city, against the top of which my head got a severe blow, it not being more than five feet high from the ground. The room was lumbered up with barrels, boxes, and all kinds of things. Amongst other things was a bustling little woman, about as high as the door, with an astounding high cap on, called Mrs. Rosaline Peck. No male Peck was on the ground.

"My first inquiry was, whether she had any fresh fish in the house. The answer was 'no!' Inflexible and unwelcome word. No fresh fish! No large delicious catfish, of twenty pounds' weight, to be fried with pork, and placed before the voracious traveler in quantities sufficient to calm those apprehensions that so often arise in indian lands, of there not being enough for him to eat until he falls asleep. 'Why, then' exclaimed my alarmed companion, 'What's to be done?' 'I calculate I've got some salt pork,' rejoined our little hostess. 'Then, madam, you must fry it without fish,' I replied. So to the old business we went, of bolting square pieces of fat pork, an amusement I had so often indulged in, that I sometimes felt as if I ought to be ashamed to look a live hog in the face. Our landlady, however, was a very active and obliging person; she said she would make us as comfortable as possible for her to do, and she 'guessed' she had a little coffee, and would make us a cup of it. Whether it was acorns, or what it was, puzzled me not a little; it certainly deserved to be thought tincture of myrrh, and, as we drank and grimaced, dear Mrs. Peck, in her sweetest manner, expressed her regret that she had no other sugar for our coffee, they having, 'somehow or other, not brought any with them.'

"Whilst we were in this repast the thunderstorm broke over us, and a deluge of rain came down, streaming through the roof in various places. In the midst of the confusion, two other vagabonds came in; one of them a ruffian-looking fellow, who said he was a miner, on his way across the indian country from Milwaukee; the other, a stupid, boorish, dirty-looking animal, said he had not tasted anything for two days, having lost his way on the prairie; and, having been overtaken the preceding night by a very heavy rain whilst making his way up a coulee or vale, had been afraid to lie on the ground, and had passed the whole night sitting on a fallen tree. Fortunately, there was pork enough for us all, and when our landlady had put the frying-pan to bed, she did the same to us by the act of blowing the candle out. Where she stowed herself was her own secret. Choosing a place between two barrels, I lay down, and drew my cloak over me; of sleep there was very little to be had, for it rained in torrents almost the whole night, and, not having pitched my camp skillfully, it poured upon me from the unfinished roof as I lay stretched upon the floor, not daring to move in the dark lest I should pull some of the articles of Mrs. Peck's museum upon me, or break some of her crockery."

When a copy of Featherstonhaugh's *A Canoe Voyage up the Minnay Sotor*, came to the hands of Mrs. Peck, she tartly replied to the traveler. She declared that her husband and son were both present when the visitor was there, that real coffee was served, that he slept on thirty pounds of feathers and as to its raining through the roof, that was all gas.

A few foundation stones on the southern extremity of an island in the Wisconsin river a short distance above Kilbourn, marks the site of the Dell House. In its time it was a famous stopping place for both travelers and rivermen. This early interior tavern was built in 1838 by Robert Allen, a bachelor, and the first family to occupy the place was that of J. B. McCuen. In 1859, in the days when Leroy Gates and Captain "Hank" Snyder were piloting lumber through the Dells, the late Orrin L. Glazier, who used to tell this story, was running rafts of lumber down the river. In the spring of that year there was on the drive a bully known as Big Johnson who was always picking faults with the weaker men and making of himself a general nuisance. One afternoon a young man crossed the rickety wooden bridge spanning the stream a short distance to the north, strode along the road through the timber, and stopped at the tavern. His clothes were of the latest eastern style, yet he carried a peculiar looking pack on his back. When he entered the barroom he gently removed his burden and carefully placed it in a far corner.

Big Johnson was there and demanded to know what

was in the pack. The mild-mannered stranger did not consider it any affair of the bully, and so informed him. This enraged Johnson who swore he would mop up the barroom floor with the stranger.

"Just a minute, friend," said the traveler, "As I came along I noticed an outside stone cellar to the east of the house and if you really want satisfaction suppose we repair to the place below, permit your friends here to lock us in together, the door not to be opened until one of us raps on the portal to be let out."

This sounded fine to the bully who thought himself more than a match for the stranger. Accordingly they were locked in the cellar, the remainder of the men waiting outside. Some little noise filtered through and in a short time a gentle tapping was heard on the door inside. On being opened, the stranger, quite unruffled, walked out while Big Johnson was found on the floor, bound hand and foot, and gagged with strips torn from his own clothes. When he was released they returned to the barroom, there to find the stranger unfastening his pack which contained a sleeping baby! He explained that his name was Arthur Jones, that he was the wrestling instructor at Princeton University. He had received word from his brother-in-law, who was a boss in the woods, that his sister had died of pneumonia, leaving the baby which since the mother's death had been cared for by an indian woman. He had come from the east to take the babe back to his home and the indian woman had strapped the child to one of her papoose boards, hence when wrapped up it made the peculiar looking pack.

Big Johnson was cured of his bullyism and many times afterward was heard to remark, "Well, you can't always tell how far a frog will jump."

One can almost see the swarms of rivermen at the tavern as they crowded about during the days when rafting was at its height, for they indulged in repeated potations and when somewhat intoxicated would relieve themselves in semi-musical tones of lines like these:

> Hairlip Sal from Rowley creek,
> She wore a number nine;
> She kicked the hat off a big galoot
> To the tune of 'Auld Lang Syne.'

Often the river was exceedingly dangerous in time of flood, and to brave the dangers of navigation with clumsily constructed rafts lumbermen deemed it necessary to fortify themselves with ample draughts before launching forth on the perilous journey. More than one unfortunate went down in the angry waters in a brave effort to bring the lumber through. Naturally the old inn was the center of much river news pertaining to the exploits of those daring souls who ventured upon the treacherous current.

Not a few of the first arrivals at Baraboo found the luxury of a night's repose in the old log schoolhouse erected in 1844, on what is now Seventh avenue; or possibly they lodged at the home of some hospitable settler, meager though his accommodations might be. In 1843 James Webster erected a building west of the north end of the upper oxbow of the Baraboo river and this place, in Lyons, was really the first approach to a hotel in the valley. Charles Armstrong, who came in 1847, says in the *American Sketch Book*:

"Just as the sun was setting we came up to a log house, over the door of which was a buck's horn. I jumped out of the wagon and, the door being open, entered. The house consisted of one large room, in the middle of which, seated around a table, were some half-dozen men in red shirts, playing cards. Finding I was not observed, I started back to the wagon, feeling alarmed for the ladies.

"At a short distance I perceived a tall, stoutly built man, and stepping up to him, I said: 'Sir, is there no other place that a stranger could get accommodations over night, only there?' pointing to the buck's horn.

"I discovered in his features an open, manly expression, and intuitively felt that we were safe. He opened his broad, frank mouth and said, 'Yes, if you will take up with such accommodations as I have in my little house, you are welcome,' at the same time starting toward the house. On entering, I found a house unsurpassed for cleanliness – in fact, one of the cleanest I ever had my foot in. This was the home of Alexander Crawford."

Concerning the inmates of the log tavern, the author of the foregoing continues:

"I afterwards became acquainted with these red shirts, and felt ashamed of myself for being afraid of them, for they were not really bad or dangerous men. The house was owned and kept by old man Webster, after whom Webster's prairie was named. He was in many respects a remarkable man, being possessed of a superior mind, yet totally deaf. But such was his power of observation that he could get the substance of a conversation merely by watching the motion of the lips of the person speaking. We had a meeting at Colonel Maxwell's store and 'Jings Adams' (that being the name by which he was designated) made a very good speech. After the close of the meeting I observed to a friend that it was a great pity Webster was deprived of hearing. He stood opposite me, and immediately exclaimed: 'Neighbor Armstrong, you say it is a deprivation not to hear. Why, one-half that is told in the world is lies, and the other half had just as well not be heard.' "

Tavern Names, Signs, and Advertisements

Such names as Green Dragon, Black Horse, and King's Arms which were common enough in Old and New England were not applied to Northwestern taverns, nevertheless there were among them designations quite unusual. Some of these came from New York and various eastern states; others where wholly original. The Rough and Ready House (later the Wisconsin), at Dodgeville, erected in 1849 by Benjamin Thomas sr., was named in honor of Zachary Taylor, the hero of Buena Vista. This inn figures conspicuously in stories of early times told by residents of the village. It is said to have been very popular as a place of entertainment and that reckless miners often spent the earnings of a month in a single night here. When the property was purchased by Joseph Hocking on election day, 1854, he was so elated that he kept a free house for a number of days. "Why should we not have enjoyed ourselves in those days," Hocking is reported as saying in later years, "mineral was easy to get, money plenty, flour worth three dollars a barrel, beef three cents a pound, pork two and a half cents, potatoes two bits a bushel, and whiskey proportionally cheap."

When Nathaniel Walton erected a tavern on the prairie at Waukesha it became known as the Lighthouse and Travelers' Home. The most numerous neighbors were Potawatomi indians and wolves. The proprietor complained that they were altogether too social.

Mineral Point in 1835 consisted of a few log cabins

and huts built with square-cut sod, covered with poles overlaid with prairie grass and earth. Bachelors were the cooks in the only place of entertainment, and in lieu of a bell or other device to announce meal time, the glad tidings were wigwagged to men at the mines by waving a white rag attached to a long pole. Soon the place was given the sobriquet of "Shake-rag," the name finally being applied to the entire settlement.

When early rivermen ran their rafts down the Wisconsin and Mississippi they returned from Galena afoot or by stage, the route being through Mineral Point, Arena, Baraboo, and beyond. The Wisconsin river was crossed by ferry, and after traveling about a mile the men came to the Setting Hen, located on Cassell Prairie and operated by Russell Bentley. First he erected a narrow, two-story frame structure. Soon business grew, and a lean-to was added on one side, and later a second on the other side. To the rivermen, from a distance, the tavern had the appearance of a mother hen brooding her chickens, hence the Setting Hen. On one side in front liquor was sold, while coffins were made by hand at the rear. More than one raftsman who lost his life in the stream near by, or neighbor who came to the journey's end on Cassell Prairie, was buried in a coffin made from boards in one of the lean-tos, while drinks were being dispensed in the other. The little rural cemetery is within sight of the cottonwood tree which marks the site of the tavern. The Red Hen, a few miles west of Waupun, was noted for its bar, dances, and physical encounters. It is of local record that one man, after a mêlée, had to be carried home from the room on a stretcher.

The Shanghai House at Black River Falls may have been named for a breed of chickens popular when the building was erected, or from a wing of the Democratic party then so designated. The chickens were tall and slim; so was the Shanghai House. A lake vessel was called "Shanghai," and a well-known Wisconsin editor also bore the title.

Sometimes colors were employed in naming taverns. The Yellow Tavern is near Watertown, the Blue Tavern stood half way between Fox Lake and Portage, while the Red Tavern, between Kilbourn and Mauston was popular when thousands were crossing the state in covered wagons to settle beyond the Mississippi.

Sometimes distances imparted convenient names, as the Six-Mile House or Riches' Tavern, west of Sauk City, the Three-Mile House in Dodge county, the Eight-Mile House north of Galena. Location not infrequently suggested names – Mount Breeze on an elevation at Sheboygan Falls, for example; and the Fox River House on the stream so named; while Lake houses were many. The Lake House in Milwaukee was appropriately named because it was first erected at Sheboygan and later towed down the lake to its new location.

Several taverns were named for John Jacob Astor, "a shrewd little foreigner who dealt in musical instruments, furs, and Manhattan real estate – except the last mentioned he never sold." The Astor House was an early hostelry at Green Bay, and a vacant building bearing the name in rafting days still stands on the bank of the Wisconsin at Sauk City.

The early tavern at Rio, Columbia county, was called the Ohio House, and Rusk's tavern at Viroqua was named the Buckeye, since General Rusk was a native of the Buckeye state.

After H. H. Deyarman had conducted the Niagara

House, the first hotel on the west side of the river in Eau Claire, he changed to another location which he named the Monongahela House, because there were several barrels of fragrant Monongahela whiskey in the cellar.

The Rutabaga Tavern, four miles from Sheboygan Falls, was so called because the proprietor was fond of that particular vegetable; while the Spread Eagle on the Sheboygan-Fond du Lac road received its designation from its "chesty" proprietor. A tavern near Janesville was known as a House with a Hundred Windows on account of its peculiar architectural characteristics. At Plover, Jesse Anson, a river pilot, constructed a tavern of the longest logs he could find. As business increased he built a section at one end, and in time made still another addition. The parts not in proper alignment had a peculiar appearance which the landlord evidently recognized, for one day when asked the name of the tavern he replied, "The Goose Horn." It was so called ever after.

The Bean Sandwich at Durand was built by Casper Hugg, the Red Lion was at Walworth, the William Tell in Oconomowoc. The Norwegian Hell at Stevens Point has memories of hard drinking and skylarking, and the Tietgen Tavern near Manitowoc was named for its proprietor who weighed about four hundred pounds and who required two ordinary chairs to be comfortably seated.

Hoel S. Wright was the founder of Wrightstown, on the Fox river a few miles above Green Bay. One day Doctor St. John crossed the stream and found the air malodorous from a passing polecat. Wright had just completed a board tavern and when the physician asked what he intended to call the place the landlord promptly replied, "Skunk's Misery."

An early hotel in Milwaukee was called Brunen Hirsch (Brown Deer), another Bohnenviertel (Bean Quarter), a third at Sheboygan the Bavarian Heaven.

Early taverners had little desire to honor redmen by adopting aboriginal names. Among the exceptions, however, were the Tonquitquioc House at Plymouth, a word applied first to a crooked river. Tonquitquioc anglicized means mullet, a variety of fish.

As early as 1837 there were seven centers of population, or settled neighborhoods, in Walworth county and each was more often called by the name of the tavern than by its proper designation. Doctor Hemenway, among his numerous callings, was a landlord and Hemenway's meant Spring Prairie. Major Meacham was a tavern-keeper at Troy and Meacham's meant Troy. McCracken's was East Troy, Bradley's was Elkhorn, Phoenix's was Turtle Creek, and so on.

In England and New England were many elaborate tavern signs, but by the time western migration had reached the Mississippi valley the desire for showy signboards on inns was feebly manifested. On Wisconsin tavern signs there were no colorful pictures of Washington, Governor Hancock, William Pitt, three crowns, horses, lions, or hats. After the Revolutionary war lions and crowns were of course no longer popular, and for various reasons most of such emblems disappeared.

Among the few represented in the Midwest may be mentioned the Eagle Hotel at Lamartine on the Military road which had for its sign an eagle with outstretched wings. The board was ornamented about

1847 and in after years was taken to Brandon where it was nailed on the outside of a wheat elevator. From its exposed altitude the wind finally blew a portion of the sign to the ground; and later the whole was consumed when fire destroyed the building.

A huge wooden eagle carved by Henry Jens constituted a conspicuous sign in front of The Eagle on the Sheboygan road in Fond du Lac. Originally the hotel was the Lewis home, built in 1848 by Robert Wyatt. With the erection of the carved sign the name was changed. That portion of the Sheboygan road in Fond du Lac has since become Fourth street.

Paine's celebrated Buckhorn Tavern west of Monroe had the antlers of a deer on a post near the roadside. Prongs usually were over the door of buckhorn taverns of which there were a number in the state, one of the most famous being north of Watertown. To this day many hotels use Antlers as a name.

A landlord at Superior erected what he considered an attractive sign, there being three parts, each illustrated:

> Beds, Board, and Booze.
> All Nations welcome except Carry.
> Coffee, not like mother made but like she drank

In the forties a tavern at Beetown had as a sign a Scotch (straw) beehive, painted by Wilson. In 1827, a few miners overturned a bee tree which disclosed a bed of mineral – a bee lead – hence the name.

Three miles southeast of Evansville stood the Ball Tavern which had a great globe to attract travelers. Leonard Martin erected a martin (bird) house in front of his tavern near Mukwanago. The Green Tree, a few miles north of Milwaukee, lured patrons by a painting of a tree in full leaf.

Many signs in the forties and fifties were square, and one, from Butte des Morts near Oshkosh, has found a permanent home in the museum housed in the Sawyer Foundation building. It reads as follows:

HOTEL
By
T. B. PETTFORD

The tavern, still standing, was erected about 1848 and was a place of entertainment for many noted men of early Wisconsin who passed up and down the Fox river between Green Bay and Portage.

At a later period it became the custom to use a single board some ten feet long, one end fastened to the building, the other to a post outside the walk. This gave travelers an opportunity to read the sign when approaching from either direction.

All that survives of the old sign at the Prairie House, near Token creek, northeast of Madison, may be seen on the lower side of the house, just above the cement about the pump at the rear door. The building was erected by Horace Lawrence, who came from Vermont in 1837, and has housed many notables, among them Jefferson Davis, afterwards president of the confederacy. Davis at the time was an officer at Fort Winnebago, Portage. Others of military rank stopped at the Prairie House in journeying across the state.

Sometimes amusing errors were made by those who painted signs. About 1845, Edwin Plummer built a tavern on the bank of the Wisconsin river west of Portage, the place being on the main stream of travel to Minnesota and the farther Northwest. There is a sandy hill near and the proprietor decided that Sand Hill House would be an appropriate designation. Accordingly he ordered these words painted upon a board eight feet long, but what was his astonishment when the sign arrived to read:

SANDWICH HOUSE

The boniface pondered a moment, then concluded this was entirely suitable and so it remained until the end of its usefulness.

In 1848 John Boutwell erected a large dwelling house at Otsego which he later converted into a tavern and which he named the Otsego House. The sign was unique in that the letter "e" had been omitted from the word "House," reading "Otsego Hous." When the proprietor was informed that there should be an "e" at the end of the word, he replied:

"Pshaw, you can't fool me. That would make it read hous-y."

Passing travelers made so much sport of the sign, however, that the owner ultimately caused it to be taken down and corrected.

Sometimes proprietor or painter lapsed into rhyme when wielding the brush. On the Mukwanago road in Milwaukee county Captain John Bell wished to call attention to the superior water in his well, hence he caused to be erected a sign with the following unusual inscription:

Stop gentlemen as you pass by,
My water tank is free,
Its source is on the mountain high,
Its course is to the sea.

Some signs were not without their amusing aspects. In 1857 C. W. Pitcher, proprietor of the Franklin House at Viroqua, advertised: "Stages call for passengers and lemonade. Board $1.00 per day." The lemonade probably had a "stick" in it.

That same year Jeremiah M. Rusk closed the Buckeye House in Viroqua and succeeded Ira Wilkins as proprietor of the North Star Hotel. Rusk advertised, "That the proprietor is thankful for the past very liberal patronage of the public at the Buckeye House and solicits a continuance of the same. Those who give him a call will receive prompt attention and find the 'fixins' in apple pie order."

Signboards on the highways were sometimes of more than passing interest. In 1844 a sign was erected between Snake Hollow and Beetown which made it anything but pleasant for the lonely traveler. Seven or eight miles from Snake Hollow the road forked and two guide boards were nailed to a tree, pointing in different directions. They were neatly and artistically painted, a fact which could but add to the confusion of the stranger. On one of the boards was the information that it was so many miles to the Nip and Tuck while the other had a large hand with a long finger pointing in the opposite direction. Below the hand was a picture of a big snake, coiled, head elevated, mouth open, eyes gleaming and apparently ready to strike. Near the hand and above the snake were the words "$7\frac{1}{2}$ m. to ———." There were several bullet holes through the board when inspected by Frank Barr. Evidently hunters had been shooting at the snake's head, usually missing it.

Here is a friendly advertisement from the Milwaukee *Courier* of February 11, 1846:

"C. S. Vail has opened his new house at Prairieville, located in the center of the village, and can be found at all times ready and willing (besides almost tickled to death) to wait on his friends and strangers who may favor him with a call."

In 1842 Edward Elderkin, in opposition to another tavern operated by Wilmot Brothers at Elkhorn, built one on the site of the courthouse. The new hostelry soon passed to Samuel Mallory who inserted the following unique advertisement in the *Western Star* of Elkhorn:

WALWORTH COUNTY CENTER HOUSE

S. Mallory takes pleasure to inform
The public that he lives at Elkhorn,
And that he has a public house in charge,
To which he invites the public at large.
Accommodations of all kinds, and good cheer,
With choicest liquors and strong beer;
Lemonade, soda beer, and Tom and Jerry,
Which gentlemen can have to make them merry.
His table is furnished with the substantials of life,
Cooked and prepared by his daughters and wife.
Myself will attend you and give you the food,
With desserts and pastry, which shall all be good.
My barn is furnished with wild and tame hay,
Which gentlemen can have for ready pay.
My oats I will sell at one shilling a peck,
And that I will have in spite of Tom Dick.
As for barn room to feed, you can have it free,
If yourself you will feed it with me;
But, as I want a part of the fleece,
If you don't feed yourself, its a sixpence apiece.
Call at the Walworth Center House, if you mistake not,
For the Elkhorn House is kept by D. C. Wilmot.
A mistake in the house you can plainly see
Is a loss of your custom and a damage to me.
My charge will be reasonable, according to times;
My attention shall be strict, and I'll do without rhymes.
I'll undergo fatigue, and be always on hand
To retain the reputation the house now commands.

George E. Graves advertised in the Milwaukee *Sentinel*, September 7, 1842, that "There is attached to this house stabling for a hundred horses, and a large and secure carriage house, built expressly for loaded teams. Emigrants wishing to go to the country will find the Great Western Hotel a desirable stopping place – as all teams bound for the interior must pass this house. Teamsters can get their meals at any time of day or night. Low prices and good fare will be the distinguishing characteristics of this house."

From the *Miners' Free Press*, Mineral Point, August 18, 1837, the following was gleaned:

"Cold Spring Tavern. The undersigned respectfully informs the public that he is prepared to entertain travelers and others at the old place in Messer Grove, – on the road from Mineral Point to Madison, – twelve miles from Mineral Point, twelve miles from Helena, forty from Madison, and fifty-seven from Prairie du Chien. Believing he understands what is necessary to render the traveler comfortable, and determined to give the business his attention, he hopes to invite a share of the public patronage. He will at all times be prepared to furnish gentlemen horses, or horses and carriage with good sober drivers to travel to any part of the country.

JOHN MESSERSMITH"

Messer Grove, July 14 (1837)

Seymour Wilcox built a log tavern, which was the first house at Beaver Dam. After it had served its usefulness he replaced it with a frame building in front of which he erected an oval sign, bearing the words The Old Stand. Still later (Sept. 12, 1848) he advertised:

"To the Traveling Public. Ward's Cottage. At Beaver Dam, Wis.

The proprietor of this House would respectfully inform his old patrons, and the traveling community at large that he has taken a new House (which has lately been rebuilt and furnished throughout) a few rods east of his old stand, where he will be in readiness at all times to attend to the wants of those who may favor him with their patronage. No effort will be spared to render the "Cottage" a desirable stopping place. The table will be supplied with the best the market affords. The barn will be stocked, and the servants attentive and obliging. He would return his thanks to those who patronized him while occupying his old stand, and would solicit a continuance of their patronage. Stages leave this house for all parts of the state. The stage office is located at this house."

Tavern Guests and Incidents

Often, indeed, days were lonely for families occupying remote taverns and there must have been general rejoicing when a stranger was observed approaching in the shadows of evening. Perhaps he was a traveler from Kentucky, clad in jeans, wearing stodgy boots, and riding or driving a shaggy old horse. At his request for entertainment, members of the household would bustle about, striving to outdo each other in acts of hospitality. There might be few luxuries in the larder but to whatever was there, the stranger was welcome.

During the winter season especially, when roads were seldom traveled, lorn and lone were these outpost taverns. For days the highway would stretch away before them without sign of track in the snow and at night the only sounds that broke the silence were the hoot of owl and howl of wolf. After darkness had curtained hill and valley, prairie and forest, what a thrill within the cabin when a knock sounds upon the primitive portal. Who comes through the stillness? Perhaps death has befallen or life is dawning at some camp by the wayside. Throw ajar the door, see whose face is revealed by the shaft of light which escapes from the feeble candle into the night! Mayhap the summons is by a traveler who has lost his way, one seeking medical aid, or merely an individual who would sit by the fire to enjoy warmth and companionship. Perhaps a stranger is discouraged and in distress, an enemy is seeking revenge, or an aborigine with blanket, earrings, and unintelligible speech, begs entrance. As the beating of waves on a rocky coast is to those who sail the sea, so a faint glimmering from a window leads to a tap upon the door by those journeying in a new land.

Daniel M. Parkinson opened a tavern on the Pecatonica in 1828, but he had no neighbors nearer than twelve miles, except a family of Oneida indians from New York state. His rude abode was the only one between Gratiot's Grove and Blue Mounds.

Jared Walsworth was the earliest settler and innkeeper between Portage and Stevens Point, locating in 1838 at Big Spring, Adams county. An indian woman was his wife and for that reason the Menominee permitted him to locate amongst them at least fifteen years before the original government surveyors appeared.

When Brigham erected his log tavern at Blue Mounds in the late twenties, his nearest neighbor on the west was at Dodgeville and on the east was Solomon Juneau in Milwaukee. At that time the population of Wisconsin was so limited, one was considered a neighbor though thirty miles away.

Who were the men and women entertained in territorial taverns? What did they discuss? What motives attracted them to the undeveloped country? What were their pleasures, their problems, their philosophies? These are among the questions to which one seeks answer, for life at that time flowed in quite a different channel from the course it pursues at present.

In early days travelers and returned soldiers often came to visit places made famous by the Black Hawk War of 1832; and since many tribesmen remained in the territory following the brief conflict, it was no unusual sight for guests to observe an indian with head thrust through the tavern door, demanding firewater. Indians frequently came to trade hides or other articles for food, beads, and baubles of one sort or another. One year when the whites raised an excellent crop of corn, tribesmen came numerously in the fall to swap muskrat hides for maize. Soon all who came were busy shelling corn, keeping at the labor until midnight, for the rate of exchange was a pint of corn for a muskrat skin. In trading indians took up only one bargain at a time, finishing before considering another. By twelve o'clock packs were depleted of furs and tribesmen returned to camp.

Picturesque scenes colored the life at some of the early taverns, especially those situated at Green Bay and Prairie du Chien. Costumes of the people ranged from army uniforms worn by soldiers and Parisian gowns of certain ladies of fortune, to buckskin garments and moccasins of indians and of those little better indeed than the aborigines. This variety and contrast in raiment produced a kaleidoscope of color, cut, and texture.

Wives of travelers and landladies conversed of homes in the east and south, of youthful comforts and joys, of cherished school days, all abandoned to penetrate the western wilderness with their husbands in the hope of improving their condition. These women who left advanced civilization for the wilds of Wisconsin and other states in the West, enduring years of hardship had assuredly their full share in developing a new country.

When the region had gained a considerable population, the traveler upon entering a tavern would be likely to find the room filled with wagoners ranged about the bar. A florid landlord usually presided over activities and in a dusky kitchen a buxom landlady, her home-manufactured gown protected by an apron of generous proportions, bustled about directing several good-looking girls. These more often than not, daughters in the family, were of valued assistance in the operation of the hostelry. At Pokerville, near Blue Mounds, when settlers poured into the taverns these maidens mingled with red-shirted miners, unknown fur-traders, and roistering teamsters in social diversions, their youth and gaily hued garments gracing the company.

Those were the days of the delightful pastime of "brag," and about the tavern there was frequently an exhuberance of this form of innocent amusement. In summer strong men boasted of the volume of wood they could cut, and in winter there was self-glorification respecting the amount of wheat they could harvest in the summer. With the absence of the telegraph, daily newspaper, phonograph, telephone, and radio, conversation was about the only escape from intellectual torpidity.

Not until the fifties did the flood of immigration break with full force in Wisconsin. Immigrants arrived in covered wagons which creaked over rough roads, through forest and swamp, all the way from New York and New England, or by tedious voyage over the Great Lakes to be welcomed at a friendly tavern at the end of a long journey. Both landlord and guest had sacrificed comfort and security for a cabin in the timber or a hut in the "oak openings," listening to voices that drew them even though these murmured of hardship and distress. It was a super-adventure – they were a part of that wonderful emergence over the eastern mountains and across the inland seas into the silence and mystery of a land to be peopled – gallant adventurers who dared to

be numbered with those whose travels should be recorded in the annals of the immortals. Their purpose
was to obtain a footing of land. Not for a moment did
they entertain the thought that their new possessions
could revert to the bear, the beaver, and the savages of
the wood. They came to adjust themselves to new conditions, to rescue the great domain which spread over
hills and prairies between Lake Michigan and the Mississippi. They were ready for whatever the gods offered
and bravely accepted responsibility with its varying
degrees of hardship and prosperity.

In the fifties the exchanges of experience regarding
money issued by banks of uncertain stability were important. The value of paper currency changed with the
days, and usually the farther from the place of issuance
the less was the worth of the medium. It behooved those
westward bound to exchange their paper for issues
which would more likely have a value nearer the point
to which they journeyed, and the same was true of bills
carried in the opposite direction. The questionable
character of money was a vital source of conversation
at almost every tavern.

The panic of 1837, too, was much discussed. In that
year when property in Milwaukee valued at ten thousand dollars dropped to one thousand dollars; when
oats and potatoes fell from one dollar and two dollars
to almost nil; when every commodity was greatly reduced in price; and when beautiful air castles suddenly
disappeared the financial crash was a favorite topic.

News brought by the stranger usually was common-
place and did not startle the occupants of the tavern.
But if he happened to have a newspaper even a month
old, what joy there was! Every column was closely
perused from top to bottom.

Besides travelers and landseekers, the clientele of taverns in the lead-mining district of southwestern Wisconsin included men interested in riches below the surface of the earth. Patrons of taverns near lake ports embraced teamsters and interior merchants, as well as others who had come hoping to find a new Eldorado; while in the reaches toward the pineries those giving impetus to tavern life were seeking wealth in the boundless forests.

In taverns standing along rough roads leading to the vast expanse of Wisconsin pine forests were heard many wonderful tales of adventure. Frequently after reaching one of these stopping places, before the winter camp had been sighted, older men would try to frighten those going north for the first time by telling them that the woods were full of "snow snakes" and other dreaded creatures. Lumberjacks would declare that snakes often hung from trees or were buried in the snow ready to leap upon an approaching victim. One timid lad while a guest at the Twin Island House became so distressed over such stories that he was near returning home when a comrade whispered the untruthfulness of the statements. There were stories also of trackless forest and lurking indian, of perilous river trips and exciting chase, all by the participants themselves. Sometimes the stories were of dusky loves of early whites – especially by those who were not averse to dallying with dark-skinned maidens of the forest.

Rough-bearded, strong-fisted shanty boys of the pineries often found taverns along the upper Wisconsin and other rivers anything but inviting as they migrated north in the fall and south in the spring. Perhaps their bunks were on the side of a wall, their beds only a coarse tick stuffed with straw or marsh hay, and their table fare of the coarsest sort.

Raftsmen were oftimes the despair of the taverners where they tarried. Apparently they had no homes and acknowledged no authority. One night at Sauk City villagers and rivermen became engaged in a boisterous battle, many more or less intoxicated. From the tavern the townspeople took refuge in a board enclosure and when the raftsmen attempted to clamber over their fingers were pounded and hacked. No one lost his life, but the morning after there were sore heads and hands.

In the taverns horse-racing and trading were often discussed. The Little Prairie Tavern near Palmyra, like many another in the state, was a horse trading center. Some old jockeys resembled David Harum in appearance, actions, and in the sharp bargains they drove.

The landlords frequently were postmasters, and to them came the community for mail, whether once a month or one or more times weekly. Peck's Tavern at Madison, Brigham's at Blue Mounds, Martin's big house near Mukwonago, and many others were post-offices which attracted callers for the mail and for friendly visits besides. In the thirties letter postage was twenty-five cents. It is related that when a resident was informed there was a letter for him he replied he had no money to pay the postage, the missive having been sent unprepaid as was the custom. He turned about, asked for a loan, half a dozen wallets came out, and soon he had the letter. There were no stamps or envelopes then; the paper was merely folded over and frequently held in place with wafers or wax.

Not unusual was it for a postmaster to carry letters about in his plug hat, as did Abraham Lincoln when postmaster at Salem, Illinois. These "two-gallon" hats were commodious enough for all first-class mail and frequently when the patron of the office desired a letter he would find it with the postmaster in field or wood or neighboring mill. At Beetown in the lead region the office was in the tavern and Samuel Varden was postmaster. The mail from Galena once or twice a week brought fifteen or twenty letters which Mr. Varden carried about on his head and the newspapers were deposited on the counter in his place. It was often said that when the postmaster's hat blew off the news was borne veritably on the wings of the wind.

The landlord usually came in to converse with his guests, to be one of the party. When the argument waxed warm, a storm of good-natured chaff prevailed. In winter one could not sit comfortably in an unheated room, hence guests, host, and dwellers in the hamlet generally found themselves part of a good-natured company. They talked about nearly everything under the sun and some of their stories still remain silhouetted against that early background. When travelers with special charm of conversation essayed to speak others in the room respected their ability and chatter was hushed.

Often groups of men who had gained state-wide reputations in politics or distinction in other fields, commingled at pioneer inns. Among notables frequenting the Hawes Tavern southwest of Madison were Judge Irvin, Moses M. Strong, Marshall M. Strong, Ebenezer Brigham, George P. Delaplaine, and J. C. Knapp. Judge Irvin was always accompanied by his famous horse, Pedro, and his dog, York.

Another group who frequented early taverns were promoters of railroads, officials, and surveyors. The advent of these affable gentry must have made great occasions for taverns, especially when the first railroad went pioneering across the state from Milwaukee to Prairie du Chien in the fifties. Wherever these functionaries halted for refreshment or entertainment for the night, the neighborhood naturally became excited and expectant. Some of the railways yet remain after an existence of more than seventy-five years, but few of the taverns of the era are standing today.

The circus in its tour over the country brought acrobats and gymnasts to inns while at hall-shows conjurers and illusionists were presented. The ventriloquist came to mystify audiences and the artful phrenologist deftly traversed miscellaneous pates to the vociferous amusement of the onlookers. All of course were made to feel at home in the hospitable tavern.

Came along the land speculator, shrewd of eye, pompous, flashily dressed and eloquent. He hovered hopefully about the tavern awaiting new arrivals and doing a "land office business" in farms and platted tracts. The itinerant preacher, pious, often mediocre, yet with prideful pretense at learning, was by no means an infrequent patron in his devout pilgrimages.

Occasionally an elderly couple, perhaps of fifty or sixty years, bound for a new location, made their appearance, explaining that since their children were grown up and married, no ties remained at home. They had clambered into the covered wagon and joined the almost endless westward ho!

History records many interesting personages whose signatures were inscribed on tavern registers. General U. S. Grant, as a salesman before the Civil war and as a visitor after the conflict, tarried at many places of entertainment in southern Wisconsin and northern Illinois. When he was a guest for a brief time at the Cliff House, Devil's lake, he was given a trip on a little side-wheel steamer which plied the placid waters. A visit also was made to Landlord Kirk's wine cellar and standing beside the general was a dainty maiden, Agatha Pearl, daughter of the Cliff House boniface, who declined to drink, whereupon the hero of many battles remarked:

"Well, I'll not take any, if the little girl doesn't."

The Cliff House holds many interesting memories. A distinguished guest was Mrs. Abraham Lincoln a few years after the assassination of her illustrious husband, while Samuel Hartley was proprietor. Quite particular was she and when shown her room in the Cliff House she returned to the office and complained to Landlord Hartley that it was not as good as she desired, saying:

"I suppose you do not know who I am. I am no ordinary woman, I am Mrs. Abraham Lincoln."

Hartley, a crusty, quick-tempered individual, is said to have replied:

"I do not care in purgatory who you are. The room you have is the best I've got and I cannot give you a different one."

Mrs. Lincoln soon after drove to the Western Hotel in Baraboo where she tarried for a short time and it is hoped was treated with greater courtesy.

Others whose names are on the Cliff House registry are Ole Bull, eminent violinist; Doctor Cronin, murdered in Chicago; General William T. Sherman, Civil war hero; Blind Tom, phenomenal pianist; Carter Harrison, several times mayor of Chicago; Marvin Hughitt, president of the Chicago and North Western Railway. The oldest part of the building was erected by E. N. Marsh in 1865 and for a time, till it became part of a state park, was owned by Colonel William F. Vilas, United States senator from Wisconsin.

Early in his residence in America Knut Hamsun, the Norwegian author, recipient of a Nobel prize, sojourned at an Elroy hotel. He was clever at drawing and to amuse himself sketched the figure of a man upon the wall of his room and, making a hole in the plastering, thrust a cigar in the mouth. When the maid entered the next morning she was much astonished. In other ways Hamsun spiced his life while lingering in Elroy.

In September, 1859, Abraham Lincoln was a guest at the Newhall House, Milwaukee, having been engaged to deliver an address at the State fair. For the talk, which was not of a political nature, he is said to have received one hundred dollars. "It was not long after tea," records A. M. Thomson, "when the rotunda of the Newhall House was well filled, and Mr. Lincoln was busy shaking hands and making pleasant remarks to the gentlemen who were introduced to him. At length someone suggested that it was a great oversight that the presence of so distinguished an advocate of the anti-slavery cause had not been taken advantage of so that he might have delivered an address upon that all absorbing topic. . . Mr. Lincoln was asked if he would not give them a little talk then and there, to which the 'rail-splitter' facetiously replied that there was no platform to stand upon, meaning that a speaker ought to be elevated above his auditors who were all standing; and secondly, that there was nothing to talk about. The first objection was soon overcome by someone going out and soon returning with an empty dry goods box for Mr. Lincoln to stand upon. . . The platform being thus speedily provided, Mr. Lincoln reluctantly stepped upon it and proceeded to deliver an address upon the one burning issue of the hour – slavery. . . I see him now as he stood there under the gas light upon his improvised rostrum, his tall, gaunt form trembling with suppressed emotion as he depicted the dangers to the country which he felt to be imminent, and the look of inexpressible sadness that at times overspread his swarthy, homely features no one will ever forget. I never saw the benignant countenance again until I looked upon it in the casket, as the remains lay in state in Chicago, when the body of the great emancipator was being taken back to Springfield, after J. Wilkes Booth had fired the fatal shot, 'heard round the world.' "

The dominating human element in the lead region prior to the coming of farmers was from Kentucky, Virginia, and Missouri, many having been residents of Illinois. With them they brought the manners and customs of the Mason and Dixon border.

During the days when there was a government land office at Green Bay, Mineral Point, or elsewhere, during those days when thousands of acres of virgin soil were being claimed by settlers, there were many land-seekers at inns along the primitive roads. Frequently it occurred that two or more individuals coveted the same unsubdued acres and this situation often resulted in an informal race to the land office. Sometimes a settler erected a cabin on a tract with the express intention of securing a title when his finances permitted, but possibly, ere he was aware, another would prepare to visit the agent. The rivalry produced amusing situations among tavern guests.

Expectant purchasers carried coin on their persons, often all they possessed. This was a source of more or less anxiety especially when in places of doubtful character. Of the guests frequenting the Buckhorn Tavern

The Western, Baraboo

Stood on Oak street; was burned November 6, 1878; a famous hostelry in stagecoach days

of Joseph Paine west of Monroe, none passed a more anxious night than M. H. Pengra while on his way to the land office in 1848. He carried with him in a shot pouch two hundred dollars in coin, mostly Mexican gold pieces. The pouch was too bulky and heavy to be easily secreted and when the owner tried to keep it in an inner pocket of his coat, the lining broke and it fell heavily to the ground. Thinking to find relief from his responsibility, Pengra retired to bed as early as possible but this did not improve the situation as Landlord Paine entered the room an hour or two later with the request that he share his sleeping quarters with him. Filled with suspicion, Pengra grasped the money pouch tightly, repose being sacrificed for the night.

In 1857 there was no jail in Baraboo; the village newspaper tells of a prisoner's treatment: "He sleeps at the Western Hotel, the best in town, eats his breakfast there, and lounges around the village, gossiping with merchants and clerks until the gong sounds for dinner, which meal he eats with as good grace as if he, instead of the county, paid for it. Afternoon and evening are spent in the same manner with the single welcome interruption of tea; and at a tolerably reasonable hour our prisoner goes to bed, not being, we fear a sadder or a wiser man. He has no disposition to run away, considering himself as he does, the best-treated man in Sauk county. We understand the sheriff proposed to him to work on his farm, but he was informed by his gentlemanly prisoner that the county had agreed to support him three months without work." This is the manner in which a resident was "punished" for stealing a cow.

Prior to the Civil war escaped slaves sometimes took refuge in taverns. Two of the most notable of these unusual guests were Caroline Quarles and Joshua Glover. The former was the first passenger on the earliest "underground railroad" in Wisconsin, the route having its northern terminus at Milwaukee. The father of Caroline was a white man and her owner, Mrs. Charles R. Hall of St. Louis, was her father's sister, therefore her own aunt. The girl boarded a boat at the Missouri city and traveled as far as Alton without arousing suspicion. Befriended by a colored man she finally reached Milwaukee by stagecoach but soon after attorneys arrived to compel her to return. By day and by night in rapid succession exciting events followed. Aided by unknown men and women friendly to the cause of abolition, she was spirited from vehicle to residence, from residence to tavern and to various stations on the "underground." A reward was on her head but after many thrilling experiences her pursuers were outwitted, she being secretly conveyed by vehicle to Chicago, from there to Detroit, and at last over the river into Canada. The extended narrative of this case gives but a faint idea, indeed, of the hazardous efforts made by those of the frontier to assist fleeing slaves.

The coming of Joshua Glover into the state in 1854 and the cognate events aroused great political bitterness and tended more to crystalize opposition to slavery than any series of episodes in the history of the commonwealth. Glover was a fugitive from the South, found his way to Racine, was cruelly beaten when arrested, taken by carriage to Milwaukee, and thrown into prison. Mounting a horse Sherman M. Booth rode with all possible speed through the streets urging citizens to rescue the colored man from jail. The door was battered down with a beam, and a dash was made with the slave for the Mansion House, Waukesha, that tavern becom-

ing the center of the excitement. In time Glover reached
Racine, was secreted on a boat bound for Canada, and
escaped to that country, never to be captured. Booth and
others were arrested and the cases were in the courts for
some sixteen years. The Booth case became nationally
known and long was the storm center of argument
around many a tavern fireside.

Unwelcome guests sometimes frightened taverners.
In the days when the fighting Finch family resided on
the east side of Lake Koshkonong, one of them was
arrested on the charge of assaulting a Norwegian. In
fact, several of the Finches – there were about a dozen
of them who had been soldiers in the Black Hawk war –
had unmercifully beaten their neighbor and chased him
from home. The act aroused the ire of Colonel Dodge
who demanded that Sheriff Bird of Dane county bring
the culprits to justice. The sheriff summoned Luther A.
Cole, then a deputy at Milwaukee, to give assistance,
and in time arrested one of the family and set out with
him for Madison. No sooner were they on the way than
word went out to Finch's confederates who rallied to
the release of their neighbor. When Lake Mills was
reached the tavern keeper was instructed to inform the
Finches, should they appear, that the officers and prisoner were on the old road to Madison, though they
took the new road. It was not long before the Finches,
ten men armed with rifles, filed into the barroom and
by way of introduction to the alarmed landlord, called
for "the best in the shop."

"Did you see three men in a wagon go down the
road?" gruffly demanded Ben Finch as he drew forth a
roll of "wildcat" bills to settle for the drinks.

Trembling with fear the taverner spoke, as if im-
parting a terrible secret, misinforming his visitors. It

was a great relief to the innkeeper and to the entire village when the desperate band went galloping the wrong way.

It cost the prisoner eighty acres of land and a term in prison for the part he played in the affair and this punishment had the wholesome effect of causing the Finches to leave the locality. The ringleader escaped to Michigan never to be caught.

Accommodations at Early Taverns

For an early landlord not to find accommodation for every stranger who appeared at his inn was deemed little short of criminal. Like an omnibus, the tavern was supposed to be elastic – always room for one more. Jocularly it was said sometimes that a place never was crowded even though "there were three in a bed and two in the middle." The average traveler was not particular as to the amount of room allotted him for sleeping quarters. It was sufficient if he found a place large enough to stretch himself beneath the clapboard roof. In mild weather he voiced no serious objection if, on account of the limited space, he was obliged to hang his feet out of the window, figuratively speaking, or permit them to be used as a pillow by a companion. It was the day of "hale fellow well met" and accommodations were provided if it was within the power of the inn-keeper to do so.

Many of these rude hostelries were like Daniel E. Bradley's place at Elkhorn; travelers never asked the proprietor to show them a room, there was only one and that embraced all upstairs. In other inns bunks were arranged, one above the other on the wall, in still others the floor at night was strewn with shakedowns for transients.

When Cyrus Church was entertained at the Van Slyke Tavern in Walworth county, he slept on a floor made of split logs while others reposed above on bark spread on poles. This bark was taken from the deserted wigwam of Big Foot, the indian for whom Big Foot prairie is named. There was no fireplace in this primitive tavern, fire being lighted at one end of the building, the smoke escaping through a hole in the roof. Not a board was used in its construction. It is said that the number of guests stowed away in the little garret of this log tavern was actually mystifying.

As a rule when a traveler rode up to a tavern he was given a cordial welcome, landlord and landlady making haste to provide the best the place afforded. During the day no guests might be within but by nightfall the house commonly was crowded and the wonder was from whence they came. At the Hawks Tavern and others located on main roads, often there would be but a single guest when the evening meal was ready to serve but by the time he had finished the other chairs would be filled.

When there were ladies in the party spending the night at a log tavern, they might be asked to go aloft by a ladder or a rough stair where they were provided with a bed behind a convenient screen, while the men found places on the floor or remained below. If a presuming fellow appeared he must submit quietly to conditions or become the butt of the rest. All were on the same level respecting accommodations. At the Wade Tavern between Sheboygan and Fond du Lac more than two hundred persons applied for lodging on a single night, many times the capacity of the place. Teamsters and others employed in the lumber regions frequently lay so close on the floors and in the garret of the Jared Walsworth Tavern at Big Springs that one could not walk between them.

When Henry Merrell in 1835, left Fort Winnebago on horseback for New York, going by way of Galena, as there was no other direct road to Milwaukee or Chicago, he stopped the first night at Rowan's celebrated tavern at Poynette. Merrell was accompanied by Captain Harris who had come from Galena and was returning home. After their horses had received care and the travelers themselves were provided with food and drink, enquiry was made as to where they would sleep. The landlady replied they would be taken care of in the other house – the tavern included two log buildings under one roof but with an open space about ten feet in width between. When they went to retire, the men found nothing in the room but a bed and one or two three legged stools. Before they fell asleep there was an unearthly squeal and grunt of hogs in the open space. With only a partition of logs between the heads of guests and animals the annoyance had to be borne with as much good nature as possible.

The following concerning the Rowan Tavern at Poynette is related by an early guest:

"I arrived in 1837, at about 11:00 o'clock P.M., on horseback. The hostler, a Frenchman, was yet up, making fires to keep those comfortable who were sleeping on the floor. After taking care of my horse, I went into the house. There was a good fire and the floor was covered with men sleeping. I asked the French hostler for something to eat; so he went into the kitchen and brought me a whole duck and two potatoes. He said that was all he could find cooked. After eating I felt like lying down. He pointed to a place between two men. I took my blanket and crowded myself into it. The next morning the teamsters got up to feed their teams and, in taking out their corn, they scattered some inside and outside the house. James Duane Doty (afterwards governor) was lying next the door in his robes. I was next to him in my blanket. A lean long old sow found the corn that the teamsters had scattered outside. This encouraged her to follow up the corn scattered inside. Finding some among Doty's robes she put her nose under him and rolled him over, when he exclaimed: 'Landlord! Landlord! You must postpone my breakfast for some time as I have not yet got rested.' Instead of the landlord disturbing him, it was the old sow."

In February, 1837, Alexander F. Pratt and Augustus Story made a journey from Milwaukee to the mining regions in the western part of the territory. They remained the first night in a log tavern at Prairieville, now Waukesha. The building was about fifteen feet square and contained one room in which were two beds. Some five or six other travelers had arrived previously and the possibility of being entertained over night seemed quite dubious. When describing the accommodations Pratt says:

"Upon inquiry, we were told that we could stay, as it was a standing rule of the country to entertain all travelers regardless of accommodations, for necessity compelled it. After partaking of a very palatable supper consisting of fried pork and bread, the two beds were properly divided among the crowd upon the floor; but, having a good supply of blankets ourselves, we refused our proportion and made our bed near the stove; and being so much fatigued from our journey we soon fell asleep and did not even awake until daylight pressed the duty upon us."

In 1838 when Robert L. Ream, an early taverner at Madison, visited Fort Winnebago at Portage, he was entertained in a tavern operated by Henry Merrell.

Sleeping quarters were limited and not without excitement, as recorded by Mr. Ream as follows:

"An amusing incident occurred that night which I cannot help mentioning. In the room in which I slept were four beds, one in each corner, and all curtained. I occupied one of these beds, and it appears the other three were occupied by gentlemen and their wives. In the night we were all aroused by a cry of 'robbers! thieves! indians!' All started up at the alarm the ladies shrieking with fright. The room was dark and, in the confusion, we ran against each other very amusingly. When a light was struck the scene was extremely ludicrous — ladies in their nightclothes looking like affrighted ghosts, some of them clinging to the wrong man; men without any nightclothes and very little of any other kind making frantic exertions to find the cause of the disturbance. The supposition was that some soldiers had been on a carousal and had mistaken the hotel for the garrison; but under the charge of Captain Low, such a breach of the regulations would never have been allowed and the cause of the alarm was not satisfactorily explained."

Ream thus tells of his visit to Rowan's:

"Rowan's wife served me bountifully with hoe cake and bacon. I then went to sleep and slept soundly until toward morning, when I was aroused by several cocks crowing simultaneously in close proximity to my bed. I did not discover until daylight that the footrail of my bedstead was the roost for Mr. Rowan's chickens."

In 1838, when the legislature convened for the first time in Madison, there were three houses where guests could be accommodated. The prices were high enough to provide reason for complaint. A guest records that six men were placed in a room only sixteen feet square.

According to Judge Knapp the charges for sleeping accommodations at the Madison House were "two pence per square foot," and the weary traveler might spread his own blanket, using his saddle or portmanteau for a pillow, rejoicing that he had so good a bed." In the American House at Madison the garret embraced most of the "school section," lodging places being defined by cracks in the floor. The floors in the Madison Hotel were covered with shakedowns almost every night. Fortunate was the man in those times who could find a bed in a cold room and frequently it was his lot to lie on the floor spoon-fashion.

Mr. and Mrs. H. S. Baird and Mr. and Mrs. William Bruce made a tour through Wisconsin in 1842 and their experiences at the American House in Madison are related by Mrs. Baird:

"Our gentlemen had not yet seen our sleeping room," she says. "When they were admitted into it the expression of their countenances was indescribable. We four could scarcely stand in it. What were we to do about lying down in it? The old proverb, 'Necessity is the mother of invention,' we found to be true. Let me describe the room. A bed, not a large one, stood with the back and head touching the walls, and the foot of the bed was about three or four feet from the other end of the room. In front of the bed against the other wall was a washstand, a trunk, and a chair, and near the door stood a very small stove.

"Just imagine us in this room, making plans for the night. We ladies were seated on the edge of the bed; one gentleman occupied the chair, the other the trunk. Of course, we ladies were to have the bed, but what the gentlemen were to do was the question. There was not room enough in front of the bed for them to lie down. A happy thought came to Mr. Bruce: 'We will spread our buffalo robes under the bed, and we can have our heads against the wall.' The gentlemen went off for the robes and we retired. They soon returned and began to fix their bed. They were a great while about it and we felt they were very awkward. I think by this time Mrs. Bruce wished to jump out of bed and help them; for the gentlemen growing somewhat impatient were not as particular in their language as they would have been under other circumstances. At last they said: 'It is of no use, these robes will not spread out.' The bedstead was so low that they could not look under it without a light, so they took up the greasy whale-oil lamp and set it on the floor. On looking under the bed a large, long box was discovered, it was made of plain boards with a cover not fastened. The gentlemen were very curious to see its contents. Two canvas-covered hams were revealed. The shouts of laughter that followed must have been heard all through the 'school section.' After the investigation the box was pushed back as far as possible and the buffalo robes were spread down. Mr. Baird being short could lie under the bed; but Mr. Bruce being tall had to lie outside on the floor. Almost as soon as they had assumed a horizontal position they were asleep; I had anticipated that there would be no sleep, as it was far into the night before quiet settled down in the room.

"The next morning the gentlemen declared they had slept well, and the day found us all bright and happy. We took a final leave of the room, not desiring to spend another night as the previous one had been. We concluded the best thing we could do was to continue our journey."

In 1841 when Mrs. Daniel Ruggles came to Iowa county she stopped in Madison, sleeping in one corner of a room thirty feet long. In the apartment were twelve beds with heads to the north and in her narrative Mrs. Ruggles remarks that the arrangement was presumably for convenience, rather than to have them toward the North Star. She slept but little that night, the chorus of snores from behind the curtain all but banishing Morpheus.

In August, 1845, Josiah Arnold, who was born in the Berkshire Hills of Massachusetts and who came to Wisconsin as a lad of but three years, made a journey from Janesville to Columbus by way of Lake Mills and Waterloo. Before reaching Columbus he inquired about accommodations at the Paddock Tavern and the lady of the house informed him that he could remain there if he took care of his own horse. Accordingly he mowed some grass for the animal from the luxurious meadow close by and stabled it in the log barn, which was well built for those times except that it was roofless and minus doors. There was no suggestion of supper, but as Arnold had eaten late in the afternoon he felt no inconvenience in consequence of that omission.

Stopping at the house was a bridal party which added to the interest of Arnold's first night in this part of Wisconsin. Mayor Fisk had recently married a daughter of Zenus Robbins, and as true love was running very rough in this case he had found it expedient to put some distance between him and his father-in-law. A devotee of the violin he fiddled away the hours of his honeymoon in careless happiness, as if he was the owner of millions instead of being penniless. Arnold at length grew drowsy under the influence of this indifferent execution of "Old Zip Coon," "The Arkansas Travel-

RUGGLES TAVERN, NORTH OF RIDGEWAY
Stone mounting block at corner of porch

LAFAYETTE HILL TAVERN, DEKORRA
Built in 1836 from timbers hewn on Pine Island; used by Scotsmen for
curling center

er," and other like melodies mixed with much billing and cooing and was shown to bed without a light. During the night landlord Paddock returned from Columbus inebriated. The thin floor was full of cracks and Arnold was entertained with the rough eloquence with which Mrs. Paddock assailed her lord for an hour or more on the economy of going to Columbus and getting drunk with a stranger in the house, the cows not brought up, and not a mouthful for anybody to eat. When Arnold awoke the next morning the light was shining full in his face through rents in the roof and chickens were roosting on a pole across the room at right angles with his bed. The breakfast of which Arnold and the happy bride and groom partook that morning consisted of tea without milk or sugar, dry bread, and stewed tomatoes.

In 1852 after the lands north and west of the Wisconsin river came upon the market, purchasers went to the government land office at Mineral Point to make entries. Many a night at the Ruggles Tavern near the Military road in Iowa county every available foot of space in the house was occupied, as many as forty persons stopping overnight in the small structure.

In early bed chambers there was no ventilation except through the door, or undersized window seldom opened in winter to admit fresh air, though the temperature without was but little colder than that within.

The foundation of the bed, except in the rudest of log taverns, was a tick filled with straw laid upon a corded bedstead, the ropes running criss-cross from pins in rails and endpieces making numerous little squares about nine inches across. Sometimes timbers would split where the pins were inserted and mortices often were rough, thus leaving generous crevices for uninvited guests. A bath of boiling water was about the only remedy for routing these pests. Ticks were not infrequently filled with musty straw and covering was none too abundant. There were no washing machines, no laundries, so sheets and pillow-cases were not always spotless. Even with such crude accommodations taverns sometimes were so crowded when night arrived that lots would be cast to determine who should be the unfortunate ones to sleep on office floor or in convenient nook selected by the boniface.

During bitter weather a warming pan – a vessel into which live coals were placed – was sometimes oscillated between sheets and blankets in order to reduce the temperature before occupancy. Even the large frame buildings erected in the fifties, those which provided entertainment for the passengers in large Concord coaches, were minus stoves in sleeping rooms except in rare cases. When George B. Smith and Colonel W. F. Vilas, most brilliant lawyer of the Madison bar, came to Baraboo to attend court they were guests at the Western. In the morning Smith, hoarse and articulating with difficulty, prefaced his argument with the explanation that: "I can scarcely speak this morning. I slept in the barn across the street last night."

Domestic help about early taverns was poorly paid, consequently often of inferior quality. Many amusing incidents are related concerning the unsophisticated individuals who were necessary fixtures. In one tavern a guileless lad assisted about the place and the first morning was directed to go to a room and arouse the sleeping guest. Coatless, with hair disheveled and candle in hand, he entered, marched to the bed, shook the man and as the latter sleepily opened his eyes, he heard the boy say, "Your time has come."

In 1856 at Poynette Hugh Jameison erected a tavern on the north bank of Rowan or Powers creek, a short distance from the celebrated Rowan Inn on the south side of the stream. For about a decade Jameison operated the place, and during that time an innocent young Norwegian, man-of-all-work, was instructed to show a man to his room, wait until he had retired and then return the light that other guests might be duly led to their lodging place. The guest after disrobing knelt by the side of the bed to perform his evening devotions. In making the sign of the cross he aroused the suspicion of the Norseman who, setting down the candle, took the other up in his arms and threw him on the bed, exclaiming:

"You bain tacking leetle too much tonight."

Menus and Manners

The question of an adequate food supply is a particularly important one to the traveler. On a journey he must transport his rations, rely on the hospitality of friends, or content himself with what is offered in places of public entertainment. Early taverns often were the only source of refreshment available to those traversing unsettled portions of the country. Menus and manners differed in many respects from dining customs of the present day.

What was the usual bill of fare in an early hostelry? With sources of supply often miles away and transportation tedious and frequently difficult the list of edibles offered was bound to be limited. Canned fruits and vegetables were unknown and arrangements for cooking and keeping food primitive. If the taverner were an alert hunter meats were abundant. Not uncommon was it to have bear, venison, porcupine, wild turkey, duck, goose, and other wild game served at table and often a variety of meats appeared at a single meal. When fresh meat could not be procured usually salt meat was available. During the winter of 1838-39 Rufus B. Clark of Walworth county alone shot ninety-eight deer so plentiful were the animals. In Green county in 1843 one hunter bagged fifty. A bear was killed at the door of the slab tavern in Reedsburg when the settlement was founded. If ammunition was not at hand game was captured by rude traps.

In the fall pork was cheap, coming from swine that

ran wild and bred in the woods. The animals lived on acorns and other natural provender the meat being worth but one dollar and seventy-five cents per hundred pounds dressed. Frequently hogs in the forest became so wild their owners could neither drive nor corral them; then it became necessary to make up hunting parties to repossess them. The farmers of Sauk prairie permitted their hogs to range on the Baraboo bluffs and more than one, shot down like deer, provided meat for the Haseltine Tavern on the East Sauk road.

Where bears and wolves were numerous it was prudent to watch swine belonging to taverns as occasionally a frightened pig bolted into an inn for protection, knocking pots, pans, and other light objects in every direction. Such an episode had to be endured philosophically as otherwise piggy might serve to appease the ravenous appetite of some beast of the forest.

In pioneer times fish could often be taken from streams with pitchforks. D. R. Burt of Grant county has left a record that with a seine he caught a wagonload of fish in thirty minutes. The sturgeon, king of fresh water denizens, was taken in all waters tributary to the Mississippi river.

Wild pigeons flew by millions, flock after flock; so many were captured in nets, knocked from trees with poles, or slaughtered on the wing that the bird has become extinct. If the landlord did not use the gun himself his purse readily supplied the table with them. Round about Waukesha during the winter of 1842-43 snow lay on the ground from November until April and wild turkeys, which had been abundant there all perished from the severity of the weather.

Wild strawberries were so plentiful in places that one scarcely stepped without crushing them. Wild plums, raspberries, blackberries, and cranberries also were abundant. Fruits were preserved or dried. The former process necessitated sugar and the procuring of this sometimes was a problem. Occasionally the fruit required more sweetening than it was worth. It will be seen that in those days of severe economy preserves were much of a luxury. Apples, potatoes, and various vegetables often were stored in pits in the earth in the fall, protected from freezing by straw heaped above. When the contents were taken out they were as fresh as when buried. By mixing shelled green beans with corn cut from the cob an indian food called succotash was produced, which became widely popular. Even to this day the combination is relished by many people.

Wisconsin was one extensive apiary – honey in hollow trees everywhere – and sugar maples grew on many hillsides. These provided sweets extensively for the table. In early days butter was exceedingly scarce; farmers were just beginning to raise stock. Great difficulty was experienced in keeping it in a palatable state. Cellars were the refrigerators, butter in crocks resting in tubs of water on cold earthen cellar floors. An ideal "frigidarium" consisted of a crude little shelter near the kitchen door over a bubbling spring shaded by willows. Springs were the controlling factors in the location of thousands of farmhouses and taverns. Governor Dodge's house, four miles southeast of what is now Dodgeville, was located beside a spring and to this day some ninety years after it still is the fountain head of a considerable stream.

Corn was one of the first crops grown, but the preparation of it for food presented something of a difficulty. Often mills were at such long distances that many devices were employed to produce meal. Some grated the maize on a contraption made by punching holes through a piece of tin or sheetiron and fastening it upon a concave board, the rough side out. Upon this the ear was rubbed and meal achieved. But grating became impossible when corn was dry, for then the grains would shell off. A crude method of preparing meal from corn was by pesteling. A mortar was made by burning a cavity in an upright block of wood or stump in which, when cleansed of charcoal, shelled corn was placed and crushed with a heavy club. Sometimes the weight hung from a bent sapling, and this simple recourse made the operation easier for the ingenious miller to do the pounding. Some used coffee mills for grinding, and other means were devised to reduce the product to a state suitable for cooking.

Going to a mill perhaps thirty or forty miles away, was an event of no little concern. Travel by ox-team was doubly slow on account of absence of roads and bridges. These conditions added much to the tribulations of early innkeepers. Ferries often were in the realm of dreams and it was no uncommon thing for teams to be delayed many hours because of streams suddenly swollen by a downpour. Such weather conditions sometimes prevailed when larders sorely needed replenishing.

A common substitute for bread was hominy, a palatable and wholesome diet made by boiling corn in weak lye until the hulls peeled off, after which the grain was cleansed of lye by washing. The corn was boiled again to soften after which it was ready for use as occasion required by frying and was very tasty. Served as a porridge with sugar and cream it was also delicious.

Lye was obtained by throwing wood ashes from fireplace or stove into a V-shaped container made of boards, water being poured over the contents to obtain the alkaline solution. A trough of lumber or of a small hollowed log conveyed the leeched fluid into a kettle. Sometimes a barrel with holes bored in the bottom was placed on inclined channeled boards. Filled with ashes over which water was poured, the same alkaline fluid resulted. The caustic liquid obtained by either manner was used not only in making hominy but in the manufacture of hard and soft soap.

Natural foods were abundant in the fall: hickory nuts, butternuts, black walnuts, and hazelnuts were to be had for the picking. These were often cracked on a flatiron commandered from the tavern kitchen and kernels extracted with thorn of tree or shrub. Smooth white turnips also were relished eaten as they were taken from the ground, and of course wild grapes and apples – the last not as palatable as the fruit from cultivated trees but used nevertheless.

Tea and coffee were luxuries and the region was ransacked for substitutes. Wheat, barley, peas, beans, dandelion roots, and browned bread were used in lieu of coffee but as soon as one tasted the beverage the fraud was detected. On such occasion host and hostess were quick to remark that the substitute was less injurious to the system than the genuine article. Sour milk and salaratus or homemade yeast yielded the rising for breads, biscuits, and johnny-cake, which were served hot when possible. Patent flour and self-rising meal were unknown. Baking powder and compressed yeast had not come into use to lighten the labors of the women who fed family and travelers in the thirties and forties.

Landlords were often able to obtain a goodly quantity of food from indians, who at times possessed a surplus of venison, wild fowl, fish, berries, wild plums, and maple sugar. These could be purchased for a trifle; brass buttons or similar trinkets being preferred to coin.

Soups of various ingredients, dandelion greens, and other greens, turtle meat, apple sauce, apple butter, cottage cheese, dumplings, meat pies, Cornish pasties, and salt mackerel were in evidence at various times on tavern tables.

Often food was obtained with unusual difficulty and sometimes disappointment confronted landlords. In 1839 when Robert L. Ream was proprietor of the tavern at Madison previously operated by Eben Peck he had an unusual experience with wolves. While returning one night with supplies from Green county he camped by the way and the hungry animals were so bold that it was necessary to keep a rousing fire the entire night to fend them off a respectful distance. As the flames leaped high he and a companion entertained themselves by singing camp meeting songs and plantation melodies. With daylight the wolves departed. On another occasion while driving to Madison from Monroe, Ream missed a bucket of butter from his wagon. Tying one horse to a tree and mounting the other he hurried back four or five miles to a point where he suspected the loss occurred only to find a pack of wolves not only had devored the butter but had eagerly gnawed the wooden bucket to pieces.

In an early day not far from Janesville, on the road to Milwaukee, stood a log tavern which in later years was succeeded by the Gravel Tavern, a building constructed of sand and lime. The floor of the former was made of split logs, rough but kept scrupulously clean by the landlord's wife, Mrs. Blood. During inclement weather not many teams passed along the road, some-

times a month intervening between arrivals of fresh
supplies for the Janesville, Beloit, or lead region. At
one time when food had become scarce a farmer returning with a load from Milwaukee brought a quantity
of bacon for the Bloods. In her delight the landlady,
who had not seen grease for weeks, picked up a slab of
the meat and with a swoop hit the floor famed for its
cleanliness a resounding wallop, exclaiming, "Thank
the Lord, there's a grease spot at last."

Considering the size of early taverns there was an
enormous amount of cooking done by those in charge
of the kitchens. When the commonwealth of Minnesota
was being settled thousands of persons came by the
Great Lakes to Milwaukee, outfitted there and moved
slowly across the state. The main line of travel led
through Portage, across the river, past numerous taverns, on westward. On the Wisconsin river a few miles
northeast of Baraboo, stands the Sandwich House, a
busy place in those days. This tavern not only was on
the route of western migration, but furnished rivermen
with food as they piloted rafts down the river. Outdoor air supplied these men with hearty appetites.
They devoured mighty cuts of beef and the landlady,
Mrs. Edwin Plummer frequently cooked an ox every
ten days. In 1847, when James Ladd became a public
entertainer at Neenah it was sometimes found necessary
to bake an entire barrel of flour into bread each day to
appease the hunger of regular boarders and transients.

Not all the cooking was done by women. When John
Andrews and Henry H. Camp operated a tavern at
Mukwonago they were unmarried and managed the
culinary department without feminine assistance.
Ebenezer Brigham at Blue Mounds remained a bache-
lor and either he or a hired man manipulated the kitch-

en utensils. Cooking was frequently accomplished under difficulties. At the Campbell House, town of Cross Plains, Dane county the landlady was forced to walk a plank to the fire in order to avoid the water which flooded the kitchen. Braving this unusual disadvantage she prepared a meal for seventeen persons, among them Captain John H. Rountree of Platteville and other members of the legislature.

Many larger taverns maintained outdoor bakeovens. These were made of brick or of stones and mortar, often the whole being plastered over on the outside to prevent rain from entering. In the oven a fire was kept burning until surrounding walls were heated, when fire and ashes were raked out, pans of bread inserted, the door closed and permitted to remain so until the food was cooked. Such ovens were apart from the house and it mattered not whether the ground was muddy and rain was falling the baking had to be done. Pies and other foods were also cooked in these ovens and were removed with a long wooden or iron shovel called a peel. At the Ream Tavern in Madison the oven was made of clay mixed with straw and the proprietor remarked that in its construction the same kind of labor and material was required that caused the children of Israel to rebel against their taskmasters. However, the oven was a success.

As years passed a greater number of food products were grown and as transportation became easier the tavern keeper had less anxiety in regard to supplies for his table. Menus had more variety though fruits and vegetables from the south were not yet obtainable. Fruits and vegetables in season, dried and preserved fruits, and such vegetables as were buried in pits were all that were served. Only after the building of rail-

OUT-OF-DOORS BRICK BAKING-OVEN
A few miles south of Manitowoc

roads – the decade prior to the Civil war – did oranges, lemons, and bananas arrive. The canning of fruits developed during the last half of the nineteenth century; cans of tin and stone jars being used at first. The covers of these were sealed with wax which if allowed to penetrate within imparted a bitter taste to the contents.

Breakfast foods in packages were of course unknown so in the forties and fifties the traveler at breakfast was served with hot biscuits, tasty corncakes, steaming flapjacks, sausage, eggs, toast, coffee. In season there was often maple syrup for biscuits and cakes; at other times honey, treacle, sorghum, or molasses made by melting brown sugar. For other meals beef, pork, beans, potatoes, salt pork gravy, and coffee were staples. A bag limit respecting quail, partridge, pigeon, rabbit, prairie chicken, deer, bear, and fish was a later development in legislation. Sometimes beef was dried; and sides of pork were smoked to preserve them. A few of the old tavern smokehouses still stand. In brine – water saturated with salt – sides of pork and portions of beef were preserved.

An example of the stress laid on meats during the early days of hoteldom is the following bill of fare at the Milwaukee House, C. Wall, proprietor, on Sunday, December 31, 1843:

Mock Turtle Soup

	Roast		
Turkey	Chicken	Venison A la mode
Goose	Beef	Chicken Pie
Duck	Veal	Bird Pie
	Boiled		
Corned Beef	Ham	Chicken Salad
Tongue	Turkey	Boiled Fsh

There were also several kinds of pie, and other desserts like those used at present.

All through the years mush and milk was popular, bread and milk and apples sweetened with molasses also constituted a favorite dish. Oysters came in tin cans, when the only refrigerator at the tavern was a convenient snowbank. Crackers from a city bakery were purchased in barrels. Salt fish was shipped in kegs and cod, one-half of a fish in a piece, in boxes.

James Ewen, landlord of the Lewis House at Fond du Lac, purchased the first celery for sale in that city. James Smith, an English gardener, grew the "decayed pieplant," as some citizens dubbed it. One of the first who ventured to eat the "truck" was Doctor D. S. Wright, who seized a bunch as it was offered for sale from a gardener's wagon and placed some of it in his mouth to the astonishment of the spectators. When the prospective purchasers smelled it they turned up their noses and walked away. Finally the hotel proprietor made bold and purchased the entire lot. Tomatoes were first known as love apples and came into use as slowly as celery, bananas, and other table novelties.

Some places where travelers were entertained in an early day were little better than wigwams of the aborigines. On the north shore of Lake Mendota Michel St. Cyr, a Canadian halfbreed, succeeded Wallace Rowan in the pioneer cabin where travelers found shelter. St. Cyr could speak English, but was illiterate. He cultivated some eight acres, raising corn and vegetables. A. F. Pratt and a companion stopped at his place in February, 1837 while on a journey from Milwaukee to Mineral Point. They found the cabin a small affair, about twelve feet square with a dirt floor, and a Winnebago woman the wife of St. Cyr. They were

weary and much relished a kind of potpie which was
served. Later they desired to know what they had
eaten and were informed that it was muskrat. The
menu did not at all disturb the landlord, for St. Cyr
pleasantly observed that white people "would just as
soon eat rat as pheasant when all were cooked together."

In 1836 when Thomas Cammuck of the Brothertown
indians visited the Westfall Tavern in what is now
Calumet county, on the Military road extending from
Green Bay to Fort Winnebago at Portage, he found
most meager accommodations. Drenched with rain he
sought breakfast for himself and feed for his horse.
Unfortunately he could obtain neither. Westfall had
gone to Green Bay, twenty-five miles away, for provisions and no meals were to be had until he returned.
Cammuck dryly remarked that such times not only
"tried man's souls but their appetites also."

In 1845 Gilbert M. Lee came from the east to Milwaukee, then journeyed across the country to Fond du
Lac where he took dinner at a little tavern about sixteen feet square the proprietor of which was a diminutive Frenchman. When the traveler sat down at table
he was confronted with the head of a large beef, cooked
whole, and was invited to help himself to whatever
portion he desired. The diner afterwards remarked
that the object before him resembled a sign one might
see in front of a pioneer butcher shop.

Tables generally were long and accommodated many
guests. As a rule individual dishes were not provided,
each person serving himself from ample tureens and
platters. The single saltcellar on a hotel table was of
ample size and into it all dipped to supply saline wants.
When the dinner bell was rung and one found his place

it was a case of – "if you don't like the greens you can help yourself to the mustard."

Notwithstanding that some tavern kitchens purveyed comestibles carelessly prepared and uninvitingly served, yet there were taverns where there were meals so delectable and delicious that guests were glad to come, happy to remain, and sorry to depart. Before the era of restraining influences respecting the sale of liquors few meals in many places were considered complete unless there was wine, whiskey or beer. Often taverns famed for excellence of cuisine specialized in some particular food. The old Spring Hotel at Madison was distinguished for its cookies and one character named Luce asked for them so often that he became known locally as the "cookie man."

Occasionally uninviting fare resulted unprofitably even to the closing of hotels. Soon after Lancaster was selected as county seat a man named Richards opened a tavern in a cabin, but patrons protested so vigorously about the food that a club was formed and a Frenchman, James Jetty, was employed as cook. This did not conclude their grievances, however, for it was discovered by a careful observer that Jetty "wept into the soup kettle." A little later the patrons were rejoiced by the advent of Mr. and Mrs. Robert Reed, who made life pleasant in the cabin vacated by Richards. Mrs. Reed was a skilled cook and the "captain" was an Englishman with jovial and sociable attributes. Sometimes he bore the sobriquet of "old human nature." At one time he had an unusual and exciting experience with a bolt of lightning. While sitting at the breakfast table there came a blinding discharge from the clouds, but Reed was "too tough for the bolt," as an observer expressed it. As he was pouring a cup of coffee cup and coffee-

pot were knocked from his hands and hurled through
the open door into the garden. Undismayed, the captain rescued the coffeepot and calmly poured himself a
cup of the beverage.

Table manners were as different in early taverns as
the early tavern is from the modern hotel. In 1836
when Henry Merrell stopped at Vail's Cottage Inn,
Milwaukee he encountered such a crowd that several
tables had to be set. When the meal was announced
there was a rush to obtain seats. Once at table the customary American celerity in eating and drinking prevailed. There was no spoon in the sugar bowl; each
guest used his own. Neither knives, forks, nor plates
were changed during the meal. The blades of the
knives were of steel and the forks two tined. Little conversation occurred each guest hurriedly appropriating
his food. Merrell thought the whole affair resembled
a feast of wild cats. Every man was for himself with
little attention to his neighbor.

J. W. Seaton, for many years a member of the Grant
county bar, has described a hotel scene in Platteville
which discloses some of the current customs. Ben C.
Eastman, one of the most prominent lawyers of his day,
whose practice was lucrative and who was elected to
congress over Judge Orasmus Cole, was a central figure
in the incident. His manners were impressive, address
agreeable, and in every way he was distinguished as a
man of culture and good breeding. "On one occasion,
however," as related by Seaton, "he made a marked
mistake in his company. He was taking his dinner at
the Bonfill Hotel, the most popular hotel in the country. As a matter of courtesy he was placed at the head
of the table where the roast beef stood and the carving
knife was laid. Ranging down the long table came

other well-known guests of consequence till it tailed out near the dining-room door where the hungry crowd was seated, which usually rushed in pell-mell to get any place available. There were great gourmands in those days as well as giants, but 'Old Bon' spread a good table and Mrs. Bonfill and her pretty daughters knew how to cook and cater to their tastes, and the latter were attractions for young men and lawyers.

"On this particular day it so happened that Sam Morris from Cassville, a noted character unknown to Ben came in as his right-hand bower and took a seat near. Ben was fresh from the east and unused to waiting on table and unacquainted with the customs of the West. Sam, with a patient eye and a watery mouth watched the tall, well dressed Yankee cut off a liberal slice of the juicy beef and place it upon his own plate and then quietly lay the knife and fork down. This was manners that Morris had not yet learned in the 'woolly West,' and he with resentment thrust his empty plate forward, sententiously saying: 'See here, young man, if you don't want that beef for your own use I would thank you for a slice.' Ben sniffed trouble in case of refusal and knuckled to the demand. He cut the meat and passed the potatoes to every man within reach of his long arms. After this introduction Ben C. Eastman and Sam Morris were fast friends – slept together in the same room, played cards at the same round table and mutually admired each other's keen wit and wonderful story gifts, which were not infrequently bandied about till long past midnight."

Peddlers and Prices

An important personage who frequently appeared at
the tavern was the peddler. He brought tinware, calicoes, laces, ribbons, linens, and even dutch ovens and
exchanged his commodities at a fancy figure for his
brief entertainment or for coin from those with whom
he bartered. At a dance or other social gathering at
the inn one heard of his coming and expectation ran
high, especially among the women and girls who delighted in seeing his wares. Mrs. Bingham in her
History of Green County gives a charming account of
one of these visits:

"It is Mr. Ludlow upon whose coming these expectations hang," she wrote. "To his energy the people are
indebted for many comforts and conveniences otherwise
unattainable. His route is from Chicago to Madison
via Rockford, Belvidere, and Monroe; and though
there are only blazed trees and indian trails to mark
the way, he makes the trip every month. In the summer he crosses the rivers in ferryboats. In the spring
and fall, when the strength of ice is uncertain, he first
walks across. If there are no signs of danger he crosses
with one horse. If it still seems safe the wagon is taken
over. His customers are always watching for him at
the appointed time. Hastening to meet him they ask,
'Did you remember my tobacco?' 'Have you brought
some pretty calico?' And he is always able to say he has
remembered and brought whatever they wish. He stops
a day or two at the tavern, entrusting his money done

up in a leather mitten to the landlady who puts it under the floor. Such is the honesty of the people, that although everybody goes to see his goods which seem to be scattered over the tavern and although in all his travels he has never had a lock on his wagon, he has never lost a single article."

Solomon Levitan, now state treasurer of Wisconsin and a Madison banker, was a frequent visitor at the Prairie House near Monroe and at other taverns in that region. While going from farmhouse to farmhouse and tavern to tavern many years ago he had an amusing experience. In haste to reduce distance he left the highway for a shorter route and as he climbed a high fence the topmost rail broke and left him high and dry, his pack on one side himself on the other. His load was securely fastened to his back and he was unable to extricate himself. The only recourse was to halloo. There was no answer and he was not able to wriggle out of his embarassing situation. Finally along came a young man off to visit his sweetheart who saved the day. Levitan generously rewarded his rescuer with a pair of new suspenders.

Patrick O'Meara, familiarly known as the "Dodgeville peddler," camped on a creek west of the village during lead-mining days and discovered ore there. The stream afterwards was known as Peddler's creek. He met with adverse fortune in mining but his name is associated with the traditions of many taverns in that region.

One of the peddlers who visited taverns in the eastern part of the state was Grandpa Boise. He trudged from place to place and sold thread, needles, scissors, thimbles, braids, buttons, trimmings, and other small articles. Uncle Ben Thorp dispensed medicines and other goods, often taking furs in payment. A harness mender frequently seen at taverns in the eastern part of the state was Valentine Heiligentag (Valentine Holiday).

But the vendor of varicolored suspenders, tawdry jewelry, highly scented soap, needles, and pins has ceased to show his wares and has forever closed his pack. Like the taverns he visited he is a part of a period in the development of the country interesting but no longer necessary, living only in the traditions of that day.

Charges by landlords varied before the upward trend of prices due to the Civil war. Measured by traveling expenses of today the amounts exacted were reasonable, in some instances low. Accommodations were primitive, food simple, so there really was scant justification for fancy figures. When landlords received but twenty-five cents a meal, with guests few, assuredly profits were small, but dancing parties and lodge functions added agreeably to incomes. If time was ample for preparation food was abundant at these celebrations. Often roast chickens and turkeys and a young pig an ear of corn in its mouth, held places of honor at table. Besides, there would be vegetables and golden pumpkin pies. Occasionally an entire lodge would arrive unannounced. At the Ferry House, Merrimack, the members of an order arrived after closing time and demanded supper. The landlord, appearing at the door explained that the family had retired for the night and that supper, therefore, was out of the question. The visitors insisted, however, and finally the wife arose and prepared a midnight repast. The price was twenty-five cents per person and the profit for that night alone was more than that for several days past so limited was the income of taverns in small villages at that time.

J. G. Knapp reached Madison in 1838 and found R. L. Ream proprietor of the Madison House, previously known as the Peck Tavern. The building had a roof of boards, was battened with slabs and was the grand resort for the aristocracy of the territory of Wisconsin. When wheat was worth twenty-five cents per bushel, eggs four to five cents per dozen, butter six to eight cents the pound, pork one and one-half cents, and oats ten cents, supper, bed, and breakfast could be obtained in the best hotel for five shillings, cigars and whisky included.

About 1828 Daniel M. Parkinson opened a tavern on the Pecatonica river; his house was the only one between Gratiot's Grove and Blue Mounds. He found that travelers often were without money and consequently not able to pay for entertainment. He says that almost invariably payment would be made at some time or other. Frequently miners came into the region, obtained credit for tools and supplies, later paying off the obligations.

In 1830 when James McCall and others came from New York to Wisconsin to locate a reservation for the New York indians, they remained at Hull's Tavern in Ohio three nights and two days on the way west, and paid for entertainment the moderate sum of a dollar and eighty-eight cents each.

To obtain supplies often involved much expenditure and effort on the part of public entertainers. At Milwaukee in 1836 salt pork was from thirty to forty dollars per barrel; no fresh meats were in market, hence not quoted at any price. Flour was from eighteen to twenty-seven dollars a barrel, price depending upon the supply and condition of the commodity. Shipped by team or boat flour frequently became wet, black and sour. Much of the time butter was not to be had and, if obtainable, cost from fifty to sixty cents per pound. Eggs were forty to seventy-five cents a dozen; potatoes a dollar and seventy-five cents to two and a half dollars per bushel by the cargo, the retail price ranging from three and a half dollars up to six dollars – decayed ones and all just as they came from the vessel. There was no white sugar until about the time of the Civil war. Brown sugar, almost universally used cost at Milwaukee in 1836 eighteen cents for a damp, lumpy variety to twenty-five cents for loaf. A barrel of salted white fish cost sixteen dollars. Prices ascended when navigation closed.

Obliged to pay such prices landlords charged from a dollar and a half to two dollars and a half per day, including room, while in private houses the rate ran from five to seven dollars per week, variation depending on the quality of room both in tavern and boarding houses. Two years later in Milwaukee flour was seventeen dollars a barrel, pork thirty-three dollars, and potatoes three dollars a bushel. Transportation of supplies to Janesville or Madison involved the use of axe to cut away brush and trees. At the former place in 1836 provisions were obtained at Chicago or Milwaukee and three dollars per hundred-weight was paid for hauling freight from those points. Flour in Janesville was twenty-one dollars per barrel, pork forty dollars, salt fifteen cents per pound, salaratus twenty-five cents, butter from seventy-five cents to one dollar and a half a pound. Frequently butter was not especially palatable even at this price. In 1839 twenty dollars was paid for a barrel of flour hauled from Green Bay to the Wilcox Tavern near Waupun which, when examined was found so hard and sour that it stood alone after hoops and staves had been removed.

Competition between landlords had the effect of maintaining low price levels. Where taverns were numerous, every boniface along the way was anxious to turn a penny by keeping travelers. About 1840 when the proprietor at Summit Corners, near Oconomowoc, was charging five shillings for supper, lodging, and breakfast with horse feed free, J. D. McDonald, who maintained a competing inn near by charged fifty cents for the same service. How he could do this and yet have a profit on the right side of the ledger remains a mystery.

Occasionally there came a traveler who artfully took advantage of the landlord's lack of adequate change. After being entertained the wily fellow would offer a large bill in payment. If this could not be broken he would depart without charge; the proprietor preferring to lose the amount rather than summon a sufficient number of persons in the neighborhood to close the transaction.

Mrs. Thompson operated a place of entertainment in the town of Sylvester, Green county, and was known for her liberal hospitality. If a stranger paid it was all right, but if he could give little or nothing Mrs. Thompson did not complain. Once ten men and one woman arrived with their teams, remained over night at the little tavern, bringing their own provisions except butter and milk which Mrs. Thompson supplied. They filled every bed in the house, all her bedding was used, and stable room given the horses, yet when a total charge of ninety cents was asked there was complaint that this was exorbitant.

Occasionally a mild-mannered boniface was forced to extreme measures to make collections. About 1856 when Seth Crowell was operating the Bay State House at De Soto boarders of a procrastinating disposition had permitted lengthy accounts to accumulate against them. Finally they were notified that unless payment was made no breakfast would be served Sunday morning. The delinquents gave the matter little attention, in fact made no effort whatever in order to see what the landlord would do. When they gathered in the dining-room on the fateful day no meal was forthcoming and it was necessary to either go elsewhere or to go hungry. This provoked one of the guests, J. H. Worden to produce a parody on Butler's "Nothing to Wear," the first lines runing thus:

> In a very small town on the principal street
> There stands a large house but they've nothing to eat.
> "Nothing to eat, sir," did I hear you say?
> "Yes, and the reason is the boarders don't pay."
> They hung round the bar, each had a bed,
> No trouble had they as long as they fed
> At the landlord's expense, without paying a red.

Remaining lines told of an interview with Crowell and the final capitulation of the boarders. The episode is still related with much mirth up and down the Mississippi.

Something of the life in a Wisconsin hotel of the fifties has been gleaned from account books and papers found in the attic of the trading post and tavern owned by Augustin Grignon and his son-in-law, Louis B. Porlier at Butte des Morts near Oshkosh. Traders, trappers, travelers, teamsters, lumbermen were entertained in the old building, which was erected in the forties and which still serves as a store on the shore of the Fox river at the "Indian Hill of the Dead." There was much travel up and down the stream, for this was the main route between Green Bay and the Mississippi prior to the advent of the railroad. Many noted persons have been entertained by various landlords in the modest old building. The charges at that time are interesting. Here are a few taken at random from the pages of the account books kept by the landlords:

1854 July 3	1 gal. whisky	.50
August 10	2 lodgings & 2 breakfasts	.75
"	8 weeks board at $2	16.00
August 29	1 dk brandy	.05
Sept. 5	1 paper tobacco	.05
Sept. 22	5 dks beer	.15
1855		
Feb. 15	ball ticket	2.00
Feb. 27	25 dks.	1.50
March 28	supr, lodging & breakfast	.63
Aug 8	vinegar 1 gal.	.25
Aug. 31	2 drinks 2 cigars	.18
Sept 5	2 lb of peaches	.20
Sept. 10.	Cr. on 1 firkin butter 109 lbs at 14 cts	15.89
Sept. 11	Wks board	2.00
Oct 9	10 cabbages at .05	.50
Oct 10	½ bbl beer	2.50
Oct 31	25 lb flour	.81
Oct. 31	3 loads wood	1.50
Nov. 4	Liquor, ball night	.25
Dec. 11	Bear skin	1.50
Dec. 11	Dinner 3 dks	.37
Dec. 15	2 cigars 10, 2 dk cherry	.20
Dec.	Cr. by 50 lbs sugar at .14	7.00

An examination of the account books of the tavern

revealed that many of the items were for liquor, that the landlord sold merchandise and accepted goods of various kinds in exchange. As noted by the foregoing, board was but two dollars per week and commodities were in most cases correspondingly low. As in taverns generally of that day there must have been lively times at Butte des Morts, judging by the account of William Catton, as follows:

1855		
Nov. 26	6 dks wky	.25
	Apples	.50
Nov. 27	2 cigars .10 apples .13	.23
	9 dks cherry	.56
	5 dks	.25
	Supper	.50
	2 cigars-liquor 2 dks	.20
	4 dks	.25
	Damage to Stovepipe	1.00

There is no indication in the records that the landlord ever was reimbursed for stock consumed or damage inflicted.

The Tavern as a Community Center

Taverns played a prominent part in the interesting movement we term human progress. Many of the determining principles of commonwealth or nation have been born and flourished beneath their roofs. In remote communities they served as courthouse, post-office, town meeting place, in truth as a center for every sort of public gathering.

The first foregathering of the legislature and the first session of the supreme court at Madison were held in taverns. When the members of the two houses of the law-making branch of government assembled at the capital of the territory in November, 1838, the statehouse was not in suitable condition to receive the solons. Members of the council met in a small room at the left side of the hall in the American House and the representatives in the basement dining room. In these two apartments permanent organizations were effected and in the basement Governor Dodge read the first message at the new seat of government. The situation that necessitated the resort to the American House provoked a resolution which led to the appointment of a joint committee to examine the capitol. The committee reported the next day that on the following day rooms for the two branches would be in readiness. It also announced that keepers of three public houses in Madison were prepared to entertain guests as follows: Madison Hotel, two rooms that would accommodate four persons each; the Madison House, two rooms that would accommodate six persons in all; and the American Hotel, eight rooms that would accommodate twenty-six persons. The territorial supreme court was organized in the Madison Hotel, June, 1838.

The tavern was the common meeting place for men when political candidates or issues were to be discussed. Here they hammered out their arguments on the anvil of debate, usually with dignity and courtesy. True, controversies occasionally became so heated that personal encounters followed, but these were less frequent than is often supposed. Political discussion in that day was apt to be more personal than at the present time. On the platform more than in the press the great questions before the public were discussed for the benefit of the voters. The political boss was not so powerful as he has become in later days and men of strength of mind and purpose were held in high regard. Money played an infinitesimal part in elections compared with later practices. A writer of that period remarks, "If we had warm differences at the polls we made them up in our private and social relations."

In the late forties the stirring issue in Wisconsin was the adoption of a constitution. Many features of the first constitution proposed and voted upon in 1847 met with serious objection; in fact, the opposition was so strong that the popular decision was adverse. A number of banks had failed in the territory, the losses had been considerable and many men were opposed to legalizing financial institutions. The greatest of the constitutional meetings was held March 30, 1847, in front of Vail's Hotel at Waukesha. The demonstration was imposing. Mukwonago's delegation led the procession with about two hundred men. Flags were numerous and A. D. Smith spoke on "Wildcat Banks." In the midst of his

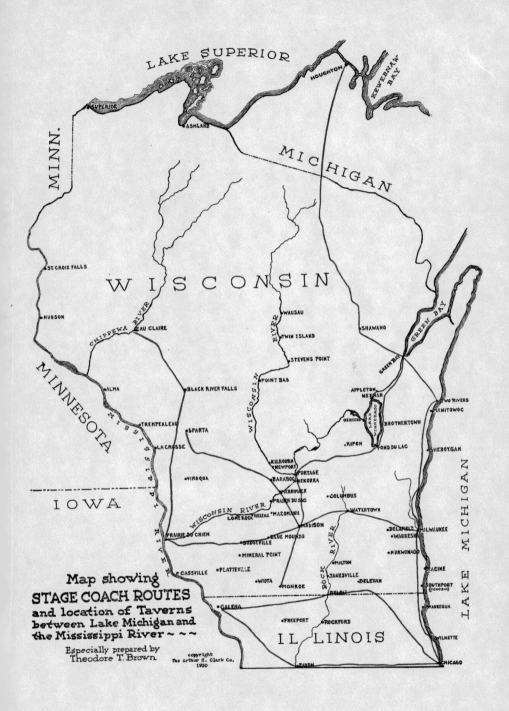

Map showing
STAGE COACH ROUTES
and location of Taverns
between Lake Michigan and
the Mississippi River ~ ~ ~

Especially prepared by
Theodore T. Brown

copyright
The Arthur H. Clark Co.
1930

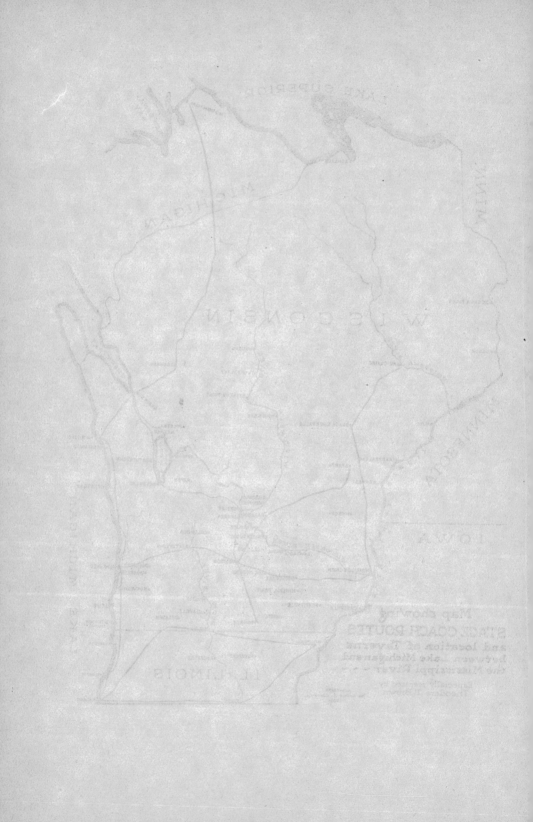

speech a coonskin was slowly lowered from the hotel and suspended in front of him. Without perturbation the speaker pointed to the pelt as a fitting emblem of the money power swinging in the breeze, hanging by its last thread, bodiless and spiritless and as the doomed man remarked upon the gallows "with but a single line between him and ruin."

The old Bruce Tavern at Waupun and the schoolhouse near it were the scenes of many amusing occurrences. In barroom and school, conventions were held and speeches made by rising politicians. At one time Judge Barber, William M. Dennis, and others held forth by the light of tallow dips. These men came from neighborhoods to the south to enlighten the residents of Waupun and while the meeting was in progress every candle was blown out by boys located near-by for the purpose. There followed a mixture of speeches both loud and strong. Nor was this all; when the meeting was over, the speakers' wagon was not to be found; thus the visitors were forced to remain in Waupun over night. They expressed their feelings in the matter in vigorous terms but their exasperation was mollified by indulgence in the universal beverage of the period.

At Cadiz in Green county, a citizen showed his indifference to the speaker at an abolition meeting by shelling a bushel of corn while the address was being given.

Religious services frequently were held in barrooms of early taverns in lieu of a more acceptable place — church, school, or courthouse. Although itinerant ministers preached from an hour and a half to two hours at a service, they usually held their audiences and themselves were untiring in their warfare against evil. These pious exhorters were apt to be more earnest than eloquent and often were more loud than logical. Weary indeed was the pilgrim who could slumber in his seat during a sermon. Hearers remained awake and trembled as the good parson hurled his thunderbolts. Hymns were "lined" by the preacher and sung by the congregation without aid of musical instrument. Organs were rare luxuries and in many localities would not have been permitted had they been available, being considered inventions of the evil one.

Preaching in a tavern was not without its surprises. In 1846 at Columbus, Elder Winchell, a Baptist itinerant, secured permission to speak in an old tavern which stood on the corner where later the wall of the Fox House surprisingly arose in fourteen days to a height of four stories. Mr. Winchell made fair sailing with the preliminary exercises and had just started on his discourse with reasonable show of regard on the part of the little congregation, when suddenly the attention of his hearers was directed toward some object in the street. Momentarily interest became more centered there. Presently one of the little company tiptoed out, then another and another and another followed, after which the rest of the flock stood not on the order of going but went noiselessly forth in a body, leaving the surprised cleric entirely alone and not yet advanced to the middle of his sermon. Bassett and Arnold, who had recently built a modest store had arrived that Sunday from the east with a stock of merchandise, and this circumstance caused the respectful stampede.

Early-day ministers were not always erudite. When Mrs. H. Elmer, one of the first five women to come to Black River Falls arrived in 1844, she conducted a tavern or boarding house, and during the summer an itinerant preacher by the name of Snow sometimes preached to such audiences as would listen. He boasted of his ignorance (not being able to read). His wife announced the texts while he expounded the word. Soon afterward he left and when next heard of was an inmate of the Iowa penitentiary for horse stealing.

Few taverns held an odor of sanctity. When the Shanghai House at Black River Falls was opened there was a dance which extended over three days and guests came on foot, horseback, and by team from a distance of forty miles. Later it was decided to have religious services in the tavern and lots were cast to determine what denomination should be invited. Dice were invoked and the Methodists won. When the minister arrived the door between the barroom and dining room was closed, services being held in one apartment while card games progressed in the other. When the time arrived for the hymns the religious group discovered there was no one present who could lead in singing. In the dilemma some one declared there was an individual in the barroom who was an excellent vocalist. The man was promptly summoned and the game suspended while he led the congregation in song.

In 1840 the Reverend Jesse Halsted, Methodist circuit rider, visited Oshkosh and preached his first sermon in Stanley's taproom. Previously, however, Clark Dickinson, from the government farm at Neenah, had occasionally visited the settlement and exhorted the people of a Sunday. His first sermon at Oshkosh, in 1838 was preached in Stanley's tavern. The initial sermon at Fond du Lac, in 1838 was by Mr. Halsted in the residence of Dr. Mason C. Darling. The building afterwards was used as a tavern. At that time the entire population of Fond du Lac was not over three hundred.

At Madison Eben Peck's log tavern served as a place of worship until a commodious barn had been erected. In November, 1838, on the invitation of Colonel Bird the first sermon was preached in Madison, the barroom of his brother's hotel being converted into a tabernacle. The service was conducted by the Reverend Salmon Stebbins, presiding elder of the Milwaukee district of the Methodist Episcopal church. Those present made up a collection of eleven dollars. ⟩

Taverns formed convenient places for voters to cast their ballots, the proprietor being compensated for meals served and drinks retailed. In May, 1839, the first election for a board of commissioners in Dane county was held at the American House in Madison, the only voting place in the county at that time. The election in 1839 in Fond du Lac was held in the Darling Tavern. The first election in the township of Waupun, Fond du Lac county was held in the spring of 1842 at the Wilcox Tavern. Eleven votes were cast. In 1860 at the first election of Abraham Lincoln, voters in the town of Dekorra, Columbia county, cast their ballots in the Wilson Tavern. Even to this day the building is neat in appearance, with fresh paint, curtains at the windows, and agreeable surroundings. The tavern now serves as a farm house, but the road leading past it has become little more than a vagabond highway.

Occasionally rivalry existed between a section of a town or between taverns for the privilege of the polling place. In the town of Vernon, Waukesha county the first few years voting occurred in a log building erected about 1841 at Vernon Center. Pressure was employed and the booth was changed to the Martin House in the southern portion of the town. Later it was transferred to the Munson Tavern in the central part. The rival factions compromised their differences and held town

meetings there for several years. Subsequently Leonard
Martin erected a large tavern on the southern edge of
Vernon and here the voters agreed to meet, being as-
sured of a right good time.

An amusing episode occurred in 1859 at the Lewis
House in Fond du Lac. One of the guests was J. W.
Partridge, who had been badly injured in the fateful
Belleville railway disaster when seven persons were
killed in an excursion train wreck. The gentleman
greatly desired to vote but was unable to leave his bed.
Inspectors refused to permit voting by proxy nor durst
the ballot box be carried to the room occupied by the
patient. It was for T. F. Strong jr. to solve the problem.
The bed was moved to the window, a ballot was attached to a long string, and leaning out of the window
so he could be seen from below Partridge carefully lowered the folded paper to the proper receptacle.

The tavern was a favorite place for town meetings. At
such gatherings there were no formal speeches, no prepared papers. The essence was practice, not theory. Men
who managed town meetings were practical and when
they spoke they spoke from experience. Varying ideas
were brought as near a uniform level as possible, the
good of the community as a whole being uppermost
in the minds of the majority. When few buildings were
owned by the public it was natural that assemblages be
held in taverns. The first town meeting in East Troy,
Walworth county, April 5, 1842, was at the tavern of
August McCracken.

In New England the community center was the meeting house, the village green, or the tavern, but in very
early northwestern communities most of their activities
were confined to the rude places of entertainment of the
day. Doubtless the cavernous fireplace and welcoming

bar with the general atmosphere of good cheer made a pleasant meeting point. Although more harm than good came from the sale of liquor in taverns where the candidate for election was expected to pass enough money over the bar to purchase drinks for all "the boys;" and generally speaking the place was not ideal for the discussion of political questions, yet rich and poor, candidate and voter, met on this common ground, where frank consideration was given political problems. Rest assured there was more interest in some proposed dog law or road improvement than in the tariff to be imposed at ocean ports.

When Captain Cram in 1839 made a report to congress concerning the harbor improvements at Kenosha the citizens of that place agreed not at all with the representative of the government and held an indignation meeting at Seymour's Tavern, the deliberations lasting throughout the day.

The Ball Tavern, three miles east of Evansville, was a favorite resort for town meetings. This inn, the site of which fortunately is marked with a memorial the original building having been moved a short distance to the east, stood on the north side of the road, the barn on the south side. Town meetings were considered holiday affairs and nearly every voter in the town was assembled on each yearly occasion. Young men would engage in baseball, pitching quoits, wrestling, and amuse themselves with various pastimes when the business of the day was suspended. Once when a meeting day was wet and rainy the crowd retired to the barn to wrestle, a favorite diversion of the time. The procedure was first to form a ring; then two opponents would engage in a struggle, the one thrown selecting a man in the crowd to take his place when the amusement would go merrily on. After a short time the individual called for on this occasion was Jesse Aller. Now Aller was a large, powerful man and his antagonist quite small. Realizing the situation Aller was reluctant to enter the ring but all shouted for him to come forward. Seeing it was useless to try to remain neutral, he finally decided to meet the situation. Stepping up to his opponent he took him by the collar with one hand, by the seat of his trousers with the other, and lifting him from the floor, held him for a moment at arm's length, then walked to the rear door where to the delight of the crowd he threw him out upon the compost heap.

Another purpose the tavern served was as a school. Here the pedagogue gathered his flock that pupils might be instructed in reading, writing, and arithmetic. There was no hurrying or cramming; each page in the book was thoroughly learned before a leaf was turned. The master was neither patient nor progressive and the rod was felt by the boy or girl who disobeyed rules. The first school in New London was taught on the steps of a tavern. In 1841 Miss Emeline Cook induced Webster Stanley at Oshkosh to build an addition to his tavern to be used for school purposes. "It was rather a breezy addition," writes a local chronicler, "six feet by ten, but despite the wintry winds, Miss Cook opened a school and instructed six or eight young hopefuls. The enterprise was suddenly arrested at the suggestion of H. A. Gallup and she engaged in the more poetical rôle of wife and housekeeper for his lordship."

When the cry of gold in California lured caravans across rivers, prairies, and mountains toward the setting sun, the Martin Tavern near Mukwonago and other like places were rendezvous for adventurers before they began the long, tedious journey to the Pacific.

What feverish excitement in those days of preparation and farewell! Guns to be repaired, animals shod, food collected, last instructions as to personal affairs, and final good-byes as the canvas-topped wagons moved out and down the winding highway. The imaginations of the merchant, mechanic, and husbandman were captivated by the stories which sifted eastward to be told and retold at every tavern by passing guest and returning traveler. All dreamed of thrilling experiences in the wondrous land of promise. From taverns wagons creaked across the continent in answer to these tales of gold. Many who bade farewell to family and friends at tavern doors early met disappointment and death. Eben Peck, first landlord in Madison joined the undaunted Argonauts only to find six feet of unclaimed earth, there to sleep in an unmarked grave. The romantic stories of these gold seekers of the late forties and early fifties ran freely through the ledgers and legends belonging to the old inns of the commonwealths to the east of the south-flowing Mississippi.

One reads with warmth and tenderness of Thanksgiving in the Northwest, inaugurated in one of these early places of entertainment. Doctor Lucius I. Barber, who came to Wisconsin in 1835 represented Milwaukee county in the legislature of 1838. One of his colleagues was Daniel Wells, jr. They occupied the same room at the Madison Hotel and one chilly morning while lying in bed the subject of Thanksgiving dinners became a topic of conversation. This moved Doctor Barber to remark, "Daniel, we ought to have Thanksgiving in Wisconsin."

"That's so," agreed Wells, "but the trouble is there are no pumpkins." The role played by the pumpkin in the Pilgrim festival was so important that a Thanksgiving dinner without pumpkin pies seemed out of the question to Wells. Doctor Barber argued that if there were a legal provision for the observance of the day, the pumpkins would be forthcoming, whereupon a resolution was drawn and Wells gave to it his support in the territorial legislature. In the lower house some opposition developed from the southwestern members because they were largely from the section where the holiday had not become firmly established. Finally, however, the resolution was adopted and from that day Thanksgiving has become a recognized feature in the life of the commonwealth.

Around the American House at Fairplay there cling memories of many a merry charivari. Fairplay is situated but a few miles from Dubuque near the boundary line separating Illinois and Wisconsin. This mining hamlet was the Gretna Green for eloping couples from both states, an accommodating minister and justice awaiting their coming. Many a time Hymen's altar was erected in the American House and when the service was not read there, more often than not devoted pairs sought quiet and seclusion in the tavern and sometimes concealment from irate parent or officer.

Perfectly natural was it for a group of young lead miners or other mischievously inclined individuals sitting around a blazing fire to welcome the news of a marriage. "Let's give them a charivari," always was the first proposal; and they made the welkin ring until the dawn of another day unless the groom generously tendered the price of refreshments to the hilarious company. The charivari was always embarrassing for the young couple but a source of delight to the authors of the bedlam and on account of their frequency more or less irritating to the owners of the tavern. On one occasion, soon after the marriage of a couple from across the state line pandemonium broke forth with unusual uproar. The landlord, determined to quell the disturbance, dashed out of the front door with a pail of water. The landlady with the same thought in mind rushed through the rear door. They met at the side of the hostelry and in the darkness the wife without investigation soused her spouse, to the vast amusement of the disturbers of the peace as the story was repeated to the region about.

Young people of the neighborhood often enjoyed parties at the tavern. Among the games that were popular were "Pussy wants a corner," "Drop the handkerchief," "Spinning the plate." All joined in the merriment. The Virginia reel was one of the most popular dances.

When plank roads began to extend in several directions, one was built from Sheboygan to Fond du Lac, others at Portage, Green Bay, and elsewhere. These facilitated travel over muddy regions when transportation was an important problem. The initial meeting to encourage the building of the Sheboygan-Fond du Lac road was held in the Wade tavern at Greenbush.

In 1862, during the Minnesota indian massacres conditions sometimes became exciting in certain Wisconsin communities because of false alarms given that "indians are coming." There would be a rush of terror-stricken settlers to the villages and naturally some of these sought the shelter of the tavern. Soon after the Sioux outbreak in Minnesota residents along the eastern shore of Lake Winnebago became apprehensive lest similar outrages should occur there. One night at Taycheedah a movement began hastily and teams were driven headlong into Fond du Lac. Soon people were flocking from every direction. Ox-teams were goaded by panicky farmers, the animals arriving with tongues lolling. Crying women and children clung desperately to the bounding, rocking vehicles. Fright, confusion, and fear reigned. Many blood-curdling stories were narrated apparently by eyewitnesses. First was a rumor that Pipe village was burning; next, the story of a mill that had been reduced to ashes; and again tales of blood-thirsty savages butchering and burning unfortunates in some other locality. Wild, crazy, and oftimes foolish fears took possession of the people. Words cannot describe the situation. Scores had seen grain stacks, cabins, barns, and other property burning and the excitement became so intense in Fond du Lac that homes were fortified. Inns were crowded and the street jammed with vehicles. Some of the more thoughtful tied cows behind the wagons in which they left their homes, others clung to worthless parcels "as if they were holding to a plank after a shipwreck." Children were crying and no one thought of eating.

Episodes of this sort are likely to have a ridiculous side. Finally a reconnoitering party was sent in the direction of Pipe village and when that community was reached the whole affair was found to be a hoax. Flowing beer at once caused the indians to be forgotten. Naturally there was concurrent delay in the return to Fond du Lac, where hundreds were anxiously awaiting news from the investigating party.

A crowning joke, however, was upon an indian. Near the Waupun road a half-breed was chopping. Observing the people fleeing to the city he ran to the highway where he begged a ride. This was too much for the excited palefaces. An indian with an ax! Teams were urged to greater speed and the poor redskin was more frightened than ever, especially as he utterly failed to obtain a ride. Finally the truth penetrated and the dusty, disgusted, and hungry travelers returned to their homes. In after years when the exodus was mentioned to some of those who had taken part in it, the excuse was offered that a few neighbors had just gone to Fond du Lac that day to purchase groceries and meet some friends at the tavern.

During a period of similar excitement near Waukesha, a family hurried from the dining table without finishing the meal; the table was there when the fugitives returned next day. People slept in the open through rain storms, and one individual hauled away a melodeon and in his excitement left behind what cash he possessed. Another family deserted the home in such haste that one of the sons, who was hunting was forgotten. When the lad returned he found the family gone, but failing to understand the sudden departure, calmly cared for the house until the absent ones appeared the following day. Horses left in barns or tied to vehicles were found where they had been abandoned by their fleeing owners. It is said the speed at which some of the frightened ones covered the distance between their homes and the city of Waukesha rivaled the race through Sleepy Hollow of Ichabod Crane and the headless horseman.

When death entered these primitive inns, often there was no minister available to conduct funeral services. As late as 1843 in the southern part of the territory, judge, attorneys, and others of the retinue of the judicial circuit traveled from county to county in performance of their duties. When court was not in session they tarried at taverns. With those who traveled the circuit of which Janesville was a part, was a poor sickly barber who plied his trade in the towns where the court was in session, his shop being a convenient corner in the tavern. When Janesville was reached this industrious individual laid down his shears forever. Concerning his funeral we have the following record:

"The next morning when the body was prepared for burial, the messenger who had been dispatched to a settlement about twelve miles away for a minister to give solemnity to the occasion, returned and reported that he had failed to find any such person. We were in a dilemma, and the town was canvassed to find a person who would undertake the office, but without success. Just at this moment, a team drove through town with a man sitting on the top of a load of bags. His clothes were white with flour; he had been down in Illinois to mill, and was going north to his home with his grist. As he reached a point in the street opposite the tavern, a man who supported himself against the corner of the house reeled out into the middle of the road and stopped the team, at the same time addressing the driver with, 'I say, stranger, can you pray?' The man sat for a moment in blank astonishment, when I stepped up and explained our trouble; he answered the question of the drunken interrogator in words something like these: 'Well stranger, you put a difficult question to me. When I lived in Rochester in New York state, I could pray. I was a member of a christian church, and in prayer meetings frequently led in prayer; but since I have been out here in Wisconsin, I have lost the habit and I do not know what kind of a fist I will make of it, but if you can do no better I will try.' And he tied his horses, put himself in advance of the procession, which was ready to move. We wound our way up the hill to a half acre devoted by the county to the burial of the dead, where the poor barber was consigned to the grave, there to rest until the last trump – no, until the county could sell the lot to the future city whereon to build a school-house."

In the Carpenter House, or United States Hotel at Portage was a hall in which "theatrical troupes used to delight the natives in the rendition of tragedies that would make a saint weep and a Winnebago indian lay down his tomahawk at the footlights." It is related that Moses M. Strong, being present at one of these entertainments was called out by the boys and responded by, "You'd scarce expect one of my age to speak in public on the stage," which called forth rounds of applause. And here, too, the young folks together with the festive old devotees of Terpsichore occasionally assembled and "hoed it down," with great animation and delight. It may be mentioned also that in the building historic tradition hath it that the first white child was born in the city – George Carpenter.

Aside from the church, husking, or other bees, the gatherings at the tavern afforded almost the only opportunity in those lonely times of exchanging opinions on the current events of the day. Here various ideas were advanced, and expression given almost to every community activity. The tavern indeed filled a highly important role in the affairs of that day.

Gayety and Weddings in Taverns

The tavern was the community center for dancing as well as other village gatherings. The special amenities that crowned the days of toil and privation of the pioneer were feasts and dances. These were eagerly anticipated and generously attended, young and old driving miles in wagons drawn by oxen to join in an evening's diversion. Younger people of course were more numerous than elderly ones. Few pioneers were over forty but all were privileged to take part in whatever entertainment the tavern offered.

At early dancing parties opportunity was afforded to study styles of dress of a dozen different years and of almost as many sections for the time did not lend itself to frequent changes of costume. People brought clothing with them from many parts of the country and this was used regardless of what others of the community might be wearing. In that day no swift running trains brought magazines into distant hamlet and neighborhood with suggestions for the making of apparel. Women danced in calicoes, men in overalls, colored shirt and boots, if no more appropriate clothes were at hand. If perchance stodgies were stiff, a resourceful farmer or woodsman might achieve terpsichorean steps in his stocking feet.

Concurrently with better times, shelves in stores filled with attractive goods and dress improved. When a dance was announced at the tavern, young women of the neighborhood arrived in silk gowns worn over swaying hoop skirts, corsages sometimes so tightly hooked that fainting resulted. Men also turned out bravely clad in baggy trousers, long tailed coats, and stovepipe hats. Beau Brummel, had he sailed the Great Lakes with the pioneers, would have encountered spirited rivalry.

Welcome was a word broad of meaning when invitations were extended for one of the old time dancing parties. People then as now enjoyed mingling and freely accepted and offered invitations for these and various social gatherings. Often the entire family went to a ball, the children being stowed away in bed-rooms.

When all were assembled in the ballroom, first came the tuning of the violin. The bow slid up and down in quickening measure as though the life of the fiddler depended upon the correct tone; then with a little flourish he would draw it delicately as though he would play naught but rippling notes. Perhaps to incline the dancers to happy mood, he might sing a few lines from an old ballad:

> When I was young and had no sense
> I bought a fiddle for eighteen pence
> And all the tune that I could play
> Was "Over the Hills and Far Away."

The traveling fiddler was the high priest at many a gathering. He always brought whole-hearted vigor to his performance. Note his eyes sparkling like dewdrops on morning grass, nerves at high tension as his body swings in rhythm to the music. His feet tap the floor or rostrum and it is his nod that sets the company in motion in the ballroom lighted from end to end with tallow candles. It matters not whether he perches on a sauerkraut barrel or is seated on an elevated platform, he is the observed of all. For the largest parties additional instruments were used, among which the bass viol and dulcimer were favorites.

The prompter was a necessary person in the dancing of square and contra dances. Next to the fiddler he was quite the most important. His business was to see that sets were full and his voice announced the opening of the dance. With a nod to the man of the bow, the instruments blared forth and the prompter with calls directed the movements of the dancers. As bar after bar of the music is played we hear him declaim sonorously, calling the changes in a quadrille:

"Head lady and opposite gentleman forward and back, dos a dos."

"Forward four."

"Four hands half around."

"Head gentleman and opposite lady forward and back, dos a dos."

"Forward four."

"Half right and left to place."

"Ladies grand chain."

A variety of dances would follow: the Devil's Dream, Irish Washerwoman, Virginia Reel, Money Musk, Old Dan Tucker, President's March, Two Dollars a Week, Cheat the Lady, Two Dollars in My Pocket, Irish Trot, Pop Goes the Weasel, and others. It was the duty of the prompter to have the different calls at his tongue's end.

At these early dances men were nearly always in the majority. At a ball at Othni Beardsley's place in Walworth county, the ladies numbered but seven — four married, three unmarried. Obviously there were no wall flowers at this affair. The party was given in the garret where the roof was so low that the taller persons were considerately accorded positions beneath the ridgepole. Busy as the ladies were keeping engagements that night, it is related that each of the three young women, ere the dancing was over, received an offer of marriage from a young farmer of the neighborhood. One of them accepted and the wedding followed within a fortnight.

Often it would devolve upon a young gallant to escort two or more ladies. On one occasion a young gentleman accompanied seventeen women, and on another two men chaperoned the entire feminine contingent to the function. Once assembled all quickly became acquainted. At Mirandeau's House, Milwaukee, dances or breakdowns were frequent in winter and here French fathers, indian mothers, half-blood children, and hired men of various breeds and nationalities danced promiscuously and heartily.

Sometimes space was small and the floor rough. At one of the early taverns in Monroe people came from Beloit and points in Illinois; supper was served, furniture was removed, the dance was on, though room was so limited that but two sets could be accommodated at one time. The merriment continued until morning. In Dodge county a party was given in a log building with puncheon floors, the timbers having shrunk until there were large crevices between. A native of Sweden attended and not knowing how to express his thoughts more precisely said he was "dancing over canals."

Except for the early Frenchmen at the fur trading centers and the southerners in the lead region, most of the first settlers of Wisconsin were from New York and New England. With advancing years other nationalities arrived bringing with them various dances. Billy Ray of Dane county played his bagpipe while the company danced the Highland Fling on tavern floor or on the green. The Irish brought their witching steps, the Germans their favorite waltzes, the Scandinavians various folk dances, until there were many movements, indeed, at these social affairs of the pioneer period.

On January 8, 1838, the first ball at Geneva was the dedicatory dance in the Warren Tavern. Dancing was on the second floor before plastering was finished, but the spring floor, pride of the landlord, was all that could be desired. One hundred men and ninety women were present and the receipts aggregated about seven hundred dollars, a great sum in those times. In 1850 when David P. Mapes opened the Ripon House, a two-story, square, wooden building, guests came from Oshkosh, Fond du Lac, Berlin, Green Lake and other places. At a later date Alanson Wood erected a brick tavern on the same site and over twelve hundred dollars was realized from the sale of tickets for the opening dance.

When invitations were promiscuous, the dance a public affair, more people sometimes came than were expected and this circumstance made it embarrassing for the landlord. The Spencer House at Evansville, built in 1844 was dedicated with a grand ball. Music was furnished by Tolles and Waite, the former playing the violin, the latter the clarinet. Landlord Grannis made preparations for fifty or sixty couples but one hundred and sixty couples filled the place to overflowing. After half of the number had eaten supper the larder was empty and trouble was brewing. Those who had not been served claimed they had paid their money and declared they would not leave until they had been refreshed. A conference was held and further unpleasantness was averted by those in charge of the kitchen cooking potatoes, salt pork, biscuits and coffee – enough for all. The musicians played ceaselessly while group by group of the dancers went to supper until all had partaken, which was not until the cock began crowing in the morning.

When the Dunlap Tavern at Waupun was constructed, the grand opening took the conventional form of a ball. Settlers came from all directions and an elaborate supper was scheduled. So many things had to be baked – chickens, turkeys, pigs, and other foods, the neighbors volunteered to aid by cooking in their homes. Fuel was cheap and all who could helped. The musicians came and the dance began – there was a jolly, happy throng. One of the neighbors having indulged in more liquor than was prudent and, knowing that his wife had a turkey in the oven for the supper, brought it over for her and threw it through the dining room window into the midst of the guests. The episode created some commotion, but a little incident like that of course could not interrupt the dance.

When people danced from early candle light until dawn of day no necessity existed for lodging the guests, but the dumb animals that brought them to the party must be fed. As an inducement landlords sometimes advertised that admission fee not only included supper but hay also. When the American House at Juneau was re-opened the affair was a marked social event in that community, the honorary committee included persons from every city and village in Dodge county. The last of the invitation reads: "Bill, including dancing, supper and horse to hay, $2."

The Sun Prairie House at Sun Prairie had no dance hall but there was one across the street. In order to avoid mud in bad weather a covered arcade or bridge was erected from the second story of the hotel to the hall over the way. This stroke of enterprise naturally added much to the pleasure of guests and to the coffers of the ingenious landlord.

Often unusual guests filtered into the dancing hall. One day there arrived at the Ream Tavern, Madison, a Teuton who had walked all the way from Milwaukee to Galena and back to the capital, carrying on his back a kit of carpenter tools. He had been induced to go to Galena for employment but being disappointed, was returning across the state to a lake port. Weary and discouraged, penniless and pitiable, he came a guest to the tavern while a dance was in progress. Hastily performing ablutions at a basin and borrowing a suit from the landlord, he hurriedly took his place on the floor. During the evening he exhibited his accomplishments by waltzing back and forth, round and round, a long time with a tumbler filled with water balanced on his head. Of course he was the cynosure of all eyes. At the Token Creek Tavern, when some twenty-five teams stopped for the night on their way to the north woods one of the drivers entertained the company by playing the violin with the hands delicately encased in gloves. Dancing masters held dancing schools in some localities. Some of these musical folk played for parties when not occupied teaching their classes. A. M. Clark made a weekly circuit of Chicago, Waukegan, Racine, Milwaukee, and Geneva. A horse attached to a dilapidated jumper conveyed him from place to place. He carried not only his violin but a rifle with which he frequently dispatched a deer along the way increasing the resources of the larders of his friends.

Fourth of July celebrations usually ended with dances. They danced on other holidays, they danced at weddings, at surprise parties and birthday festivities.

Nearly every one save a few connected with certain churches, enjoyed the diversion and sociability of dancing parties. Not only did they dance on the rough floors of log taverns and upon spring floors in the more pretentious hostelries, but in barns, breweries, and leafy groves. To the uninitiated, spring floors were a novelty. They were laid independently of the joists in such a fashion that "under the feet of dancers it yielded like thin ice." The Buena Vista at East Troy, the Smith Tavern at Mukwonago, the early taverns at Rochester, Waterford, Loganville, and other places had spring floors. Even to this day the family occupying the Smith Tavern gives an annual neighborhood party in the old ballroom on the third floor. When a corpulent gentleman stepped upon one for the first time in the famous old tavern of J. D. Sarles near Union Grove, he threw up his hands, stopped the music by exclaiming in alarm, "Hold on! Your floor's got the ague."

Although pioneer dancing may have been more spirited than graceful, more agile than dignified, yet there was real beauty in many of the movements of dancers at those early gatherings as they followed the music of the minuet or threaded the intricacies of an old time quadrille. It must have been an evening of especial note when Commissioner Bird and his wife led the Virginia Reel or Hunt the Squirrel at the old Peck Tavern in Madison.

> 'Twas music in the sinner's ear —
> 'Twas life and health and peace.

At last as dawn approaches, the prompter steps from the platform, the fiddler places his beloved instrument in its case, and the revelers with only the moonlight shining on the snow to guide them, turn happily homeward.

FIRST HOUSE IN MADISON, WISCONSIN

Built in 1837; landlord, Eben Peck; later sold to Robert Ream; first wedding at the capital took place here

A wedding in a tavern was the most interesting event in the monotonous routine of the lives of a landlord and landlady in frontier days. With eager anticipation they looked forward to the arrival of the guests, the preparation of the bounteous meal, and the endless joking. Often obstacles were placed along the line of travel to embarrass the groom and his bride. Journeying to or from the tavern they might find a tree felled across the road, a grapevine stretched athwart their path, or other tantalizing contrivance to delay them.

After the ceremony there was likely to be an exciting hunt for the whiskey bottle or a charivari with all its attendant bedlam. If the participants were not averse to dancing, there would be music and terpsichorean enjoyment from early evening until morning.

The bride's trousseau was simple; her costume a calico dress, cowhide shoes, and Shaker bonnet, with such humble accessories as the household could furnish. Her dowry frequently was a feather bed.

Sometimes it was necessary for the groom to obtain a license in one place, horse in another, and buggy elsewhere. Minister or magistrate often came a distance of thirty or forty miles and after the ceremony there was more traveling to enthrone the bride in her new home and to return animals and vehicle to their respective owners. If horse and buggy were not available, oxen and wagon were used or the journey made on horseback.

The first wedding in Madison was in the Peck log tavern. The ceremony took place on April 1, 1838, and Simeon Mills writes of the happy event as follows:

"The bridegroom was Jairus S. Potter, a long, lank, jack-knife carpenter, as the saying was, a term to designate a mechanic who could do good work on a poor job, and he always used large words in small places. He was familiarly known as Long Potter, to distinguish him from a namesake known as Short Potter.

"The bride was Miss Elizabeth Allen, a tall, angular young lady, who found her way west, and filled the position of maid-of-all-work in the Peck House, where the ceremony was performed.

"During the day the parties continued to work at their usual occupations and when night came, supper being over, and the dishes cleared away 'time' was called and the loving pair, matched but not mated, were soon in place. The room was decorated with the early flowers of spring, such as wild tulips and hyacinths, which were found in great abundance on Dead [Wingra] lake hill, and nothing was lacking to make it a first-class affair; but because of peculiar characteristics of the day, it was unanimously voted there should be no fooling on this solemn occasion.

"The presents were not costly nor numerous, but they were unique and useful in a young family in a new country; prominent among which might be mentioned a milking stool, an empty champagne basket with rockers attached, and a fishhook and line labeled, to supply the family with suckers. The ceremony was performed in the most primitive style by Eben Peck, Esq., who had been appointed a justice of the peace a few weeks before, and this was his first official act.

"Of the friends who gathered to grace the occasion, about nine or ten were called 'Ribs,' while those not so designated numbered some twelve or fourteen. The ceremony over the cry was 'On with the dance!' And inspired by the thrilling music of the violin in the hands of Luther Peck, a younger brother of the landlord, the dance went on and 'joy was unconfined,' until the mor-

row's sun was well up to light home the retiring
guests."

In 1841 in the Wilcox log tavern, occurred the wedding of William G. McElroy and Lucinda Collins –
the first marriage at Waupun. The service was read by
Doctor Mason C. Darling, physician and taverner at
Fond du Lac. In describing the event some years afterward a pioneer wrote as follows:

"The wedding day came; the woods were a frozen
poem written by invisible fingers. The earth was wrapt
in its winding-sheet of snow, but in our little cabin the
light flickered grotesquely from the fireplace on the
unhewn rafters. There was no useless array among the
bridal party, no satin dress dotted with stars, no jewels
spangled on the bosom of the bride, no bracelets encircled her arm, nor did any veil fall from the back of
her head to hide the simple evergreen that shone in her
hair. . . The ceremony over, I can see the white cloth
placed on the table, and on it a plate or two of biscuits
almost as white. Then I see a big gobbler, fattened for
the occasion, and almost smell the sage with which the
stuffing was sprinkled. Then came a bowl of pickled
cabbage, a dish of baked beans, a plate of boiled beets
fantastically decorated with cloves, and after that the
crowning dish of all – a glorious jelly cake, well seasoned with ginger and molasses plentifully spread between the layers for jelly. The day after the wedding
the wedding party proposed a journey to Lake Emily,
where the bride's parents resided, which lay twelve
miles distant through roadless woods and prairies. And
what was their chariot? A magnificent sled. By what
was it drawn? A magnificent yoke of oxen. With what
was it enshrined? A magnificent bundle of clean straw,
and on this the beautiful bride and her attendant sat as

dignified as did Cleopatra when surrounded with all that wealth could purchase."

On another occasion a couple came from Dodge county to be married at the Wilcox Tavern, which was located in Fond du Lac county eighty rods from the boundary line between the counties. After the wedding party had assembled it was found that the magistrate had no legal right to perform a marriage ceremony outside the confines of his own county. To relieve the embarrassing situation the bride suggested that all promenade the eighty rods, crossing the line into Dodge county, and have the rites performed there. The suggestion was followed and the service was read under no covering except the sky; then all returned to the tavern for the feast.

Joseph Hall, a justice of the peace of Walworth county and Lydia M. Warren of Hubbard were to be married on January 26, 1846. Barnabas Snow, who had been engaged as the magistrate was snowbound thirteen miles away when the hour for the ceremony arrived. Since the prospective bridegroom was a justice of the peace, a guest suggested the couple marry themselves, which they did. The magistrate said taking the lady's hand, "I take this woman to be my lawful wedded wife," and so forth; while the bride returned with "I take this man to be my lawful wedded husband."

In the Brigham Tavern at Blue Mounds was solemnized a wedding that was amusing in some respects. The marriage – the first in the town – was that of E. B. Erbe and Anna Christina, both from one of the Scandinavian countries. They had planned to be married in their homeland before sailing for America, but since they resided in different provinces the cost of the ceremony would have been forty dollars. On account of this great expense they decided to wait until they should arrive in Wisconsin. The ceremony was performed by Esquire Dale in the Brigham log tavern at Blue Mounds, the charge being recorded as thirty cents for the certificate, with treats for all present at the nuptials.

In that early day more men than women braved the privations of the west; hence there was a dearth of brides. This circumstance accounts for the brevity of courtships. In 1844 when one of the most respected citizens of Waukesha was traveling toward Milwaukee, he met an attractive young woman journeying along the highway. The lady inquired the distance to her destination and was answered properly. He then desired to know if she had a husband and family to follow, to which she replied in the negative.

"How long before I can reach Mr. N—s house?" she asked.

"In two hours if you keep steadily on," he answered, adding the question, "How long before you could get married?"

"In two hours if I had the opportunity," she archly replied.

"Good!" exclaimed the would-be suitor, "It's a bargain." It is recorded that they were wed immediately after this whirlwind courtship and lived a happy, prosperous life. The fact that the gentleman was tall and possessed a good figure may have had something to do with the prompt acceptance of the lady.

In the town of Spring Grove, Green county, a young man proposed to a fair girl the evening he was introduced to her, and they were married the next time they met. Later he explained his haste by saying, "It was the way then to do things up pretty quick, and as I had to work out of doors as much as any of the men nobody needed a wife more than I did."

Occasionally young folks were so anxious to be married that they disdained to avail themselves of a log cabin. John Douglas of Token Creek, near Madison, once united a couple seated in an open buggy beneath the shade of an oak tree. A current chronicler remarks that it is reasonable to suppose the young people were made happy even though the service was romantic. In early times it was now and then more difficult to catch a justice than to be caught by one.

Courts and Brawls in Taverns

Courts frequently convened in taverns. Before court-houses were erected the most convenient places for the administration of justice were these houses of entertainment. Quite often judge, jury, attorneys, witnesses and others assembled in the barroom where cases were decided with as much deliberation as in the costly county buildings that arose in after years.

In 1837 a tavern was built at Jefferson, and in the barroom the first session of the circuit court was held by Judge David Irvin. In this primitive room the bachelor jurist did not hesitate to improvise rules for the government of subordinates, which attracted no particular attention at the time but would be considered extrajudicial in these days. Judge Irvin was an unusual character, a queer compound of ability and eccentricity, who would adjourn court in order that those assembled might go fishing, thus reducing the pressure on the taverner's larder. Once while he was holding court at Prairie du Sac, the cry of "Bear!" was raised in the village and all hurried from the courtroom in order to bag bruin.

When Wayne B. Dyer was managing a tavern several miles southeast of Portage he was appointed county clerk, the person elected failing to qualify. When he asked the officers who had been chosen by the voters where he should locate his office, there being no court-house in Columbia county at that time, they replied, "Carry it in your hat." The first meeting of county officials was held in the Dyer Tavern and the landlord carried the business of the county on his head for a year or more. Eventually the county board settled on the Low Tavern, or Franklin House, as it was called, situated about halfway between the Fox and Wisconsin rivers at the portage. Here before a great Franklin stove Judge Irvin administered justice in his usual abrupt and autocratic way. Territorial laws were in force at that time and the members of the jury were paid in specie before leaving; some of them came without a cent, dinner and supper in their pockets, and departed with several dollars. They felt richly rewarded. The Franklin House was erected and operated by Gideon Low, a former officer of Fort Winnebago. The hostelry stood within sight of the fort, close to the trail taken by Red Bird and other historic spirits associated with the famous crossing between the rivers. What excitement there must have been in the old tavern during the session of court! On occasion some playful member would don the landlord's superannuated uniform, thrust into the extra space two or three pillows and, with rattling sword, cause the boniface to hurry down stairs to find out what was wanted.

About 1844 an amusing episode occurred at the Hawks Tavern in Delafield. Hull, a horse thief, had been arrested as he was selling a team stolen at Kenosha to Landlord Barber of another inn. When the prisoner was brought before Justice Jacques he said to Landlord Hawks, "You will please act as counsel for this man, Mr. Hawks."

"Very well," replied the landlord, "but if I act, I shall clear him."

"With that I have nothing to do," answered the justice. The prisoner was in another room, the constable sitting in the doorway to block entrance or exit. During the trial the officer fell asleep and Hawks appreciating the situation, slipped to the rear, beckoned the prisoner to come quickly, took him outside and tipped a large drygoods box over him. Soon Hawks was in the courtroom again looking as meek as Moses and when called upon to defend the prisoner took up a copy of the statutes, held the volume upside down, and gravely said:

"Whereas, it is further enacted, that when a prisoner gets forty rods the start of the officers of the court, he shall in such case be cleared, provided he runs fast. Therefore, in accordance with the law in such cases made and provided, I ask the court to discharge the jury."

This caused a general laugh. The justice ordered the constable to bring in the prisoner, some one gave the officer a punch to awaken him, and he at once began running about to find the thief. Everyone joined in the vain search.

After all had retired for the night, Hawks gave the man his supper, and told him never to show his face in that community again. Naturally the criminal was grateful and rewarded the landlord with a heavy gold ring which the boniface wore to his dying day. Both the landlord and the justice would often tell of this case and when the justice detailed the incidents he would close by saying that it was a novel method of winning a case but one, nevertheless, which he could not conscientiously recommend to the legal fraternity.

After costing the litigants more than a thousand dollars, a large sum in that day, a suit was finally brought to a conclusion in a Walworth county tavern. Elias Hicks hauled three logs, one black walnut and two poplar, to a mill owned by Christopher Payne. At that time it was the custom for the proprietor of the mill to notify the owner of logs as soon as they had been converted into lumber in order that the property might be removed to avoid possible loss from theft or danger of its being taken away through error. If the lumber remained on the ground at the mill, it was supposed to be at the risk of the owner. Hicks, notified by Payne to remove the lumber, failed to appear, but later demanded his property. However, he received neither boards nor satisfaction. Suit was brought in the court of Justice Dwinnell, who awarded the plaintiff six and one-half cents damages, thus throwing the costs of the action on the owner of the mill. The case was three times tried in a higher court, the jury thrice failing to agree. The judge at last became so weary of hearing about the logs and the lumber that he threatened to strike the case from the docket. Friends of the litigants finally persuaded the plaintiff and defendant to compromise, and this was effected by the son of each flipping a copper, the best two out of three to win the action. It was further agreed that the winner was to treat the crowd at the tavern bar. Surrounded by a throng of anxious onlookers, a son of each litigant threw the coins. Payne won, but in reality he lost since he was called upon to sponsor a generous round of drinks for the thirsty group.

Sometimes when landlords served as justices of the peace, they "made the law subservient to the circumstances of the case." This may be said of Adam Smith, an early taverner a few miles east of Madison. On one occasion the offender was a thief who was ordered to pay the penalty by walking through tenacious Dane county mud to the scene of the depredation, make a suitable apology, return to the justice, and suffer the humiliation of a reprimand. At another time Smith threatened to chastise two neighbors who, despite his suggestion, would not come to an amicable agreement. Justice Smith was of large proportions and it behooved those who came in contact with him to submit to his dictum, else a painful fate might await them. One day a stranger, big of build and full of confidence, stopped at the Smith Tavern, was bountifully refreshed, yet refused to pay the proprietor, claiming he was without funds. Although Smith was known far and wide for his hospitality, he did not propose to be outdone by a stranger. In the midst of a heated discussion the impostor boldly walked away, Smith following. A physical encounter ensued at which the superiority of Smith was quickly manifest. The vanquished guest was brought back and a search of his person disclosed three hundred dollars in gold hidden around his waist. The muscular boniface not only made the elusive stranger liquidate fully, but as he called it, defray the legal expenses of pursuit, capture, and return!

Landlords of that day sometimes acted as mediators. In the summer of 1837, the day that Jameson Hamilton rode into Willow Springs, Lafayette county, Tuttle Baker, charged with stealing a horse was receiving rough treatment while helplessly tied. Backwoodsmen and miners were making life miserable by jeering and otherwise mistreating him. Hamilton picketed his team, strode into the group of men surrounding the criminal, learned the occasion of the punishment, and denounced the conduct of all present. He declared that no matter what the man had done, it was shameful to behave toward any human being as they were doing. Finally the ire of D. M. Parkinson was aroused and he stepped forth.

"Stranger," he said, "if you do not mind your own affairs, I'll give you some of the same sort; this man is a thief and a rascal and has got to be punished."

Parkinson had hardly finished before Hamilton threw off his coat and the two men began fighting furiously. In the heat of the battle, Isaac Chambers, an early landlord at Willow Springs, rushed upon the scene, recognized an old friend in Hamilton, and succeeded in getting the belligerents separated. Explanations were made, the men shook hands and ever after were friends. Strange as it may seem the families of Hamilton and Parkinson occupied the same cabin the following winter.

Not always the blind goddess but Judge Lynch sometimes administered justice in and about early taverns. About 1836 when the Denniston House was being erected at Cassville, a discharged soldier was employed to cook for the company. One evening it was discovered that some clothing, together with a razor had been stolen from a workman employed in constructing the building. Suspicion fell on the cook; a committee examined his effects, the property was found, a court was organized, the alleged criminal was provided with counsel and a fair trial given. After the evidence had been submitted the jury pronounced the prisoner guilty and he was sentenced to receive twelve lashes on his bare back, the punishment to be administered by the man owning the stolen property. After the whipping the cook was ordered to depart and that was the last seen of him in Cassville.

An amusing incident occurred in the Carpenter

House which stood just south of Portage. The third story of the hotel was used as a courtroom and after one of the cases had been heard the jury failed to agree, so the twelve men were locked up for the night. The bailiff dozed on a lounge placed in front of the door. Mrs. Carpenter, a forehanded woman, always inaugurated the preliminaries of her breakfast the night before it was to be served, and aware that the landlady had something good below, two of the jurymen carefully lifted the lounge to one side and all passed down and obtained a lunch. They returned quietly to the room, replaced the lounge and asked its occupant if he also would not like a meal. The joke tagged the bailiff as long as he lived.

Rivermen rarely missed throwing ropes from their rafts over the snubbing posts at Prairie du Sac, for at the tavern of Steinmitz and Fief, probably the first place of entertainment in the region, they were sure to find something to warm the cockles of their hearts. Especially welcome was this when the trip down the river had been made in weather filled with dampness and chill. Travelers often came from Madison to the Sauk village to board a boat for Prairie du Chien and they invariably partook of the generous hospitality of this tavern. The place was of course the rendezvous of the community, where all sorts and conditions of men were wont to gather to discuss the ever green subject of politics and the latest gossip of the locality.

One day there came to the river Abe Wood, terror of territorial times. A bold, brawny individual was he, vitriolic in temper when his will was opposed, and rarely indeed did any one seek a quarrel with him. Many there were in the Baraboo region who hated him but none ever questioned his courage or assailed his militant reputation. There was a merry clinking of glasses in the taproom of the Prairie du Sac inn, when suddenly a head was thrust through the door and an excited voice exclaimed: "A bear! A bear!" Down went the glasses and in an instant every man was hurrying into the open. It developed that two worthy citizens were working on a farm near by when one of them noticed a bear trying to mount the fence surrounding the field in which they were occupied. Shouting to his companion to hasten for aid, Tabor, who had discovered the animal, busied himself in keeping the creature from scaling the enclosure by use of a pitchfork which he happened to have in hand. When the bear attempted to ascend the fence, Tabor would give him a thrust through the openings of the rails, an exciting performance attended with some danger. He was kept busy for several minutes, for the bear was as determined to gain the field as the farmer was that he should remain without.

The comical performance was at its height, as hatless and breathless the convivial loiterers at the tavern tore along the road and across the field to relieve Tabor. The bear was quickly dispatched by one of them and Abe Wood, among the first to arrive upon the scene, stepped up with several others to remove the skin from the carcass. No sooner was the hide separated from the beast than Wood leisurely folded it and throwing it carelessly across his shoulder, marched back to the bar with the trophy. Now Tabor had expected nothing less than the bear skin. He it was who had discovered the animal and he had played a stellar rôle in the opening of the exciting drama. The longer he thought of the matter, the more he became convinced that the property should belong to him. He was undersized, no match for Wood in a muscular encounter, yet he determined that come what might, he would have that pelt.

Hastening to the tavern, he paused a moment outside the door. The rumble of voices and the clinking of glasses were plainly audible. He stepped within. There lay the coveted skin in a corner where its bearer had carelessly tossed it. Tabor's decision was quickly made. Striding to the pelt, he spread it upon the floor with the assurance of ownership, then straightening his body to its meager height and folding his arms upon his heaving breast, he spoke in no uncertain tones:

"If any man here thinks he has a better right to this hide than I have, let him take it."

The eyes of the company turned from Tabor to Wood. For a moment the situation was tense. The little man was no match for the "terror." With one stroke of his powerful fist Wood could cause a stampede. The tableau offered a conundrum for the company. Suddenly the big fellow threw back his head and emitted a boisterous roar of laughter. The spectacle of a diminutive individual like Tabor throwing a challenge to him was farcical. The atmosphere cleared. Tabor took the trophy without objection and landlord and roisterers continued their jests and libations.

By the time the tavern had taken its place in the development of the Northwest as a means of settling controversies, dueling had become obsolete. Fisticuffs, however, still were in fashion and never was there any difficulty in finding reasons to wage war by using the clinched hands. Saturday in the mining region was fighting day. In their personal encounters men did their utmost to injure each other, and this was accomplished in such heat and haste that there was no consideration of Queensbury rules. Frequently biting and gouging were savagely employed.

The Exchange Hotel at Wyocena was a stirring place while the railroad from Milwaukee was under construction, the dispensing of liquor adding not a little to the chances of controversy between patrons. One night a member of the construction crew and the landlord became engaged in argument and results were immediate. The railroader drove a blow into the landlord which sent him over the stove. The innkeeper, bounding up, seized his gun and sent enough shot into the fighter now in flight to disable him. Friends of the wounded man transmitted a communication to the proprietor that they were coming back to wreck his place. Forthwith came the answer that if they did it would be necessary for them to be carried away on stretchers. The landlord was not molested.

At the same hostelry J. C. (Shanghai) Chandler was sometimes a guest. Chandler was an irritable, eccentric, somewhat intellectual editor who at one time and another owned weekly newspapers at various places, was frequently in his cups, and enjoyed any diversion in which there was a mixture of levity whether or not at his expense. He was accustomed to wear a "two gallon" hat, and one day at the Exchange Hotel made a wager of a pint of brandy that a bibulous friend could not put a bullet through the hat at the distance of a few paces. The beaver was perforated and Chandler paid the debt with as much pleasure as if he himself had done the shooting.

When William A. Fields was landlord of the Token Creek Tavern, located a few miles from Madison on the road to Portage, there once came to his place by stagecoach an individual who was anxious to "rassel."

TOKEN CREEK TAVERN

From an old tintype. Ella Wheeler Wilcox's father stands on upper veranda with a violin under his arm

He was going strong: he was like King Canute when he challenged the tide.

"I have flung every man who tackled me all the way from Stevens Point to Token Creek," he loudly boasted, and after refreshing himself liberally at the bar, he turned, and in a lordly maner exclaimed:

"Is Token Creek folks cowards?"

Uncle Grafton, a friend of Fields, was standing beside the landlord, each aged more than sixty years. Both eyed the swaggering individual and the proprietor said:

"Grafton, can we stand that?"

With a wink Grafton replied: "I was just thinking I might go back twenty-five years if he says any more."

"Your chance is good," replied the bully, throwing off his coat. The next instant the fellow was standing in an old-fashioned, deep woodbox on his head. After this brief encounter, the bully, humiliated, extricated himself from his embarrassing position, bathed the sides of his bleeding face, and departed completely humbled.

The jumping of claims provoked many fights, especially in the lead region. Frank Baer, writing of the Beetown Tavern about 1844, tells of an encounter which resulted disastrously to one of the participants. The best dressed and most courteous person at the tavern was Samuel Varden, who usually acted as "figurehead" – that is, he sat at the head of the table and did the carving. He also acted as postmaster and carried around the fifteen or twenty letters, which came from Galena once or twice a week, in his high silk hat until called for by the persons to whom they were addressed.

One morning this immaculate individual appeared on the streets dressed as though to attend a party, with "boiled shirt," stovepipe hat, and pressed clothing. On his way to the diggings he remarked to Baer they were good, that they had been jumped by Brewer and some others. He added that he was determined to have his rights if he had to wade through blood to his knees. Baer was invited to accompany Varden, but excused himself, stating that he would come later. Only a few moments elapsed before a man resembling Varden returned to the tavern, his boiled shirt, stovepipe hat, and broadcloth coat demolished and himself covered with blood; his eyes were nearly closed, his face badly discolored and swollen. He had met Brewer and had been badly whipped. Such in the forties were the methods of settling differences.

Sometimes fighting episodes were the result of feuds of long standing between groups of men, at other times the encounters would arise with almost no apparent cause. Little things would assume undue proportions, and if words or fracas failed to clarify the situation, the matter would find its way into the courts. Generally, however, difficulties were settled without delay by physical adjustment. Arrests were not made and not infrequently the hardy principals would depart declaring they had spent a most enjoyable evening.

Practical Joking at Tavern Gatherings

The barroom of an early tavern was a cheerful place. The care-free company that gathered beneath the tavern roof was keenly alive to jokes, sallies, pranks – anything in fact offering diversion, and the landlord could usually be counted upon to make merry with the best of them. Wary ones were tricked, wags lured the unsophisticated to positions of embarrassment, roistering bullies engaged in combat, the victim in all cases standing treat for the remaining members of the group.

Nicknames for persons or things were evolved, some of which clung for years, bogus wedding cards were mailed, a doctor was sent post-haste only to find his services unnecessary. Horses, cows, fowls, and other property mysteriously disappeared nor were returned until the expressed anxiety of the owners had afforded a generous measure of amusement for the idlers. Honest citizens were sued for false indebtedness, charges of theft were brought against innocent persons, the names of young ladies were used on invitations sent to youths to attend husking-bee or candy-pulling never planned. Sometimes such a riot of joking would overtake a neighborhood that the nerves of the entire community would be on edge. Occasionally an individual would refuse to accept a joke good-naturedly. For such further tantalizing was in store. A broad vein of waggery ran through the life of the time and to almost everyone the fun was acceptable. Golf and motor cars were yet to appear to aid in relieving monotony.

Many stories are told of the rollicking bachelors whose rendezvous was in the old hostelry at Oconomowoc kept by Charles C. Wilson, famed joker and raconteur. When phrenology was coming into vogue a shabby individual stopped at the inn and enquired of a bystander:

"Hever 'ad a lecture on phrenology 'ere?"

Receiving a negative reply, the stranger vouchsafed the information that "lecturing and examining 'eads" was his business and that he would like to give an evening's entertainment if he could get some one to assist him in posting bills. This detail was readily adjusted and arrangements were made for the lecture. When night fell a number of lively spirits assembled to enjoy the program. The speaker had not gone far in his delineation of character before he proved himself a fraud and this group of jokers decided to give him a fitting send-off. A stout youngster jumped up, seized a dog by the hind legs, swung it around, knocking Mr. Phrenologist heels over head in the evolution. As soon as the would-be lecturer recovered his breath, another candidate was perched on the stool before him, to whom he assigned a character befitting a saint. This circumstance so incensed his hilarious auditors that they seized the reader of craniums and jerked him into the barroom of the tavern. A soap-and-whiskey slide was a species of amusement peculiar to those days and to this the stranger was introduced. The rules were simple: a victim was laid on a table or counter, smeared with soap and whiskey, and slid briskly back and forth, finally to be shot into space at his peril. If he went "straight" he was not hazed again, but such good fortune seldom befell the victim. In this instance poor "Phreno" called lustily to the landlord for protection, but of course the boniface was absent. His tormentors rough-housed him again and again until his body resembled a still or soap factory. At last, opening a door they shot him into a hillside alley from whence he arose filled with anger and mortification, ejaculating as he disappeared: "I calls such treatment ha hinsult."

Prairieville, now Waukesha, was famous for its frolics. The leader of all the practical jokes and hilarity in general was Alex. Randall, as he was known before he became governor of Wisconsin and later postmaster-general of the United States. His companions were Harrison Ward, Charles R. Dakin, Andrew E. Elmore, E. M. Randall, William A. and Samuel H. Barstow, A. F. Pratt, and others. It was said that when three or four of these worthies met at a tavern not the Lord but the Old Nick was with them. For many years whenever any one was the victim of a practical joke, Randall and his pals were blamed. Few in public or private life in the locality escaped them.

At Janesville and elsewhere was an organization famed as "The Thousand and One." The origin of this bogus fraternity is given in the following lines:

'Twas at the foot of Mount Aetna,
  Just at the setting of sun,
Our order sprang into existence,
  And was christened 1001.

There registered at one of the early hostelries in Janesville a stranger who announced he was from Boston and was a lecturer on astronomy. He had been in the village but a short time when a member of The Thousand and One confided to him that he could not expect an audience unless he became a member of the order. After some persuasion the man agreed to join. In the meanwhile, bit by bit, portions of his history had been obtained and when the hour for his initiation arrived these fragments pertaining to his private life were arranged in order for reading. All this was a prelude to what was to follow. The patron saint of the organization was said to be Confucius, and numerous questions covering the stranger's personal record were read at the initiation by one of the members, answers being given by another worthy follower of The Thousand and One who impersonated the great moralist. The affair took on the semblance of a spiritualistic seance, the cult being highly popular in that day. The candidate, seated on a box blindfolded, soon became disturbed; his life, it seemed, was to be wholly revealed. He pleaded to be permitted to finish the story himself. Whether the spirit of Confucius or the victim should complete the chapter was finally decided in favor of the mystified candidate who, upon reaching the end of his narration, was elevated in a blanket until every muscle and sinew was sore. The initiation was concluded by the victim being dropped, battered and bleeding, through a chute into the room below. Next morning he hastily departed.

On another occasion a mechanical genius with a patent three-wheeled buggy, a novelty in its way, appeared at a Janesville tavern. Such a contrivance in the town provoked the amusement of the sensitized members of The Thousand and One. A few of those belonging to the lodge borrowed the queer invention, broke it – part of a plan – and awaited developments. In good time some one approached the stranger and cautiously hinted that by becoming a member of The Thousand and One he could ascertain who was responsible for wrecking the vehicle and probably obtain recompense for the damage wrought. Had the visitor been filling Hamlet's galligaskins, he would not so readily have taken up with the proposition but have gone his way without protest. Instead he fell into the trap. His fate was similar to that of the astronomer from Boston and his departure as abrupt.

Another merry scene was enacted in an early inn when the first member of the legislature was elected from the Port Washington district. His name was Solon Johnson and he was slender of body, lank in limb, standing more than six feet five inches. He is said to have been kindly and magnanimous but somewhat eccentric, with a sense of humor revealed in various drolleries. He went about his daily duties, slovenly in dress, but sometimes appeared upon the street in a suit of the latest cut and a plug hat. A short time before the legislature convened Johnson made a trip to Milwaukee where he purchased a suit of broadcloth and high silk hat. He managed to transport the toggery to his home without creating comment and decided he would not appear in the new clothes until ready to depart for the capital. But it became known to the home folk that the apparel was stored away awaiting the date of departure. A hurried caucus was held, Wooster Harrison presiding, and a scheme was concocted and resolutions adopted whereby it was unanimously agreed that his honor should be compelled to get the new suit wet or stand treat for his friends at the tavern bar. Wooster Harrison, or General Harrison, as he was familiarly known, was a red-blooded Yankee, a clever story-teller, with a fund of wit that made him in demand as an entertainer. He was appointed a committee of one to wait upon Johnson to ask him to don the new suit, then to appear with him at a certain location. Harrison called according to plan, directing the conversation to the election of the representative and his prospective jour-

ney to Madison. He congratulated him upon the honor
the district had bestowed, spoke of the responsibilities
that awaited him at the statehouse, and of the confidence
generally felt in his ability adequately to represent
Washington county. At last the subject of the new
clothes was broached. Johnson with good humor readily agreed to the suggestion that he invest himself in
the recently purchased clothing. Harrison was compli-
menting him upon the fine appearance he would make
in legislative halls when hurried steps were heard in
the hallway and an excited voice asked for Mr. Johnson.
The legislator opened the door and the agitated messenger entered, apparently almost out of breath.

"Are you Mr. Johnson?" he gasped.

"I am," answered that gentleman, "What can I do
for you?"

"A friend of yours is badly hurt," was the reply. "He
wants you to come to the tavern at once."

"Who is it?" Johnson questioned.

"I don't know," said the wary messenger, "but they
told me to tell you to hurry."

"You had best go at once," advised Harrison, and in
a moment, with the bearer of the exciting news, they
were hastening to the hostelry. There they found a number of men gathered. When Johnson inquired who had
been injured, the group gave him the laugh and added
three cheers for the solon. It dawned upon Johnson
with this that he was the victim of a joke and turning
upon the wily Harrison, he exclaimed: "You old
rogue! This is another of your diabolical tricks." Assurance came from the crowd that he was not mistaken.
Yielding to the inevitable, Johnson returned: "Well,
boys, you have earned your treat. Landlord, they all
drink at my expense." Port Washington voters declared

this to be satisfactory. They had viewed their respected representative in his gala garb and had enjoyed a brimming treat. That was enough for the day.

Even the shrewdest of landlords was sometimes deceived. It is said that Innkeeper Wall of Milwaukee was once duped by an individual from whom a quantity of tea was purchased, the price paid being ninety dollars. Some of it was then sold at a marked advance, but customers soon discovered that each box was partly filled with tanbark, enclosing a small tube under the testing hole. Since there was no tea in the box except in the tube all purchasers were victimized, Wall with the rest. Wall considered this one of his best stories.

One wintry night a number of men were seated about the stove in the barroom of the North Star Hotel at Viroqua. While conversation was proceeding pleasantly, C. C. Brown came in with a bag beneath his arm. Asked what he had in the package he replied, "powder," at the same time tearing off a corner and throwing it into the stove. There was an explosion and the exits were crowded, none knowing but that Brown was either drunk or crazy and might toss in the whole bag. One by one the guests returned to learn that Brown was resting comfortably by the fire and that the whole affair was merely a joke.

The brick hotel at Delavan was a hostelry where circus folk congregated and they were given to much levity. When one of their number became hopelessly intoxicated an animal cage was wheeled from the winter quarters and the victim dumped in, the exhibit being displayed in front of the hostelry. Upon the cage was this placard, "Most peaceable lion in captivity." Those passing on Sunday morning were greatly amused, and not until the man had become sober enough to realize his predicament did a friend come to his relief and open the locked door.

In Rutland, Dane county a taverner sold whiskey and groceries to add to his revenue. One day a neighbor came, purchased a pound of crackers, and then asked if he could exchange them for a drink of whiskey, stating that he had changed his mind.

"Yes," said the landlord, "that'll be all right."

The customer drank the whiskey and moved toward the door.

"Hold," exclaimed the boniface, "you've not paid for the whiskey." Whereupon he was informed that he had been given crackers for the drink.

"Then I want pay for the crackers."

"But," said the man as he disappeared through the door, "you have the crackers."

While building the addition to a house for J. and L. Childs, the first tavern in Milwaukee, some laughable incidents occurred, as related by Buck in his *Pioneer History of Milwaukee*. The men employed and others who came to the tavern, slept in the third story of the small part, all in one room reached by two flights of box-stairs. The sides of the room were not more than four feet high while the roof was only a few inches from the top of the beds, six in number, ranged along the wall. There was one small window at each end of the room, which in hot weather was a veritable Black Hole.

Among those occupying the room was an Irishman, Mike Connor, who had a hereditary dislike for negroes. One hot night in July as Buck and Parker, stopping there at the time, observed Mike sleeping alone on a bed it was proposed to have some fun at his expense. Parker returned to the kitchen, blackened his face with soot, came back, and quietly got into bed with the unsuspecting Mike. When all was ready the sleeper was awakened and Buck inquired where the negro came from. Mike gave one look at the blackened face, sprang from the bed, striking his head on the rafter, the force of the blow felling him to the floor. While crawling underneath, in order to escape, he cut a gash in his scalp on the sharp edge of the bedrail, and otherwise made much commotion before regaining his feet. He then gave one more look at Parker's face, slipped downstairs in a twinkling, and was seen no more till morning, having passed the night beneath a workbench in the new portion. Afterwards Mike is said to have remarked to one of his companions,

"Be gorra, I jist thought it was the devil, sure and no mistake!"

Parker contracted the not unusual habit of remaining out late at night and for the benefit of the Yankee, Buck one night arranged a noisy reception. As previously explained, the sleeping chamber was reached by two flights of stairs, the doors at the foot of each opening into the room from which they originated. At the top of the first flight one chair was placed on another, and atop of the whole several pans, shovels, tongs, and other articles. A log chain was placed on the upper flight in such a way that when set in motion it would roll down on the unsuspecting victim. When Parker returned there was first a crash, then the rolling of iron, with the result that the man soon was thirsting for revenge. The lesson cured Parker of his nocturnal habit.

Not uncommon was it in pioneer days for an individual or group to give vent to pent-up feelings by mounting the tavern table and ambulating the length of it. Destruction of the dishes was of minor importance, it seemed, when affairs came to such a crisis that a scene of this character was enacted.

In early Wisconsin the two political parties were Whig and Democratic, the latter in the majority. In 1840 when William Henry Harrison was elected president and John Tyler vice-president, the territory had no voice in the choosing. Yet there was the liveliest interest in the result of the election. Democratic orators and newspapers cast jibes at Harrison, calling him "a poor man – too poor to have wine on his table; so poverty-stricken in fact, that he was compelled to live in a log house, hunt coon for meat, and wash it down with hard cider."

During the campaign of 1840 coonskins were used as banners, hard cider was consumed in staggering quantities, and log houses were prominent on floats in political parades, a barrel of hard cider standing invitingly by the door. The cry of hard cider and coon meat turned voters, not from the presidential candidate, but toward him; and his victory was complete.

The Whigs of Milwaukee announced that on December 15, 1840, they would celebrate the victory by holding a barbecue, invitations being sent broadcast. At least two thousand persons foregathered from all parts of the territory, the leading Whigs being present to enjoy the flow of oratory and the novelty of dining at the Milwaukee House on an animal roasted *al fresco*. The invitation was so attractive that the opposition also assembled in great numbers, and this circumstance resulted in a deplorable failure of the program. Sylvester Pettibone, a prominent Milwaukee Whig, provided not an ox, but a cow for the occasion. This fact greatly amused the Democrats, and their ironic observations at the expense of the Whigs were as entertaining to the onlookers as they were irritating to those taking part. To add to the discomfiture of the Whigs there were no apples in the territory at that time, and in order to manufacture cider for the feast everything approximately suitable but the fruit of the apple was used.

Harrison Reed, editor of the Milwaukee *Sentinel*, was master of ceremonies for the feast spread in the Milwaukee House, but he evaded the cider substitute, so fearful and wonderful were its reputed ingredients. The "ox" was hung on a pole and a fire kindled on all sides. Respecting what happened that evening the following has been chronicled by an old settler:

"Alas, for the hungry Whigs! While they were soaking their toasts in champagne, and such like liquids to make them soft, the crafty west-siders came and stole their ox, carried it to Kilbourntown and had one good square meal. This so enraged Mr. Pettibone who furnished the animal, that in order to be avenged, he got upon the table and walked the entire length, making children's crockery of half the delft upon it in less time than it would take a stuttering man to count six. The effect of this promenade upon the assembly was electric. Fred Wardner immediately ran out and slid down the hill on East Water street in a champagne basket; W. A. Webber, not to be outdone, rolled down in a hardware cask; and several others played circus, to the great amusement of all the little boys."

Thus closed the first political barbecue in Milwaukee – a humiliating failure on one hand, yet producing no end of mirth for Democrats.

There was a time at Sauk City when friends and neighbors gathered in a grove each year to indulge in a day of sociability. Here the disciples of Bacchus brought forth kegs of amber fluid, and frequently tarried longer where the beverage flowed than near the orator of the day. Once at the time of this annual celebration a circus rolled into Prairie du Sac, a village located a mile from Sauk City. No sooner were the arenic folk at liberty than some of them headed for the broad Wisconsin river, the surface of which gleamed like molten silver in the June sunshine. After enjoying a plunge in its cool waters they threw themselves on the bank. Soon were heard the martial strains of a brass band borne on the summer air. A passing citizen who was interrogated concerning the occasion of the music, replied that this was the day of days in these parts — the day of the joyous June picnic.

The circus people, filled with curiosity, determined to find out more about this famous entertainment. A constantly increasing procession of farmers and their families was passing and the circus folk fell in with them, joining in the enthusiasm as they all traveled toward the picnic grove. The crowd grew as they neared the site of festivity. With every beat of the big drum volunteers were added, so that soon the knights of the sawdust ring were central figures in a hilarious throng. The day lay before them. The circus would not exhibit until Monday and the kinkers, wind-jammers, freaks, sword-swallowers, dog-boys, and side-show barkers bounded along to the scene of revelry with rising spirits.

As the spigots turned and the amber fluid flowed, the crowd increased faster than Falstaff's "men in buckram." One or two cooling draughts and the acrobats fell to performing marvelous feats, perilously twisting and turning in an imaginary ring until the amusement of the multitude knew no bounds. Keg after keg was rolled up and the entertainers were showered with invitations to partake freely. They accepted with alacrity and it was not long before the air was filled with sounds as strange as were the earlier muscular activities of the performers. Their agility, what there was left of it, was now more amusing than ever and their daring amused as well as enthralled the audience.

The drummer for convenience had placed his instrument slightly at one side of the hilarious throng. On noticing the drum, a brilliant idea entered the woozy brain of one of the kinkers. Quick as a flash, flipping one foot in the air, he tumbled the instrument on its side and with a bound turned a sommersault upon it, thrusting both feet through the tightly stretched head. This impromptu feat ended the acrobatic performance at the grove. Soon after, gathering themselves together, the merry Andrews marched gaily, if not in soldierly manner, toward the Empire House at Prairie du Sac, emitting a continuous "oomp, oomp, oomp" as though beating an aggregation of imaginary drums, as they ambled along. Thus they filed into the old tavern. The leader, looking neither to left or right, marched straight into the dining room, turned the moveable seat at the end of the extended table, and stepped waveringly upon the chair; when without hesitation he strode the length of the table amid the din of breaking queensware, every inebriated individual in his train following. Dining-room girls dashed to the open and their cries brought tavern loafers to the scene. Having delivered themselves of this inurbane incivility, the erstwhile picnickers, now unable to distinguish the hour on the face of the tavern clock, dropped into insensibility. Later they paid for the damage and departed from the quiet village of Prairie du Sac, declaring that never had they so enjoyed themselves.

During roistering river days a woman daintily

mounted a table at a small celebration in the tavern at Onalaska and stepped gaily from one end to the other. The episode was the talk of the time up and down the river. Her escort gallantly "paid the shot."

After Mr. and Mrs. Eben Peck disposed of their celebrated tavern, in Madison, they took up their residence in Baraboo, and sometimes travelers were entertained in their home. Abe Wood, a terror in that region during territorial times, became murderously mad at one of the residents. To avoid combat the offender dashed into the Peck double log house, Wood following with all possible speed. The pursued individual tarried not but dashed through to the woods. Wood made a hasty search of the house, then in fury leaped upon the table standing in the open space between the joined cabins, the dishes crashing with every descent of his ponderous boots. Mrs. Peck, little and fearsome, could only stand aghast at the wanton destruction.

Conviviality at Taverns

In decades prior to the Civil war, whoever liked might make liquor and so plentiful was whiskey that it was sold at from twelve and one-half to twenty-five cents per gallon, or three cents a drink over the tavern bar. People drank socially, not in the manner of the moonshiner with jug secreted in barn or cellar. Many landlords did not hesitate to raise a mug with their tipsy patrons, in fact some of them craftily encouraged the use of intoxicants as thereby revenues were increased. It is related that one artful boniface was in the habit of inviting "chair-warmers" to loiter about until a stranger appeared when he would introduce them one by one, as his friends, thus augmenting the number of "rounds."

A distillery existed in almost every neighborhood and a bushel of corn or rye would purchase a gallon of intoxicants. Whiskey was easily the favorite beverage and it was freely provided at tavern, at home, at barn raising, and at all social gatherings. Even women would take a little, sweetened and diluted with water. Intemperance, not temperance, predominated and naturally, most landlords of that day were venders of strong drink, this not affecting their standing in the community.

The first recorded license for a tavern in Wisconsin was issued May 13, 1823, at Prairie du Chien to John Brunet. Soon after licenses were granted to John Dispouse and James Reed, also residents of Prairie du Chien. These taverns were small yet, no doubt, rich in human interest; unfortunately, only legends remain of them. In 1825 the first tavern at Green Bay was licensed in favor of Judge John P. Arndt, who had come from Pennsylvania to the frontier village the previous year. At that time Wisconsin was a part of Michigan and the licenses fell under the jurisdiction of that geographic division.

At Madison a tavern license in 1839 cost twenty dollars and for other parts of Dane county, twelve dollars. A grocery license to sell liquor was thirty dollars and the proprietor was not permitted to sell less than one quart in quantity. On December 14, 1839, a tavern license valid for a year was granted to William T. Sterling for his place of entertainment. In 1844 in Grant county, at that time one of the most thickly populated counties in the state, there were ten tavern licenses and eleven grocery licenses for the retail of liquor. Five were in Potosi, four in Platteville. Groceries specialized principally in "red liquor."

During the thirties and longer, a license to sell liquor in a grocery at Madison was four times the sum required for a tavern. About 1838 Abner Nichols, a former Mineral Point taverner and owner of a stage line, in partnership with Jacob George, erected a building at the capital and applied for a tavern license. Because beds were not in evidence or for some other reason, license was refused and forthwith Nichols proclaimed that if he was not permitted to operate under a tavern license, he would run something "worser." Sans license the "worser" began business and operated for some time. Here men could drink as much as they pleased and in the dark cellar they could deliriously grapple with an imaginary animal, whose horrid den was there.

In some communities there was no regulation, and

whoever desired could make and sell liquors without restriction. About many a tavern bar of a stormy night there were assembled the neighborhood farmer, garbed in homespun; the prosperous squire, always conscious of his dignity; the tired traveler, welcome purveyor of distant news; and the parson, who had precious little influence when political debate became the storm center of conversation. All came to lend eager ears to happenings of the neighborhood, to meet new arrivals, and to exchange opinions. By laying a few pennies on the bar when he entered, an individual felt free to make himself at home in the tavern as long as he liked. From the hum of conversation he could glean fragments of news, could listen to the reading of the New York *Tribune* or such other journals as might filter into the West, could enjoy the roaring fire although quarters might be so crowded as to forbid him a seat next to it, and by packing his pipe from the pouch of a new-found friend, could contribute his portion to the cloud of smoke which darkened the room.

There is evidence that some Wisconsin forebears saw little that was derogatory in combining the pleasure of the table with their pursuit of christianity. In the forties Joseph Stowe opened a place near the Four Mile House, not far from Fond du Lac. He not only maintained a place of entertainment but provided a hall where religious meetings were held. The Stowe Tavern was temperate but there was a whiskey tavern at Seven Mile creek, the proprietor of which had been a member of a church but had strayed from the straight and narrow path. When religious services were being held at Stowe's, the proprietor of Seven Mile creek sent word to the Methodist minister that he wished to unite with the church. The preacher announced services would be

held where liquor was sold three miles away, and the
date of the meeting was circulated throughout the
neighborhood. When the day arrived a large congregation assembled. After the sermon the pastor asked those
who desired to unite with the church to come forward.
The landlord was one of the first to present himself and
when interrogated as to whether he was willing to
abide by the rules of the church, not to indulge in
drunkenness and not to purchase or sell intoxicating
liquor, unless in a case of dire necessity, the boniface
hesitated. The preacher informed him that he was at
the fork of the road and must take one course or the
other – there could be no middle ground. Still he wav-
ered. The cleric argued the case fully and earnestly,
quoting scripture to sustain his position. The sale of
whiskey was the impediment, the tavern-keeper liked
his liquor and the profits therefrom, so the church failed
to receive the influence and support of the landlord, and
the landlord failed to have the religious organization
sanction the sale of intoxicants.

Although there was some movement toward temperance, yet the use of liquor was scarcely less than
universal. Those who shunned raw whiskey frequently
consumed their quota in the form of bitters. Many
medicines of that day had a base largely alcoholic and
these were taken in liberal quantities, not only by temperance folk, but by habitual drinkers. Frequently there
was an eye-opener in the morning, an appetizer before
noonday and evening meals, afterwards a little stimu-
lant to aid digestion, and a nightcap before retiring.
With some individuals there was not a little pride in the
capacity for consumption. At barn-raisings, husking-
bees, and various other gatherings a jug was in evidence, and occasionally tippling occurred at funerals.

Usually liquor was taken straight, but occasionally its rasping quality was modified by the addition of molasses. The story is told that an odd character who in the fifties lingered about the bar in the Ferry House at Merrimack, would take a glass, pour in a little liquor, add molasses, taste it, declare there was too much sweet, add more liquor, sample again, and continue the process until the vessel was full to the brim before he swallowed the concoction. In order to make liquor "cut" the throats more vigorously, red pepper or other ingredients were added, especially in the lumber regions. Occasionally a barrel was emptied, a plug of tobacco nailed to the bottom then refilled. After the tobacco had remained in the barrel for some time there was a peculiar reaction in the liquor which a woozy individual seemed to relish, although the next day he was not able, perhaps, to put on his hat.

There are some amusing episodes in connection with these old groggeries. One winter day three men brought three loads of tanbark to Baraboo, selling the product to Andrew Andrews who operated a small tannery. On the way home they stopped at the "last chance," the Burlin Tavern to gain internal reinforcement before continuing their way in the rigors of the boreal night. They shook dice with Robert O. Hall for the drinks and in due time they had imbibed enough – at least so thought the young man in charge. It was growing late and Hall finally informed them that he would shake no more dice nor serve more drinks. They insisted. Again and again he refused and at last they decided to carry away the bar. Realizing three to one were too many for him, Hall ran for his father, proprietor of the establishment. The two were able to eject the trio before they had ripped fixtures from the floor. After the vandals had squared accounts in court there was little left of the forty-five dollars they had received for three loads of tanbark.

Nigger Dick, a character at Baraboo prior to the Civil war, once performed a daring trick at the Exchange House on Water Street, conducted for a number of years by Volney Moore and others. The central figure in this episode was on his way to Sauk City for the June picnic, expecting to make the journey over the bluff astride a horse. The day was hot and the Senegambian decided to have a cooling draught before departing on his long ride. When Dick thrust his dark countenance into the room and made known his wants he was refused. Wheeling about, he strode to his horse tied to a post, untied the strap, swung himself into the saddle, and rode daringly into the office, to the serious detriment of the furniture. With this bold act he apparently had the individual in charge of the bar completely buffaloed, for the desired potation was immediately forthcoming.

Neillsville claims to have won its place in the commonwealth as the result of an unusual occurrence. Neillsville and Staffordville were rivals for the honor of the county seat. Joseph Smith had visited the former place to obtain lumber for the Mormon settlement at Nauvoo, Illinois, then others had located at Neillsville, giving the settlement some little importance. A ballot was to decide which of the two places was to be the seat of government. When the election came there was a general holiday. Each hamlet possessed a bar where firewater was sold and each proprietor ordered a liberal supply of the beverage from La Crosse in anticipation of much drinking. The two hamlets were only a mile apart, a stream flowing between. Unfortunately for

FIRST HOUSE IN FOND DU LAC

Built in 1837 by Mason C. Darling; used as a temperance tavern; preaching service held here in 1838; election held here in 1839

Staffordville the whiskey failed to arrive at its tavern
and there was no bridge across the creek – just a fallen
tree over which even a sober person might find his way
with difficulty. With a burning desire for refreshment,
Staffordville voters filtered into Neillsville and before
the day was over were able to navigate only indiffer-
ently. Not one with his unsteady feet was able to nego-
tiate the wobbly log across the stream, so Staffordville
lost the election, and Neillsville became the county seat.

The first tavern at Fond du Lac, the Fond du Lac
House, was operated by Dr. Darling. In 1838 he closed
the Fond du Lac House I and opened a temperance
place called the Fond du Lac House II. In the same
village Theodore Herbert, a French blacksmith, built
a residence, also a shop and forge. Soon his wife began
to entertain such travelers as would not patronize a
temperance house, and naturally whiskey was sold.
Liquor was purchased by the barrel, Mrs. Herbert
being the first woman to sell intoxicants by the glass in
Fond du Lac, although nearly all the settlers had whiskey not only to drink if they so desired, but to barter
with indians. Business grew rapidly for the Herberts
and the husband soon abandoned hammer and tongs,
built an addition to his house and joined his wife in
dispensing liquor. By 1847 the Frenchman and his wife
had accumulated sufficient means to erect the Exchange
Hotel, three stories high and by far the most imposing
structure in the town at the head of the lake. Due to the
large size of the building the owners were called fools
and bullheads, but the venture was successful. The wife
had quite as much to do with the growth of the hotel
business as her husband.

The Byastoper Tavern, some miles southwest of
Waukesha, was a popular rendezvous. Seldom did a

bridal couple escape the honor of a full matured charivari that had its origin around the bar of the old hostelry. A small cannon, horse-fiddle, a few cowbells, and tin pans constituted adequate means with which to make such an affair first class in every way. A staple sold at the place was "squirrel whiskey," so called because after an individual had taken three drinks it was said that he was fired with ambition to go out and climb a tree. The house was not large but customers were many. Often when a patron felt drowsy from drink, he was given a bed but after becoming unconscious would be shunted to a place on the floor and another accorded the bed. In the morning full rate would be collected from every one for the night's lodging.

The most painful incident in the legislative records of Wisconsin had its finale in a drinking bout at the Monroe House in Monroe. Early in the session of the legislative assembly in 1842, Governor Doty submitted the nomination of Enos S. Baker to be sheriff of Grant county. There was a strong disposition to table the nomination. The governor's action was upheld by his neighbor, Charles C. P. Arndt of Green Bay and among those who led in opposition was James R. Vineyard of Grant county. The differences led to a personal altercation between the two members, finally resulting in Arndt striking Vineyard and the latter shooting and killing the former. Vineyard was expelled, found guilty of manslaughter, and a change of venue was taken to Monroe, where he was acquitted. At the close of the trial Vineyard received his friends at the new Monroe House and entertained them so jovially that the night was not soon forgotten.

The excessive use of liquor met with some opposition early in the history of the territory, as the following will show: At a meeting of citizens of the village of Milwaukee, held at the Bellevue Hotel, on Thursday evening, August 18, 1836, for the purpose of adopting such measures as might be deemed expedient to prevent the evils resulting from the excessive use of ardent spirits, A. S. Hosmer was unanimously called to the chair, while William N. Gardner was appointed secretary. The object of the meeting having been lucidly explained by the chairman, and the subject discussed by those present generally, on motion of E. Easterly it was

"*Resolved*, That a committee of six be appointed by the meeting to seek out and report to the proper authorities all the violations of the laws regulating the sale of ardent spirits that may hereafter occur in this town; whereupon, the following persons were appointed a committee: Solomon Juneau, Isaac H. Alexander, J. K. Lowry, W. R. Longstreet, Dr. William P. Proudfit, and S. W. Dunbar."

"The Baraboo Whiskey War," the only war that Baraboo ever experienced, began in the barroom operated by Michael Kornel in the Wisconsin House, which stood at 136 Fourth avenue, at the present time the location of the Al. Ringling theater. During the spring of 1854 a great temperance wave engulfed the village, the leading spirits in the movement being the Reverend W. Cochran, pastor of the Congregational church, and the Reverend W. H. Thompson, Methodist minister.

At the time there lived in Baraboo a hard drinker who was a good citizen when not in his cups. He was an habitual patron of Kornel's bar in the Brick Tavern as the Wisconsin House was then called, to the sad neglect of his family; and at a desperate moment he made an attempt to take the life of his wife. The proprietor of the bar was besought to refrain from selling rum to this individual, but the appeal was unheeded. At last death intervened and the grave closed over the inebriate. The following Sabbath the Reverend Mr. Thompson became savagely eloquent over the sale of liquor in the village, then numbering about one thousand persons, and said he wished "to God the thunderbolts of heaven would shiver the Brick Tavern and its contents, animate and inanimate." Attorney Pratt a few days later said that he would be happy to see "all the liquor in the village poured into the streets." Indignation gathered momentum as the days went by. An impromptu meeting was held and a few zealous women decided to attack with berserker fury. A writer in describing the scene says:

"Hark! There's a sound of devastation – a sudden unloosing of liquid devils. The barroom of the Brick Tavern is in the process of female invasion. Fumes of liquor infect the air. Rye, Bourbon, and Fine Old Tom meet a common fate, and are rapidly absorbed by the parched earth in front of the hotel. The whilom dispenser of these evil spirits is wrapped in slumber; for it is early morn and none but sober citizens are abroad. The righteous work of destruction proceeds so quietly that his repose is not disturbed. In disposing of the empty bottles a corrugated schnapps is deposited in an ancient drygoods box in which a reveler of the previous night has taken lodging. The breaking of the fallen bottles does not molest him, but there is a familiar smell about it which brings him to his feet with all the alacrity of a toper invited to drink; and he looks upon the strange scene and weeps."

After the visitation at the Brick Tavern, the band of women marched to a place nearby where they found the proprietor had sensed trouble and prudently locked the door. The visiting women made a proposition to purchase his wares, but while he hesitated to set a price an entrance was affected at the rear, and there was a quiet turning of faucets which soon flooded the floor. By the time they reached French Pete's the news of the revolution had spread throughout the village and a crowd gathered upon the scene. As one of the women attempted to gain the entrance to Van Wedell's saloon she found the way blocked by a patron, who was caught by the waistband and rudely jerked aside, the suddenness of the attack causing some of the fastenings to give way. Deputy Sheriff Chapman advanced and began to read the riot act, calling upon the crowd to disperse. Addressing one of the ministers, he said, "Mr. Cochran, you disperse!" The man of cloth calmly informed him he did not know how.

Some days later a number of the ladies were escorted to Sauk City by Sheriff Munson that an impartial trial might be held. However, the case was remanded to circuit court, the women returning to Baraboo under protection of the officer. When the case was called by Judge Wheeler the damage was fixed at one hundred and fifty dollars which was immediately paid, thus ending the Baraboo whiskey war.

In Dodge county a group of women led by Mrs. Breman attacked the Dan Benjamin Tavern where liquor was sold, with destructive results. The astonished owner of the place gazed ruefully upon the wreck of his worldly possessions and manfully admitted that the demolition was just.

Opposition to liquor took other forms. About 1842 Newton and John S. Capron built a distillery at Lake Geneva, but the miller, Charles M. Goodsell, refused to grind corn for them. This caused much excitement

as non-temperance farmers expected to sell their crop
to the distillery, there being no other market within
many miles. Those enraged over the situation employed various means to induce the miller to change
his mind, but to no purpose. Finally the matter was
taken into court, judgment was obtained against the
miller, this was appealed, and the case dismissed. Costs
were never paid. At the next session of the territorial
legislature Goodsell rode to Madison where he insti-
gated the enactment of a law which exempted millers
from grinding grain for distilleries.

In the late forties and even earlier, temperance so-
cieties became active and temperance taverns were frequently found by travelers. The McCracken or Wright
Tavern at East Troy, the Ripon House at Ripon, the
Ephraim Wilcox Tavern at Wilmot, and the New England House at Janesville were among those which had
no bars. Duty J. Greene at Albion, where J. Q. Emery,
Governor Knute Nelson and others attended an acad-
emy, maintained a rigidly dry house. When General
Dodge visited Kenosha (Southport) in 1841 and every
available vehicle was pressed into service in his honor,
the distinguished indian fighter gave his address at
Whitney's Temperance House, a building of hewn logs.

Resentment was met by ministers who spoke at temperance meetings in taverns and elsewhere. The Reverend Mr. Cutting Marsh, an early missionary did not
hesitate to enter the place where reigned the individual
with the cloven foot, although displeasure was sometimes manifest because he was bold enough to attack
King Alcohol in his lair. Once after speaking at Beaver
Dam, he discovered the next morning that his horse's
tail had been cropped, giving it much the appearance

of Tam O'Shanter's mare after the wild ride over the bridge with witches in close pursuit.

The temperance movement was slow in growth. Although more money was spent for intoxicants than for religion or education in early days, the people progressed, nevertheless, and left to posterity a heritage more substantial than the customs of the time would indicate.

Ghosts and Gaming in Taverns

Many a mystery is mingled with the traditions of old taverns and of course there were stories of ghosts that mounted the silent staircases and peered from dark passageways. In barrooms of some of the ancient buildings the clinking of glasses is said to have been heard on windless nights and through the windows of empty chambers shadowy forms have seemed to be passing and repassing in the dusk of evening. Possibly the "galloping ghost," which is said to be connected with the old Ferry House at Merrimack, owes its origin to some unrecorded crime committed during rafting days. Certainly the worn relic had a sufficient aggregation of years to its credit to make it appear likely that it may have survived any number of bloody deeds, although there is no record of even one having occurred under its roof. Those associated with the life of the village for many years declare there is no more reason for spooks infesting the old tavern than for the ghost the imaginative old woman saw when walking to Fakenham – first she heard a short, quick step behind, on looking around she beheld a four-footed monster, which, after the poor woman had fainted, proved to be a donkey following her in the night.

Strange tales are told of the old Dell House which stood where waters go roiling through the Wisconsin river dells. Rough and ready rivermen engaged in many a combat at this tavern during pinery days are said to have hidden all evidence of their crime in the waters of the swirling stream. This is not an improbability. No wonder the old raconteurs solemnly affirm that ghosts were in possession of the place from the time the last glass was filled until fire effaced the ruin.

The Layton House, built long ago in Milwaukee by the founder of the Layton art gallery, stands near a cemetery not far from the well-known tavern at Hale's Corners which has been under the management of the Dreyfus family for two generations. The Layton House was erected in 1844 when there was much passing along the Janesville plank road and about it there was established an ox and horse market. Now the grim brick structure filled only with haunting memories of past activity is falling into decay, and on account of its location the timorous sometimes imagine they hear weird sounds from within which they attribute to ghosts.

On a corner of the public square in the village of East Troy stands a cobblestone structure which dates from the beginning of Wisconsin's statehood. A mystery enshrouds this hostelry. For three quarters of a century or more the walls of the old building have kept their secret, and, now that all the participants are dead, there is little likelihood that it will ever be discovered. Samuel R. Bradley, a Milwaukee boniface, moved from the lake port to East Troy where he secured a site and erected the Buena Vista House. It was a dream of this taverner to construct from glacier boulders a building that would surpass anything of the kind in the state. From highways and byways, from fields and fences, from lake shore and stream bed, diligently he toiled gathering cobblestones for the edifice. Week after week he could be seen with his horse and wagon selecting and hauling the material which one day was to be

MELCHIOR HOUSE, TREMPEALEAU
On the Mississippi; built with a brewery at one end

FERRY HOUSE, MERRIMACK
Near the north end of the ferry across the Wisconsin river. This building
was begun in 1847; moved to its present location about 1852

his monument in the community. His search for stones of proper size led him across a nearby lake, the boulders being brought by him to the shore in a rowboat and hauled to the site he had selected. When completed the building stood three stories high with an additional half story to be used as a ballroom. An attractive feature of this was a spring floor which was popular at the time. The unusual structure was finished soon after the battle of Buena Vista in the war with Mexico, and the proprietor named his hotel in honor of the victory achieved by American troops. There was a magnificent banquet and ball; many attended from the eastern section of the territory, among them being a number of distinguished guests.

At the time of the completion of the hotel there was a mortgage on the property, but in less than three years this was canceled. Soon after the debt was liquidated Mr. and Mrs. Bradley departed leaving the impression that they were going to England. Neighbors wondered but no word was received from them and the mystery of their disappearance never was solved. Why did they desert their home? What became of them? Did they throw themselves into the lake completely hiding a tragedy? Were they murdered, their bodies buried in an unmarked grave? Did they depart to begin life anew across the water under an assumed name? For a time the Buena Vista House stood vacant, then squatters took possession. People came and went, queried and wondered, but no word was forthcoming from the Bradleys. Days crept into months, months into years, years into decades, yet the cobblestone structure retained its secret. There is no one living in East Troy now who remembers the Bradleys. Only the building and the name in the village records remain.

The razing of old taverns has sometimes solved neighborhood mysteries. At Liberty Pole in Vernon county, where Jeremiah M. Rusk was wont to pass when driving a stage, stood a large three-story tavern erected in the fifties by E. Alexander. Here many travelers were entertained. For years after the structure had served its purpose and after most of those who had any association with it had passed into the beyond, the building became a tenement, and later was torn down. During the process of wrecking a human skeleton was found in the debris and this circumstance caused no little excitement. It developed upon investigation that William Gray had been a guest at the tavern while teaching school hard by, and had used the skeleton while pursuing medical studies. His ambition to become a doctor of medicine having waned, Gray turned his attention to other things and secreted the bones in a dark recess of the inn where they were to be exposed later to awaken wonder in the neighborhood.

What became of John Whare? He was an Englishman by birth and a glass blower by trade, who after pursuing his vocation in New York for some years moved to Madison and became the proprietor of the Plow Inn, located on the Monroe Street road. The old tavern still stands, a substantial red brick structure two stories in height and through the years its capacity has been increased by two additions. A busy place it was in times past but at present it reposes quietly in a grove of stately trees. Rough days were those when Whare and his family moved to the Plow Inn. Gruff teamsters were common and reckless young fellows were among the lead haulers who often sought entertainment at the tavern. Such an individual as Whare was well able to manage these drinking, fighting, fun-loving adventurers. He was a short heavy man with a quick temper and had the reputation of never refusing to fight. In some of the encounters it is said that the tavern furniture suffered severely. Not only was Whare hot-headed in his dealings with guests but with members of his own family and because of his irascibility they stood in wholesome fear of him.

At dinner one day a son said or did something that aroused the anger of his father when with a sudden blow the landlord knocked the youth across the room. As quickly as the boy could recover he seized a huge bowl of gravy from the table and half drowned his parent with the greasy contents. Angered beyond control as he sought to free eyes and hair from the sticky mixture, Whare reached for a shotgun and dashed to the door, but the discreet boy had fled to the deep wood at the rear and was not to be found. After some years Whare disposed of the inn and supposedly returned to his native land leaving his family in Madison. No word ever was received from him and the riddle of his fate never has been solved. Since then others have resided in the inn. Neighbors covertly pass along the legend that a guest of the ancient hostelry, killed in a drunken brawl in John Whare's day, lies buried in a dark corner of the lawn which surrounds the tavern.

Other taverners also have disappeared into an obscurity that never has been dispelled, among them Eben Peck of Baraboo. Peck was a landlord at Madison, but about 1840 was attracted to an undeveloped waterpower on the Baraboo river. After removing to this location restlessness again possessed him and he set out for the gold-fields of California. No word was received from him after his departure, but from various sources information filtered back that he had succumbed to disease on the way, that he had been killed by indians, that he had reached his destination but soon after had died. Communication in those days was slow and uncertain and it is not surprising that little is known of many a traveler who set out to cross the continent. Peck's widow resided among the Baraboo hills for half a century after his disappearance.

Landlord Cooper at Reedsburg had such an unsavory reputation that for years he caused many whisperings in the quiet village. All suspicious characters seemed to gravitate to his place and when an officer once searched his rendezvous stolen property was found. However, the mystery which clings about the old tavern concerns a dead man. One night there came to the hostelry two or three evil looking characters who gave stern injunction to all about the place to keep away from the vehicle in which they were traveling. However, one individual possessed such a bump of curiosity that he decided as soon as opportunity offered to make an investigation. After all had retired and silence reigned, the fellow crept slowly to the wagon and in the dim light began to feel about for the contents. He had not proceeded very far before he came upon something which aroused his curiosity, and to his horror found it was the body of a man, cold and stiff. He was so frightened that he was unable to sleep during the night, and when morning came, hesitated to divulge his experience for fear the secretive travelers might wreak vengeance upon him. Not until they were far away did he disclose what he had discovered. Then it was too late for an officer to attempt to investigate. Who was the dead man, why was he being transported in secret and who were the strangers bearing him along the road in this mysterious manner? Never was the secret revealed.

In tavern days great personal liberty prevailed. Population was sparse, and prior to the coming of the courts there was little restraint regarding behavior. Gambling in taverns was not beyond the dignity of the early judges, according to an account by Alexander F. Pratt in *The Judiciary of Wisconsin, 1837-1838*. Judge William C. Frazier of Pennsylvania was appointed for the eastern district, and when he arrived in Milwaukee of a Sunday evening in June, 1837, he became a guest at Vail's Tavern. Soon he met some Kentucky friends who invited him to a private room that they might quietly indulge in a game of poker. Colonel Morton, register of the land office, and others were there – all friends of Judge Frazier. According to Pratt, "they commenced playing for small sums at first, but increased them as the hours passed, until the dawn of the day, the next morning – when small pots seemed beneath their notice. The first approach of day was heralded to them by the ringing of the bell for breakfast. The judge made a great many apologies, saying among other things, that as this was his first appearance in the territory, and as his court opened at ten o'clock in the morning, he must have a little time to prepare a charge to the grand jury. He therefore hoped that they would excuse him and he withdrew from the party. The court met at the appointed hour, Owen Aldrich acting as sheriff and Cyrus Hawley as clerk. The grand jury was called and sworn. The judge with much dignity commenced his charge; and never before did we hear such a charge poured forth from the bench! After dilating upon the laws generally, he alluded to the statute against gambling. The English language is too barren to describe his abhorrence of that crime. Among other extravagances he said, that 'a gambler was unfit for earth, heaven or hell,' and that 'God Almighty would even *shudder* at the sight of one.' "

Gambling was on open diversion in taverns of the lead region during early mining days. In 1844 two gamblers journeyed from Dubuque to Beetown, and as soon as they arrived at the tavern they informed the landlord they desired to open a bank and have a little game. In one corner of the room stood a large horn. This was seized by some one, thrust through a broken pane in the window, and a terrific blast was sent reverberating among the hills. At once miners flocked from every direction, some on the run. Most of them had Mexican dollars or French five-franc pieces, which soon were stacked on the edge of the table in the center of the room. All money was metal, and the game continued throughout the night. There were a number of fights but no one was killed – just a few black eyes when day dawned. During the earlier part of the night the visiting sports managed to acquire possession of most of the money, but by morning the miners had recovered some. When one of the miners went "broke" he took a tallow candle, ascended to a large chamber above, peered into the faces of the sleepers rolled in blankets or buffalo robes until he located a friend whom he would awaken to borrow a few pieces for further participation. This might occur several times during a night.

The popularity of poker in Carter and Giblett's Tavern at West Blue Mounds gave the place the sobriequet of Pokerville, and the remnant of dilapidated buildings that marks the location of the hamlet is so designated to this day. When the two proprietors erected their building they began playing poker, and during the halcyon days of lead mining, in fact from 1846 to about 1860, the little round chips made a noise that was reminiscent to various guests in the village. For about a quarter of a century poker was the "leading industry" of the place and many miners parted company here with their hard-earned accumulations.

In the lumber regions, too, gambling made short the night and poor the purse. At the Goose Horn Tavern, at Plover a sport from Galena named Curran prepared one of the rooms with lattice above the gambling table and a wire leading to his chair below. He had a son who looked through the lattices above and telegraphed important information to his tricky father through the secret wire. A riverman, often a guest at the Goose Horn, tells of another gambler coming from Milwaukee, and when the two pitted their ingenuity and skill across the table one night, the stranger lost forty thousand dollars, not knowing of the informatory wire.

Telling of their experiences at Uncle Ab Nichols' celebrated tavern at Mineral Point, Alexander F. Pratt says:

"There were all kinds of fun, sports and music going on in the room. After sitting awhile, we removed the bandage from our eyes, washed them, and found that they were much better. (The bright snow had affected the optics.) Such a sight as presented itself to our view we never saw before or since. It seemed that the miners were in the habit of assembling there on Saturday nights to drink, gamble, and frolic until Monday morning. The house was composed of three or four log cabins put together, with passage-ways cut from one to another. This was the only public house in the place. The barroom in which we were sitting contained a large bar, well supplied with all kinds of liquors. In one corner of the room was a faro bank discounting to a crowd around it; in another a roulette; and in another sat a party engaged in playing cards. One man sat back in a corner playing a fiddle, to whose music two others were dancing in the middle of the floor. Hundreds of dollars were lying upon the tables; and among the crowd were the principal men of the territory – men who held high and responsible offices then and now. Being pretty much worn out by our journey, we expressed a wish to retire. The landlord showed us through a dark room and opened the door of another, in which two men were also playing cards and a third lay drunk on the floor. The landlord set down his light, seized the drunken man by the collar, and dragged him into the next room. He soon returned and informed us that we could choose between the two beds – there being two in the room – and bid us good night. We sat down on the side of the bed, and began to figure in our mind upon the chances. We had several hundred dollars in our pocket, which we had brought with us for the purpose of entering land. We imagined that in case they should get 'short' they might call for our 'pile.'

"After studying a while we threw down the outside blanket and quietly crawled into bed with all our clothes on except cap and boots. We had a good bowie knife in our belt and a pistol in each pocket; we clasped a pistol in each hand, and in this way we lay until daylight; and a longer night we never wish to see. When daylight made its appearance we got up; our roommates were still playing cards. On going out to the barroom we found that the crowd had mostly disappeared; there were here and there one or two asleep around the room, and all was still. The next day our companion

(Mr. Story), who had been visiting some friends near-by, came around. We entered our lands and returned to Blue Mounds, where we laid in a store of provisions and left for home, which we reached in four days, having learned the way, the fare, the manners, and customs of the miners, and having seen enough of traveling in a new country to last us from that time to the present."

Tavern Tragedies

Taverners sometimes were called upon to perform the duties of surgeons, physicians, nurses, and undertakers. Lack of hospitals in rural communities often made the matter of accidents and diseases, especially contagious diseases, most serious for both hosts and guests. One cold night in the little barroom of the Ferry House at Merrimack, entertainment of a distressing and unexpected nature was provided. J. H. Ela had come to Wisconsin with Landlord H. M. Jones and family, and after arriving had married a sister of Mrs. Jones in the parlor of the old tavern which occupied a commanding view on the bank of the Wisconsin river. Following a day spent in hunting deer on the Baraboo bluffs a few miles away, Ela returned to the tavern with his feet frozen. It was not long until one of the toes caused excruciating pain and in a paroxysm of misery, the agonized man implored some one to remove the offending member. There was no physician in the place, the night was cold, the situation desperate. At the suggestion of the proprietor a block of wood was placed on the floor, a hammer and chisel provided, and the sufferer was instructed to place his foot on the timber. Then the chisel resting on the toe, was smartly struck, the member dropped, the victim fainted! It was necessary the next morning to bundle the patient into a sled and rush him to Lodi, where Doctor E. H. Irwin deftly completed the operation and removed two other toes.

Robert L. Ream, while operating a tavern in the first log house built at Madison, was called upon to fill the office of both nurse and undertaker during his incumbency. In the summer of 1838 a workman named Gallard fell from a scaffold breaking his leg and an individual named Simons was prostrated with typhoid fever. It was necessary for the landlord to serve as nurse. During the same summer a man named Warren, employed on the new capitol, was killed by lightning near the tavern, and since he was a boarder and there was no undertaker near, it was to be expected the landlord would assist at the burial.

A rueful occurrence was that at the Platteville House in 1843. Miles M. Vineyard died from cholera in the hotel, and at the request of the widow the coffin was opened that she might have a last look at the face of her husband. The number of deaths which followed caused a panic in the village. The place was quarantined against the surrounding country and about half of the five hundred persons residing there were afflicted with the malady. The Platteville plague did not abate until the next year. Sometime after the disease had subsided, Isaac Hodges and George R. Laughton journeyed to Galena, where they were guests at the American House. There they met J. Allen Barber, who knew of the quarantine and spread the alarm. The guests went to Landlord Rosette and demanded the expulsion of the men. Night was at hand and he could not well dismiss them, but when they descended the stairs in the morning they were informed they owed the hotel nothing and that they must leave at once. Other guests were muttering threats so openly that the men decided to depart.

At the Stagg Inn, Mineral Point, a waggoner stopped

TAVERN AT JOHNSTOWN CENTER

East of Janesville; dance hall extends across the second story; lead haulers, teamsters, and travelers stopped here

EMPIRE HOUSE, PRAIRIE DU SAC

Where traveling circus people were entertained

his team in front of the tavern, tied the horses to a post, entered, asked for a room, retired, and died from cholera before the animals had been removed. At another time while William Terrill, father of Mark Terrill who operated the place many years, was the proprietor, a woman suffered quick death with the same disease. She came to the inn one day, did the washing, hung the clothes upon the line, returned home, died from cholera, the funeral procession passing the tavern while the clothes were still fluttering in the wind. On account of the deadly nature of the malady burials took place immediately after death. These scourges came and went, taking prodigious toll in suffering and in human life.

In a tavern on West Water street, Milwaukee, near the present City Hall, where Heinrich Nunnemacher was the proprietor for some time, cholera was fatal to many. During the years of pestilence the place was known as the *Schweizer Heimath zu den Drei Bundes Brüder* (Swiss Home of the Three Union Brothers). The tavern was frequented by emigrants from Switzerland and Germany, and during the fateful period of the disease there were not a few deaths among the boarders and transient guests. As many of these who died had no relatives in this country, landlords often took charge of the personal belongings of the departed, including whatever money he possessed. By this means their riches rapidly increased.

Where several roads meet at Johnstown Center, a few miles east of Janesville, there stands a rambling old tavern which belongs to the days when lead was hauled by teams from mines in western Wisconsin to lake ports. This was a favorite stopping place and in rainy or bitter weather teamsters rolled themselves into

robes or blankets upon the floor of the barroom or large
"school section" (a room without bedsteads, where
every one could help himself to the best there was, as
was done on the school sections of land covered with
timber) and in this way would pass the night. One cold
evening a physician was summoned to the Johnstown
Center Tavern to see a patient. When Doctor Harman
Gray entered the room filled with men rolled up in
blankets and buffalo robes, he warmed himself by the
roaring fire, and asked for the patient. An individual
silently suffering on a table in another part of the room
was indicated. The doctor, wending his way among the
sleepers on the floor, reached the sufferer and when he
drew back the buffalo robe exclaimed: "Great Heavens, the man has the smallpox." Those in the room
sprang up as one man and crowded the exit. The victim
of disease was removed to a cottage where he received
care from another who at one time had been ill with the
malady and therefore was immune.

Sometimes hostelries were convenient points for giving first aid to the wounded following a political riot.
A proposed state constitution was framed during the
period from October to December, 1846, and great excitement prevailed throughout the territory. On account of many varieties of opinion, turbulent meetings
were a popular method of expressing approval or dis-
approval of the product of the convention. Naturally
there were free fights, opposing chairmen at meetings,
high-handed proceedings, and other manifestations far
from gentle. Friends and opponents of the proposed
constitution formed torchlight processions, marching
through the streets with bands playing and flags flying.
In Milwaukee two processions clashed, blazing torches
on the ends of sticks descended upon heads, clubs were

wielded and weapons of various kinds laid many victims low. Not only were there bruised heads, but clothes were stripped from wearers and in other ways bitter sentiment was evidenced. Long Smith, a contractor, was brought to the earth with a blow, and J. R. Treat, a blacksmith who weighed three hundred pounds, slid beneath a friendly wagon to avoid the violence of the storm. The wounded of this exciting affair were carried into the nearest hotel, where their injuries received attention. So bitterly was the constitution assailed, that it was rejected and another drafted for ratification.

About halfway between New Lisbon and Necedah stands a rude memorial bearing the following inscription:

"Mrs. Salter killed here by the indians, June 13, 1863. Two indians, Jo and Jim Dandy killed by Salter and buried here. This ax handle (impression of an ax handle is in the concrete of the concrete memorial) killed two indians and Mrs. Salter. Puck-a-gee."

At the time of the tragedy the Salter Tavern on account of its location was frequented by river men returning from trips down the Yellow river, the Wisconsin, and the Mississippi. After reaching Saint Louis or other river ports where their journey ended, these men would embark on a boat for La Crosse, board a train from this point to New Lisbon, and from the railway station return to the lumber mills of the Yellow river or the upper Wisconsin by stage or afoot. Lumberjacks more often walked than rode, for they could travel as fast along the sandy roads of the region as a conveyance drawn by one or more teams. Since the Salters sold liquor their tavern was a favorite stopping place for roistering mill and rivermen as they trudged through miles of desolate road in the heat of summer or through the blasts of winter.

On the day marked by the memorial, Salter was away from home. Returning he was shocked to find his wife murdered and two Winnebago, Jo and Jim Dandy, lying at the scene of the outrage so intoxicated as to be totally insensible. It was supposed the redskins had come to the Salter Tavern and asked for liquor. Being refused, they had wreaked vengeance with an ax handle upon the helpless woman soon to become a mother. The landlord outraged at the awful deed is said to have seized the ax handle and dispatched the two tribesmen and not satisfied with this, severed the heads from the bodies and placed the ghastly relics on hop-poles by the side of the highway as a warning to other indians. Later these were taken down and with the bodies buried in the sandy soil. There is nothing near the rude memorial to indicate the location of the tavern nor to mark the graves of the tribesmen.

Until 1923 there stood on the north side of the road, a mile west of the village of Mount Horeb, a tavern where murder occurred, during a charivari. Only scattered pieces of plaster, stone, and other hardened material now remain of this place once familiar to travelers on the Military road. The tavern was operated by David Holton, quick-tempered, stony-hearted. A granddaughter, said to have been an orphan, was a member of the family and when the girl was eighteen years of age the taverner arranged her marriage with a stock-buyer, Jesse Williams by name, aged some forty-five years. If the bride-to-be voiced any objection on account of the difference in age between herself and the stockman, or if there was opposition to the match from others, none of it had weight with Holton as the two were married by a justice of the peace, Oliver or Ole Heg, at the time a tenant on the Holton farm.

When the youths of the neighborhood learned of the wedding, they planned a charivari. On the night of September 11, 1866, some twenty young fellows assembled under the light of the harvest moon and created a bedlam of noise in honor of the newly wedded couple. Prolonged pandemonium brought forth no reward to the group of energetic performers and when some of them knocked at the tavern door the landlord refused entrance. The revelers were not to be baffled, however. A council was held and two young men, Theron Eusebius Dryden, who resided on a farm nearby, and a son of Ira Isham, opened parley. They stood on each side of the entrance when Holton, suddenly throwing the door ajar appeared, gun in hand and without warning fatally shot Dryden and wounded Isham. Onlookers were horrified to observe Holton, after he had fired, seize a stick of wood and brutally club Dryden. The young fellow's comrades carried the victim, mortally wounded by the load of shot, into Heg's rooms where he died four days later.

The murder caused great excitement. It is said the funeral was the largest ever known in the locality. Holton was arrested, gave bail for his appearance in court, jumped his bond, was re-arrested in Illinois, eventually was tried in Madison, but after several disagreements was acquitted. W. F. Vilas, afterwards United States senator, defended Holton and is said to have made part of his reputation as a lawyer in the case.

The ruins of a wall is all that remains of an old tavern in which the Ehle family perished on a bitter night, February 16, 1886. The hostelry stood near the main highway between Sheboygan and Fond du Lac –

the old plank road – and just east of the north-and-south line which separates two counties bearing the names of the cities just mentioned. The tavern was a large building and in the days of the rumbling stage-coach had sheltered many a guest; in the barn across the way horses almost without number had been given protection at night. Long before the disaster befell the Ehle family the last coach had passed and the rural structure had lapsed into use as a farmhouse.

The circumstances of the fire and the important suit which followed, made the tragedy one of unusual inter-est. Altogether seven persons perished; Abram Ehle, aged eighty-two, whose wife had died the previous year, James A. Ehle an only son, born in 1841; Helen Taylor Ehle, wife of the latter born the same year as her hus-band; their three children, Flora Maria, Abram Tay-lor, and Mary Belle, all born between 1876 and 1880 inclusive; and a Mrs. Kinney.

A young man who made his home with the family was out the evening before, returning about ten thirty o'clock. When he arrived there was a light in the room occupied by the elder Ehle in the western part of the house and all the others had apparently retired for the night. The roomer came into the house through the woodshed, entered the kitchen and retired in an adjoin-ing room. Some two hours later he was awakened by the barking of the family dog in the shed, scented smoke, opened the door into the kitchen, was met with flames which scorched his hair, jumped through a win-dow without lifting the sash, found himself in the wood-shed, and escaped with only the clothing worn at night. All others in the building perished.

The elder Ehle, who resided with his son and fam-ily, owned the property and had made a will bequeathing one hundred and sixty acres to his son during his life. At the son's death the property was to pass to the three grandchildren, each to receive one-third of the land, two north-and-south lines dividing the farm into three equal parts. After writing his will the elder Ehle purchased one hundred additional acres but failed to make a new testament or attach a codicil to the one already signed and witnessed. The increase in the estate and the uncertainty respecting the rightful heirs, due to the sequence in which the members of the family died – as frequently happens when lives are lost in a shipwreck at sea – rendered a clarifying suit necessary.

The old gentleman was wont to have a fire in his room during the boreal season and was also in the habit of arising during the night, lighting a candle and taking liquor or medicine or both. Due to the peculiar circumstances of the case the court decided that the old gentleman perished first; that his son – who was heard by the young man to utter a cry about the time he opened the door into the kitchen – died next; that the wife and three children next succumbed; and that Mrs. Kinney, who slept farthest from the place where the fire originated, was the last to expire. These conclusions were deduced from the evidence regarding the point where the flames began, the direction of the wind, and the position of the bodies in the ruins. The case had final hearing in the state supreme court, which held that, since the children died last the property must go to the next of kin, the two grandparents. A beautiful memorial standing on the south side of the little cemetery at Plymouth, marks the last resting place of most of those whose untimely death came so tragically on that midwinter night more than a generation ago.

Within taverns or within the shadows of them, many

shooting affairs have occurred. During July of the same year in which James R. Vineyard shot Charles C. P. Arndt in the territorial legislature at Madison, Enos S. Baker, formerly sheriff of Grant county, whose appointment led to the tragedy in the capitol, had become involved in a lawsuit. J. T. Mills was the opposing attorney. Mills, though small of stature had a caustic tongue, and some of his utterances were so bitter that Baker concluded the only justice for the lawyer lay in the cowhide. The fiery little lawyer resented the punishment, sprang into the office of Doctor Rickey, seized a gun, bolted into the street and meeting Baker, told him to defend himself. The former sheriff carried a revolver and as he drew it, Mills fired shot into the hand holding the weapon, then fled to the hotel nearby. He took refuge in the parlor where were several ladies, and thus the affray ended. At the subsequent trial the attorney was acquitted.

The first house, a tavern and saloon at Dunnville in Dunn county, was erected in 1840 by a man named Lamb. The following year he sold the property to his brother-in-law, Arthur McCann, a sawyer in one of the local mills. After the conclusion of the transaction, the two played at cards in the tavern, drank freely, began to quarrel, and finally McCann shied a weight at Lamb. The latter repaired to the cabin of Philo Stone nearby, loaded a rifle, returned to the home of McCann, called him out and, as he appeared, shot him dead. The murderer fled and nothing was ever after heard of the fugitive. Philo Stone took possession of the tavern, and his wife, a full-blooded Chippewa reputed to be a good housekeeper, became the mistress of the hostelry.

In 1839 at the Astor House in Southport (Kenosha), resided two men whose past troubles cemented them

together in close friendship. With a burden or worry
from domestic infelicities and other sorrows which
weighed upon him, one of them, Brown by name, had
come to Southport from Kinderhook, New York, and
had soon after made the acquaintance of George Rodg-
ers Barlow, familiarly known as Scip. Misfortunes,
too, had befallen the latter and his sympathies were
easily aroused. He must have been of a somnolent in-
clination, however, for one day while shingling a roof
he fell asleep and fell to the ground, breaking both
ankles; and when nearly recovered he hobbled to the
lake where he drowsed off on the wharf, plunged forward into the water, and was not rescued until almost
drowned. The two men sat at the same table in the
barroom and occupied one bed in the tavern. One
stormy night lightning struck the inn and the fluid
descending the chimney, instantly killed Brown as he
slept. When morning dawned, Scip gazed awesomely at
the dead body of his friend and overcome by the fear
that a bolt might strike twice in the same place, hurriedly left the Astor House and never again was a
guest within its walls.

The Buckhorn Tavern (the antlers of a deer fastened
to a post as a sign) was a familiar stopping place
located a few miles west of Monroe and was operated
by Joseph Paine, a careless, quick-tempered type of
pioneer who in time sold the inn to John Bringhold.
Paine's pugnacious attributes soon made difficulty, a
quarrel over a boundary line between farms ensued,
and instead of submitting the matter to the courts,
Paine decided to pursue a course of his own with
tragic results. As Bringhold was placing the rails on
what he declared was the line of division, Paine appeared and at the point of a gun ordered him to cease

operations. This was refused, there was a report, and Bringhold fell to the ground dead.

Paine soon was made prisoner, was confined in a room in the courthouse – the only jail in Monroe – and later was taken to the American House for safe custody. Quickly he picked the lock of his room, mounted a horse, and dashed away. He procured a second steed from a relative, a third from George Paine, crossed the river at McGregor and ultimately reached California. When morning came, the sheriff found his prisoner gone and never saw him again. After the shooting Paine declared he had not intended to kill his victim. Few remain who recall Paine or even the site of the frontier hostelry.

Tragedies sometimes befell gentle guests entertained at these primitive places. In the early fifties a young girl recently arrived from Germany, stopped at a Plymouth tavern for the noonday meal, while walking alone from Sheboygan to her relatives who resided near New Holstein. It was late in the afternoon before the girl left, and the landlord called her attention to the fact that she was fully seventeen miles from her destination. He urged her to remain until the morning but she answered that she was not afraid, so continued the journey.

Early the next day while a New Holstein resident was driving oxen through the almost unbroken forest toward Plymouth, the cattle suddenly shied at something by the roadside. Upon investigation the driver was horrified to find the bloody tracks of a human being roundabout a beech tree, a few scattered bones, and remnants of a bundle of clothing here and there. Hurrying to the nearest habitation, he brought others to the scene. After careful examination the conclusion was reached that the young girl had met a bear with cubs, that the cubs had perhaps approached the lone traveler in a playful way, that in attempting to drive them away the girl had irritated the mother, which had then turned upon her with ferocious consequences.

Murders were committed in the tavern which stands on the main street in Dodgeville, in the Stagg Inn at Mineral Point, and in various other public houses about the state. Then there were lesser tragedies, those disappointments and sorrows which come to almost every household, in virtually all the hostelries here and there along the highways of the commonwealth. From the foregoing it must appear that there was much of agony and grief in a land full of opportunity and promise.

Last Days of the Taverns

During the Civil war taverns were important rallying and recruiting points, many stirring scenes being enacted in and about them. The band was stationed at the tavern, here animated addresses were made, enlistments recorded, drilling done, and here farewells were said when young recruits marched away. In time some of these returned to the tavern, wounded and broken in health, or perhaps without life to be laid away on the flower-covered hillside. Others never returned.

The Tyler House at Platteville witnessed many pathetic episodes as young patriots from that region went to war. A tablet on the building now occupying the site states that more than a thousand enlisted there, an unusual number for a rural community.

A squad of Civil war recruits at Freer's Tavern in Delton (now Mirror Lake) occupied one room in which were twenty beds, two in a bed. They indulged in pillow fights and other forms of mischief, till by the time the soldiers were ready to leave Delton every bed in the room had been wrecked, the men sleeping on the floor.

In the neighboring town of Fairfield a few miles distant, dwelt a southern sympathizer, locally known as the "copperhead." Setting out with his team one morning to drive to Delton, as he neared the tavern he encountered the members of Company E, Twelfth Wisconsin volunteer infantry, famed for its destructive pillow engagements and later for bravery in sanguinary conflicts in Dixie. The soldiers led the disloyal Fairfieldite to the tavern barn, where they invited him to salute the American flag. He refused. Angered, they promptly ordered him at the point of their muskets to salute. Again he refused. His obduracy aroused them to rude action. Quickly a line from a harness was around his neck and he was given to understand that sterner measures were in store should be continue in his refusal. The man was no coward. He stoutly stood by his convictions, and for a third time declined to make obeisance to the national emblem. A crowd now gathered and excitement was running high. Suddenly the strap about his neck tightened and the victim swung off his feet. After a moment he was again commanded to salute, but still was inflexible. The anger of the soldiers and of others who had assembled to witness the proceeding now exceeded all bounds. The exasperating fellow found himself swinging in space with cries of "Let him hang!" ringing in his ears. At last when the victim realized the situation was serious, he yielded and finally was released. The episode created endless discussion, and the lesson to the "copperhead" was enduring. Not until long after the last gun had been fired on southern battle fields did he, disgraced, humiliated, reappear on Delton streets.

The Central House at Reedsburg was erected in 1856-1857 by Alba Smith, and for many years was known as the Alba House. Prior to and during the Civil war the proprietors of the Mansion House and the Alba House were bitter rivals. Democrats gathered at the former hostelry to learn of important events, and Republicans at the latter. Both had commodious dancing halls and in them the opposing factions assembled

TYLER HOUSE, PLATTEVILLE

Used as a recruiting station during the Civil war. A tablet on the building now occupying this site (Third and Main streets) states that more than a thousand men were here enlisted, 1861-1865

for their festivities. It is related that a young lady was
invited to attend a ball on an evening when there was a
party in each tavern. Her sympathies were strongly
with the North, while those of her escort were with the
South. On the way to the village the lady had the fore-
thought to enquire:

"Are we to dance at the Alba House?"

"No, we're going to the Mansion House," was the
reply.

"Then I'll go home," she commanded, and home the
young man was obliged to take her.

High in the Baraboo bluffs by the side of the stage
road which extended north from Prairie du Sac, stood
the Haseltine Tavern. During the early sixties the
report became prevalent that a Confederate flag was
being displayed there; so one evening some friends in
Baraboo loyal to the North decided to investigate. Under cover of night they passed out of the city, across
the little bridge spanning the west branch of Draper
creek, along the road to the foot of the bluff, up the
long slope past the spring where the blackhaws ripen,
and through a wooded section to the tavern. All
marched into the barroom, but no confederate flag met
the eyes of the expectant group. If one was about the
place it had prudently been secreted or destroyed. The
fruitlessness of the excursion was somewhat assuaged
by the drinks which freely went round at the expense
of the landlord.

One night a woodsman driving a team on his way to
the pinery stopped at the Token Creek Tavern. He was
from Illinois, was a southern sympathizer, and seemed
unaware of the intense loyalty of Wisconsin. During
the evening he thrust his head into the barroom of the
hostelry and shouted: "Hurrah for Jeff Davis!" As one

man the group around the bar rushed for the stranger. Leaving his team behind, the fellow dashed across a field and into the wood, the excited men in pursuit. His return was delayed far into the night, when he cautiously appeared, took his horses, and by morning was miles away.

The frame building at the intersection of University and Randall avenues, Madison, was a place where boys in blue "lifted high ones" during the Civil war. The tavern under the management of Peter Newman was noted for the size of its steins. Camp Randall was not far away, and at the bar of the old hostelry the young soldiers were wont to linger until taps summoned to bunks. To add to the pleasure of those who tarried in the tavern, a dance hall was provided in the basement, and on the outside was a long shed where a bowling alley afforded diversion during seasonable weather.

After the close of the Civil war and the coming of the railroad the hand of change was far more active than in any previous age, and this was keenly felt both by tavern and stagecoach. After the advent of the "iron horse" places of entertainment along main highways rapidly declined, first in one direction then in another, and there seemed to be no new sphere of usefulness for them. There is no doubt the swifter mode of travel which so greatly expanded in the sixties and seventies, was the greatest factor in causing landlords to remove their signs. The market was brought nearer the producer and long distance transportation by team practically disappeared from the highway. Distance also was greatly reduced for the traveler by the appearance of the passenger train.

While many a landlord fully realized that the railroad would ruin his business, yet he was willing to contribute liberally toward its construction.

The refusal to pay a small amount ended the business of entertaining at the Spring Green House, a log tavern which stood about a mile north of Spring Green and operated in early times by Smith Love and his wife. In front of the place was a large sign which proclaimed to the public that entertainment might be found within. One evening a stranger on foot stopped and the next morning was handed a statement of account containing three items:

Supper _____25c.
Lodging _____25c.
Breakfast _____25c.

The stranger, declaring that he had no money, hurried down the highway. This so enraged the proprietor that he proceeded to level the sign. About that time a neighbor came along and asked Love what he was doing. Straightening up and pointing down the highway, he said:

"Do you see that galoot going down the road?"

"Yes."

"Well, he refused to pay his bill."

With that explanation, the landlord continued the task of converting the sign into kindling wood. The non-payment of a bill of seventy-five cents actually ended the business of this old time tavern.

In 1857 John Meyer Levy built the Augusta House, La Crosse, and was receiving rent from a tenant when, in March, 1862, the building was swept away on the flood tide of the Mississippi. At North Bend, in Jackson county, a hotel met a similar doom when a rush of water came down the Black river.

An earlier tavern at Helena suffered a more exciting fate. After the battle of Wisconsin Heights in 1832, the soldiers marched to the hamlet to cross the river in pursuit of Black Hawk. When the indians reached the stream after their defeat near Sauk City, part fled overland and the remainder endeavored to escape down the Wisconsin. To enable the whites to gain the opposite side quickly, and for the remaining few to attack the indians on the river, the tavern at Helena was feverishly pulled apart and converted into rough rafts. The whole region was ablaze as the indians advanced and every available aid was invoked to overtake the fugitives.

Alva Culver later erected a tavern at Helena, the favorite crossing place of raftsmen when they were slowly finding their way from Galena to the pinery north of Kilbourn. There was also a ferry there much used in the days of early travel. Later when the railroad was laid a mile away and a new village came into being, the tavern was moved to a location near the railway station and became the first place of entertainment in the second Helena. Subsequently the building passed to William Bartlet who tore the structure apart, loaded the material onto flat cars, and with the furniture took the property to Iowa.

A tavern at Okee, between Baraboo and Madison, suspended operations in an amusing way. In 1859 during the height of lumbering in that region J. N. Fellows opened the hostelry, and when business was no longer profitable on account of the decline in lumber production, he sold to a taverner named Ober. The new owner was a young man who came to the place with a keg of beer, expecting to sell meals and drinks to those who came from a distance for lumber sawed at the mill.

Last Stagecoach on Eau Claire-Black River Falls line

Ober and his wife drank the beer, and had no funds with which to purchase an additional keg, so the business failed.

Failure was invited when men were not adapted to the business. In 1851 Michael Banfiel and Frank Callen opened a tavern on the road from Neenah up the Yellow river, and since neither of the men were married they had to play the parts of both landlord and cook. So reckless was their way of doing business that they soon disposed of the inn to Doctor Bronson. The latter added music in an endeavor to win customers, but he learned soon that something more substantial than notes from a fiddle appealed to woodsmen.

The coming of the railroad revolutionized modes of travel and houses of entertainment. In their day the stagecoach and the tavern were powerful factors in the development of the country, performing services that were a necessity of the time. The older generation regards with endearing memories the social hours spent in the tavern, but that institution has ended its career, fulfilled its destiny. Occasionally, one stands by the roadside deserted, dilapidated, neglected, forlorn, weatherworn and storm-battered, only a suggestion of its proud and useful self, now merely an interesting relic of pioneer times. Ghosts of other days people it – shades of those entertained, spectral forms of idlers who made it their daily haunt. The landlord has smiled upon his last guest, has related his last tale. The gaping fireplace long ago consumed the last stick from the pile at the rear, the clinking of glasses and bottles has long since ceased in the old barroom, the fire beneath the soap kettle has died out, the festoons of dried pumpkin have disappeared from behind the kitchen stove, and the old well-sweep, which brought forth buckets of cold water to refresh the weary, has fallen to decay. Winds of winter have carried away the ancient shaved shingles and corroding rust has destroyed the links holding the weather-beaten sign.

The humble names of these early hostelries, the honest effort of bonifaces, and the human interest incidents will live, perchance, in song and story long after their exact locations have been forgotten. As one visits room after room in those still standing, there is a whisper of the words of Tom Moore:

> I feel like one
> Who treads alone
> Some banquet hall deserted.

The generations which the tavern and stagecoach served have all but passed, giving way to a civilization whose interests cross and recross in a maze of mechanical inventions and industrial relations. The world is vibrant with romance, yet no longer does manifestation come through the medium of the stagecoach and the tavern.

Index

Index

2225